THE MEDIEVAL PARK

The Medieval Park

New Perspectives

Edited by Robert Liddiard

WIND*gather*
PRESS

The Medieval Park: New Perspectives

Copyright © Author(s) 2007

Published by: Windgather Press Ltd, 29 Bishop Road, Bollington,
Macclesfield, Cheshire SK10 5NX

Distributed by: Central Books Ltd, 99 Wallis Road, London E9 5LN

British Library Cataloguing-in-Publication Data

A catalogue record for this book is available from the British Library

ISBN 978-1-905119-16-5

Designed, typeset and originated by Carnegie Book Production, Lancaster

Printed and bound by Cambridge Printing

Contents

List of Figures

Abbreviations

....

BL	British Library
Bod. Lib.	Bodleian Library, Oxford
CChR	Calendar of Charter Rolls
CCR	Calendar of Close Rolls
CIM	Calendar of Inquisitions Miscellaneous
CIPM	Calendar of Inquisitions Post Mortem
CPR	Calendar of Patent Rolls
CRO	Cumbria Archive Service, Cumbria Record Offices
CRR	Curia Regis Rolls
DNB	*Dictionary of National Biography*
HALS	Hertfordshire Archives and Local Studies
HCCAHBR	Hampshire County Council Archaeology and Historic Buildings Record
HMSO	His/Her Majesty's Stationery Office
LDB	Little Domesday Book
MCO	Magdalen College, Oxford
NRO	Norfolk Record Office
NYCRO	North Yorkshire County Record Office, Northallerton
OE	Old English
OFr	Old French
ON	Old Norse
SMR	Sites and Monuments Record
SRO/B	Suffolk Record Office (Bury St Edmunds)
SRO/I	Suffolk Record Office (Ipswich)
TLS	*Times Literary Supplement*
TNA:PRO	The National Archives (formerly the Public Record Office), Kew, London
TRE	Tempore Regis Edwardi (in the time of King Edward)
WBA	West Bretton Hall Archives
WYAS/L	West Yorkshire Archives Service, Leeds Office
YAS	Yorkshire Archaeological Society, archives, Leeds

Editor's Preface

A collection of essays on the medieval park seemed appropriate at this time for a number of reasons. First, the editor was aware of a number of scholars from different backgrounds working on various park-related topics and considered that the subject might be better furthered by, rather than the results of these researches being published piecemeal in various scholarly journals, the combination of these results in a single volume. Second, discussions with several of the contributors revealed a general feeling that parks were worth a re-examination, as (certain publications aside) the subject had not received a detailed treatment for a considerable period of time and several significant issues required reassessment. It must be stressed, however, that this volume in no way reflects all aspects of current research on parks, nor does it include contributions by all researchers currently working on parks; rather, it is intended to illustrate the diversity of approaches to the medieval park and give some idea as to the conclusions being reached by a range of scholars working in the field. It is hoped that the papers included in this volume will serve not only to illustrate the variety of current work, but will also act as a stimulus to debate and further research.

I would like to thank a number of people who made this collection of essays possible. First, thanks must go to Stewart and Anne Farquharson for permitting the generous use of 'The Garret', without which this volume could not have been completed. The production of this volume took place during a period of study leave, for which I thank Professor John Charmley at the University of East Anglia. Richard Purslow embraced the idea with his usual enthusiasm, Nigel Liddiard provided valuable technical support and Sarah Harrison provided the clearest editorial advice. A debt of gratitude is also due to the authors of each of the chapters, who showed considerable patience during the final stages of the editorial process. Finally I would like to thank Sarah, Georgie and Edward for all their support over the past year.

Robert Liddiard
University of East Anglia
December 2006

A note on measurements

Measurements are given in imperial units. A guide for conversion to metric units is provided below.

Miles to kilometres: multiply by 1.6093
Acres to hectares: multiply by 0.4047

Introduction

....

Robert Liddiard

For sylvan beauty and variety of timber, few landscapes
can compare with an English deer-park.

(Whitaker 1892)

Parks are familiar features in the modern landscape and today the word
conjures up images ranging from children's playgrounds through to animal
sanctuaries and science research stations. Although such parks are obviously
far removed from those of the Middle Ages, the idea of a separate place for
recreation or some kind of specialised activity set within real or conceptual
bounds arguably reflects a hazy memory of a long-lived conception of the park
as a place of particular significance within the countryside.

To landscape historians parks are perhaps best known for their role in the
rearing and management of deer, an activity that gave the park a specific
status throughout the medieval period and was also responsible for its most
popular appellation historiographically: the 'deer park'. While parks' primary
functions as game reserves and hunting grounds are well attested and have
recently been restated with some force, scholars have demonstrated that parks
were always far more than mere preserves for deer. The contribution of parks
to the wider economy of medieval England as locations for grazing, timber
production, arable farming and industrial activity is well documented and,
more recently, the roles of the park as a place of recreation and contemplation,
and as the pleasurable backdrop to the noble residence, have occupied the
attention of researchers. In order to reflect the multiplicity of uses to which
parks were put during the Middle Ages this volume will use the term 'park'
rather than 'deer park'. To do so is not to downplay the importance of deer
management to the economy of parkland; rather, it is to reflect the broad
range of activities that took place within enclosures that, in medieval sources,
are normally referred to simply as *parcus* (Stamper 1988).

The study of parkland touches upon a range of topics central to discussions
of medieval society. Parks were, of course, private seigneurial areas and a study
of their construction and development offers some insight into lordly attitudes
to demesne and the constitution of aristocratic status during the Middle Ages.
Imparkment often required the extinction of existing rights over what were,
frequently, large areas of countryside, ensuring that the effects of park creation

were not simply confined to the aristocracy but were felt throughout medieval society. If the primary function of the park was that of a game reserve then the lordly control of resources, and their consequent denial to others, found expression not only in park creation and aristocratic hunting culture but also in illicit poaching and park breaking. In the early fourteenth century, when parks occupied their greatest spatial extent, an area possibly as small as just 2 per cent of England was imparked (Rackham 1986, 123); yet it is clear that parks exercised a disproportionate impact on the *social* landscape of the countryside (Figure 1).

While the importance of parks to the medieval economy has long been recognised, there are significant aspects of the subject that are only partially understood or which invite reinterpretation; as the author of one recent study has commented, the medieval park 'remains unevenly studied and, in many quarters, under-appreciated' (Mileson 2005a, 19). The unevenness of study is arguably a reflection of the fact that much of the literature on parks is regional in scope and, therefore, it is not always immediately clear where the broader significance of this type of work lies. Perhaps this is why there have been remarkably few efforts at a general synthesis of park development in medieval England; it is telling that there have been few attempts at a single-volume history of the park from the eleventh to the nineteenth century since E. P. Shirley's *Some Account of English Deer Parks* in 1867 (*cf.* Lasdun 1991). The essays brought together here hopefully demonstrate the potential gains to be made from both a national and a regional approach to the medieval park – and how the two approaches are far from being mutually exclusive. The first part, 'Approaches to the Medieval Park', examines a series of conceptual issues concerning the place of parkland within the medieval countryside. The second part, 'Parks in the Landscape', comprises a series of case studies intended to offer insights into particular problems or provide informed accounts of park development in specific areas.

It is also to be hoped that the papers brought together in this volume have more than just an academic interest. At the time of writing there are probably more deer in the English landscape than has been the case for centuries, a situation primarily due to an upsurge in the planting of woodland and wildlife conservation policies that have, often unwittingly, provided an excellent habitat for native and new deer species alike. Issues of deer conservation and culling are currently exercising government and have even attracted the attentions of the national press (Mitchell 2006). If, in the modern countryside, the issue of deer management currently has much relevance, then contemporary debates cannot help but be profitably informed by an understanding of practice in the past (Figure 2).

The first chapter re-examines the long-held idea that parks were important status symbols within medieval society and were anxiously sought after by parvenus. If it is a truism to state that the park was a status symbol in medieval England, it is also true, as Stephen Mileson points out, that the idea is one that is simply asserted, rather than argued in detail. An examination of the motivations of park builders as a group provides a more tangible approach to the sociology of park creation in medieval England. Mileson demonstrates that park ownership was more restricted that might be thought to have been the case: by the late thirteenth century it is unlikely that more than 20 per cent of gentry families owned a park, a situation that is unlikely to have significantly altered in the succeeding two centuries. Costs of maintenance and upkeep ensured that park-making was only ever a realistic possibility for those individuals from wealthy gentry families and above; hence Mileson plays down the idea of the widespread diffusion of parks down the social scale during the course of the Middle Ages. Nevertheless, the expense of park creation ensured that a certain degree of exclusivity was associated with park ownership and thus made possession of a park attractive to particular social groups. Therefore, emulation clearly played a part in park creation, and may be seen most clearly, perhaps, in cases where parks formed part of a wider residential scheme. While social climbers do indeed account for a significant number of new parks created throughout the Middle Ages, such examples must, however, be placed alongside those individuals who chose not to mark their new position by creating a park and those long-established families who imparked as part of a general process of estate improvement. As an explanation for imparkment, therefore, 'status' can only go so far; the motives for park creation are best approached at a detailed local level.

Mileson's conclusions concerning the link between the status of the park and the noble residence raises a broader issue of the extent to which, during the Middle Ages, parkland was actively manipulated in order to heighten the aesthetic appeal of residential surroundings. The close association between parks and the great buildings of medieval England has long been recognised, but the extent to which residential surroundings were 'designed' in a modern sense is more open to debate. Landscape historians, in particular, have recently emphasised the close spatial relationship between (mainly) secular residences and associated parks, especially in those instances where parkland lay immediately adjacent to suites of accommodation and where the topographical relationship suggests that the park was intended to be 'viewed' (Herring 2003; Taylor 2000).

This topic is discussed in the second chapter, in which Amanda Richardson reviews the evidence for the 'landscape approach' to the medieval park through a study of royal palaces, where, if it is to be found anywhere, landscape 'design' should perhaps be most evident. By the fourteenth century, the golden age of the park, English kings clearly favoured an arrangement in which their residences were enveloped or completely surrounded by parkland. Considerable care is evident not only in the location of park and residence but also in that of park lodges and in the visual approach to the main buildings. 'Little parks' are apparent from at least the mid-thirteenth century, and some visual significance was clearly attached to them: they enjoyed a particular spatial relationship with grand apartments or lodgings and appear to have functioned more as gardens than 'conventional' parks. The desire to make the residence magnificent, therefore, certainly extended into the wider parkscape.

FIGURE I.
Staverton Park,
Suffolk, a rare
survival from the
medieval countryside.
It remains open to
question, however,
whether the intensely
managed landscape
of the medieval park
looked anything like
the relic landscape we
see today.
G. BATTELL

If parks assumed a special significance within the medieval landscape then this was usually due, at least in part, to the keeping of deer within their bounds. This, in turn, raises the thorny issues of the definition of the park and the status of the medieval park as a hunting landscape, the latter in particular proving a source for disagreement and debate (Rackham 2002; Mileson 2005a; Pluskowski this volume). The modern use of the term 'deer park' implies a utilitarian purpose (albeit usually with qualifications) and, as has been pointed out, there is some difficulty in envisioning hunting taking place within the confines of what were, in the majority of cases, relatively small enclosures. It has been suggested, therefore, that many parks are best regarded principally as venison farms: breeding grounds and places where hunt servants or parkers could take deer when venison was required for occasions such as feast days (Birrill 1992). While management practices akin to 'venison farming' are well documented, so too, however, are hunting expeditions in parks (see Mileson this volume), a situation that has led to the widespread use of the modern term 'hunting park'. Such a term is, if anything, more problematic than 'deer park', in as much as it implies that such parks had one exclusive – in this case, recreational – function, a situation that is unlikely to have been the case even at those parks of the highest status.

Part of the difficulty in defining the precise status and character of the park in the medieval countryside lies in the diverse character of parkland itself; the evidence points to a great variety in medieval practice and credence should also be given to the idea that the concept of the park underwent considerable revision in the period from the Norman Conquest to the Reformation. Questions over the status of the park as a hunting landscape, in particular, must necessarily be closely linked to debates over exactly what did or did not constitute hunting in the Middle Ages. Certainly, hunting *par force de chiens* (the chasing down of a single deer over the course of a day and its ritualistic killing and dismemberment) and its variants were simply impossible within the bounds of a park (Almond 2003, 73–82). This was not the case, however, for 'drive' or 'bow and stable' hunting, where animals were steered towards stationary hunters who then dispatched the quarry from pre-prepared positions or hides (Cummins 2002). Historical sources made it clear that this latter method of hunting was practised in English parks; indeed, it may have been the norm. Documentary sources also attest to the practice of coursing, where a single animal or a small number of beasts were chased along a defined course. Coursing is known to have taken place at Windsor during the fifteenth century, but the extent to which it was common elsewhere is unclear. The possibility that it was widespread is, however, suggested by the recent archaeological identification of a late medieval course at Ravensdale in Derbyshire (Taylor 2004) and by stray documentary references, such as that made in 1311 to coursing in the park at Burgh-next-Alysham in Norfolk (CCR 1307–1313, 324).

The problematic issues surrounding the status of the park as a hunting landscape are discussed in this volume, albeit from different perspectives, in two closely linked papers by Naomi Sykes and Aleksander Pluskowski. The primary function of parks as animal enclosures barely needs stating but, as Sykes points out, it is curious that, historiographically, accounts of park

FIGURE 2.
Fallow (*Dama dama*) bucks. There are probably more deer in the English landscape now than has been the case for centuries and deer management represents a considerable challenge in the modern countryside.
IAN D. ROTHERHAM

development have usually focused on the activities of those men and women who built and experienced them, with the park species themselves often tangential to mainstream analyses. The zooarchaeological approach to parks attempts to offer a corrective to this bias, centring as it does on the function and meaning of parks as investigated through the study of faunal remains. The study of the changing representation of taxa in the archaeological record can shed important light on the development of parkland. In particular, the pre-Conquest period is characterised by a limited range of species, probably a reflection of specific forms of Old English hunting practices and game management. Later medieval assemblages, in contrast, exhibit a greater range of species and, from the twelfth century onwards, increased instances of exotic beasts. From a zooarchaeological perspective, the origins of the park – at least in its most characteristic medieval form – would seem to lie in the twelfth century, rather than in earlier periods.

The conceptual development of the park over the course of the Middle Ages is central to Pluskowski's contribution to this volume. While park creation is frequently placed within the context of hunting as a practical activity, the hunting of wild animals also occupied an important place in the psychological world of the aristocracy, whose perceived authority over the natural world found expression in a range of material culture. The care taken in the organisation of the park ecosystem was not simply concerned with the management of game; the park was a space where the potential for *control* of the landscape was considerable and, consequently, there was a clear relationship between the physical organisation and the ideological conception of the park. During the later Middle Ages, partly as a result of an absence of wild deer populations, park-based hunting took on a greater significance, as did the visual relationship between park and residence. As such, there was a distinctive 'social ecology' of the park, with the park occupying a symbolic liminal position between the enclosed landscape of the garden and the unbounded, wild, landscape of the forest.

While medieval parkscapes may have represented an important part of the imagined landscape of the aristocracy, parks were also economic units that formed carefully managed areas of the lord's demesne. The archaeological remains of features such as boundary banks, lodge sites and ponds are familiar signs of past management, but the physical remnants of parkland in the form of surviving flora can also offer enormous potential for shedding light on past practices. Ian Rotherham, in Chapter 5, discusses the ecological dimensions of medieval parks and draws particular attention to the importance of former parkland as an ecological resource today. Unimproved grassland, veteran trees and dead wood provide valuable habitats for a range of flora and fauna, but the complex ecologies that exist today are a reflection of complex histories and will require careful management in the future.

If the ecology of parkland, both past and present, is a tangible reminder of the importance of parks in the modern countryside, the second part of this volume examines the significance of parks in the medieval landscape. The range of evidence for parks occupies much of Stephen Moorhouse's discussion of Yorkshire. What emerges most forcibly from his chapter is the complex range of uses to which parks were put during the Middle Ages. The evidence for this complexity lies scattered in archives and across the landscape and, in order to arrive at a full picture of how parks were utilised, multi-disciplinary research is essential. The results of a holistic approach to the medieval park are considerable. The use of the park as a hunting landscape involving a variety of game is amply demonstrated by evidence for standings, kennels, traps and snares; yet an emphasis on this aspect of the park draws attention away from other important activities, such as mining, mineral-working and quarrying. Parks were also important as a grazing resource for non-game stock, something that appears to have become more pronounced in Yorkshire during the fifteenth century.

Although not always the best unit of study for landscape history, the county-based survey provides a mechanism through which national trends can be tested and evaluated. Anne Rowe's examination of the relationship between parks and woodland in the heavily imparked county of Hertfordshire is a case in point. The national association between parks and woodland is well known but, as Rackham has pointed out, there are significant variations to the general pattern (Cantor and Hatherly 1979; Rackham 1986). In Hertfordshire, while there is a close correlation between woodland and parks at a local level, there were clearly other factors at work in determining the overall distribution of parks across the county; there were significant areas which, despite containing large reserves of woodland and wood pasture, did not see high levels of imparkment. The explanation for these differing levels of imparkment is found not simply in the distribution of woodland, but is rather more closely linked to the tenurial geography of the county.

South-west Hertfordshire was characterised by relatively large manors that had, at an early date, come into the possession of major ecclesiastical houses. Numerous documentary sources attest to the wooded character of this part of the county, yet park creation was limited; the presence of extensive ecclesiastical lordship appears to have retarded park creation. In the east and north of the county, by contrast, in a landscape characterised by high levels of population and smaller manors, parks tended to occupy the classic interfluve locations and were created by secular lords wishing to enclose pockets of woodland.

If Rowe's work on Hertfordshire represents an example of the complication of a general national model via a local case study, then Rosemary Hoppitt's chapter on Suffolk parks has considerable implications for another national issue, that of rates of imparkment and, in particular, the problems inherent in relying over-much on the records of medieval government for estimating growth in park numbers. In Suffolk, two broad phases of imparkment are suggested by 'state' documents: from 1086 to the end of the fourteenth century, and the sixteenth century. It may be an obvious point that the increased number of documentary references to parks from *c*.1200 is connected with the fact that many of our principal sources only survive in any numbers from this date onwards (Clanchy 1979), but where earlier documentary evidence exists, the dates of known parks can often be pushed back into the twelfth century or earlier. Even in the absence of documentary material approximate dates of imparkment can be suggested on the basis of the known development of the regional landscape: thus in Suffolk it is probable that, on the basis of topographical evidence, the twelfth century saw a greater rate of imparkment than documentary sources would suggest.

In a much-needed corrective to the general model of park development, which owes a great deal to work carried out in the English midlands, Angus Winchester discusses the particular regional characteristics of parks in Cumbria. The nature of Cumbrian parks was determined in part by the physical landscape of the uplands but also by a distinctive pattern of lordship and land tenure. In general, lowland parks in Cumbria were associated with major baronial castles and were in place prior to 1300. The lords responsible for these castle parks also claimed extensive hunting rights over neighbouring uplands and often created parks in areas of private forest. These 'forest' parks were more numerous than their 'castle' counterparts and a possible context for their creation is suggested by a retreat in the extent of hunting rights over the uplands as a result of peasant colonisation. A chronological development also seems apparent, in which large areas known as 'hays' seem to have given way to smaller 'parks'; this, again, may have been a response to a decline in the extent of baronial hunting grounds. Significantly, the term 'park' appears to have embraced enclosed woodland (wood pasture and coppice) and also demesne stock-rearing farms: thus, 'a convergence between wood and pasture, but not necessarily deer, appears to have been central to the concept encapsulated in a "park"' (Winchester this volume).

The aim of this volume, as stated in the Preface, is to draw attention to a range of recent work on the medieval park and, in so doing, signal a number of potential avenues for future research. It is significant that, as the reader will note, in the essays brought together here there are sometimes subtle differences in interpretation or emphasis. The origins of the English park, the precise status of parks within the medieval landscape, the medieval concept of the park, the different regimes of parkland, the regional character of the park and park development all await further explanation and discussion. But whatever differences in emphasis are apparent between individual contributors, this volume serves to highlight that the potential benefits to be gained from further work, be it local, national, historical, archaeological or ecological, are many and varied. In 1953, towards the end of his pioneering discussion of relic parkland, O. G. S. Crawford noted that 'virtually nothing has been done' to elucidate the study of parks in England (Crawford 1953, 196). Fifty years on, the cumulative efforts of a range of scholars have changed the situation considerably and it is to be hoped that this volume not only reflects the results of five decades of research, but also helps to stimulate a further stage in the historiography of the subject.

PART ONE

Approaches to
The Medieval Park

CHAPTER ONE

The Sociology of Park Creation in Medieval England

S. A. Mileson

On 31 October 1302 a small delegation of men, including sub-escheator Nicho-las de Wedergrave, took seisin of Huntington Castle (Hereford.) and went hunting in the castle park (TNA:PRO C145/61, No. 1, m.6; *CIM 1219–1307*, 508–10). Their task at Huntington was to complete a formal take-over of Humphrey de Bohun's estates and obtain the fealty of the tenants for their royal master, Edward I. Humphrey's father, who had died a few years previ-ously, had been one of Edward's chief opponents and the marriage between the old earl's son and Edward's daughter, Elizabeth of Rhuddlan, and the entail of lands associated with it, was an important part of the king's efforts to link the great fiefs to the royal family. This was a policy aimed at enrich-ing himself and his kin, but was also, necessarily, an assertion of royal power (*DNB*, vol. 2, 771; McFarlane 1973, 261–7). Given these circumstances, the deputies' hunting foray may seem a purely incidental activity, perhaps even a rather frivolous one, but, according to an unsigned report written by one of them, it was actually carefully conceived with this larger situation in mind. As the writer put it to the king: 'because there is a fine ('beau') park, we hunted barren does ('deymes baraignes') therein the better to publish and solemnise your lordship ('seigneurie') and seisin before the tenants and people of the country' (Figure 3).[1]

Such a record of an individual hunt is rare enough in itself, but this epi-sode is lent particular interest by its apparent use as a theatrical vehicle for propaganda. Here we seem to have a carefully thought-out attempt to use a game reserve to reinforce the king's new control over a power-centre of one of his great tenants-in-chief, a place made more significant by its position on the edge of the Welsh March, where Edward had striven to underline his authority in the 1290s (Davies 1987, 377–9). Beyond the specific circum-stances, this hunt also seems to be highly suggestive about the more general symbolic role of parks and hunting within medieval society: it appears to fit in well with the modern idea that part of the motivation for the creation and maintenance of parks in the Middle Ages was the desire to assert or reinforce lordship and high social standing – or, to put it simply, that parks were status symbols.

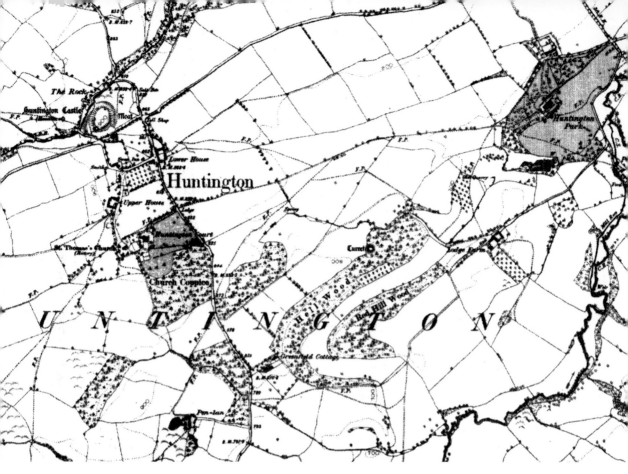

On the other hand, for all its potential implications for the social meaning of parks and hunting, this case has its share of complexities. The idea that hunting in fine and public style within a park might signify lordship is plainly expressed, but even if this hunt really was a planned effort to demonstrate royal power (rather than an administrators' jolly), we cannot be sure how far it would actually have carried real social resonance for those who witnessed it. The outcome of the hunting trip also suggests that creating the desired impression may well have been far from straightforward: in the event, the party did not manage to catch any deer, 'but only took a hare in returning to the castle'. The whole exercise thus seems to have been a flop, and perhaps rather an embarrassing one given the kind of message about royal power that these men were apparently trying to put across. And quite what should be made of the reference to barren does is unclear. Was it anticipating the accusation that they had been heedless about preserving the deer herd? Or was there some other more symbolic meaning, clearer to a medieval audience than to a modern one?

These kinds of questions and uncertainties are symptomatic of the difficulties which surround our understanding of the cultural role of medieval parks. Some recent work has begun to develop a more nuanced and sophisticated approach to the meanings that contemporaries from various social groups may have vested in parks and the hunting and other activities that went on within

FIGURE 3.
Huntington Castle, with the medieval park to the south-east.
HEREFORDSHIRE SMR

their bounds (Marvin 1999; Johnson 2002; Herring 2003; Liddiard 2005). An important aspect of this has been to investigate how ordinary people – apparently the mainstay of the audience at Huntington – may have looked on reserves which so often interfered with their traditional land uses. Yet the central issue of how far park creation was informed by conscious efforts to project high status still remains uncertain. The idea of parks as status symbols remains in many ways incompletely articulated, having been more often asserted than argued in depth, and the heavy emphasis on status assertion in some more general historical accounts can appear somewhat simplistic and lacking in explanatory power (*cf.* Birrell 1992, 126). Some of the more pragmatic uses to which parks were put seem to have little to do with display and this, in turn, may raise questions about the significance of status in the initial decision to impark. How, it might be asked, did status assertion relate to the range of possible motivations influencing park-makers, from the enhancement of hunting opportunities to the control of woods and pastures and, perhaps, the facilitation of their economic exploitation?

One of the most significant barriers to a clearer understanding of the social role of parks is that the sociological context of park-making remains only superficially explored, especially when compared with the much greater volume of work devoted to uncovering the form, utilisation and landscape setting of parks themselves. The people behind parks – those kings and lords who actually had them created – clearly ought to be close to the heart of any attempt to understand these important features of the medieval countryside, yet many questions about these men and women (mainly men) remain unanswered. While the broad outlines of the distribution of park ownership are fairly well established, the extent to which this ownership moved down the landowning scale, and precisely when, remains open to debate. More significantly, active park-makers have seldom if ever been looked at as a group to try to discern whether they shared any common characteristics which might help explain their motivations. This chapter offers a fresh examination of the proposed link between parks and status assertion, looking more closely at park-makers themselves.

The ideation of the park as status symbol

The medieval perception of the park as a status symbol has long been accepted as one of those firmly established historical 'facts', and the repetition of this idea has done a great deal to shape modern thinking about these enclosures (Chisholm 1911, 924; Rowley 1986, 129; Dyer 1994, 20; Harriss 2005, 154, 225). Indeed, an emphasis on display has underpinned almost all comments made about the social character of parks and park-making, no doubt because it appears to offer an overarching explanatory tool encompassing other, more particular, motivations. The supposed status-reinforcing quality of parks has been seen as an attraction for all sorts of individuals, including kings and great lords, although it is often thought to have been especially important to social climbers and parvenus, who may have had a special interest in asserting their high standing through the adoption of a particular lifestyle (Cantor and Hatherly 1979, 78; Bond 1994, 134, 139; Carpenter 1992, 180; Williamson and Bellamy 1987, 70–1; Liddiard 2005, 106–7; Britnell 1997, 192–3; Richardson 2005, 14; Harriss 2005, 225). A preoccupation with status assertion is particularly evident in the field of landscape studies, where scholars have increasingly focused on the apparent integration of parks with castles and manor houses to create a kind of extended stage for gracious living and conspicuous consumption (Richardson this volume).

This concern with display tends to be reinforced by much modern historical, art-historical and anthropological literature, which posits the reinforcement of social standing through the acquisition and use of expensive possessions and the pursuit of activities closely associated with high-status social groups (Blockmans and Janse 1999; Coss and Keen 2002). Parks have been explicitly linked to other possessions interpreted at least partly as status symbols, such as tombs and chantry chapels, with their strong chivalric imagery (at times taken up by those with limited claims to significant military service), and, above all, castles and houses themselves and their associated seigneurial features, such as ponds, dovecotes, orchards and warrens (Carpenter 1992, 225–34, 240–1; Coulson 2003, 74–7, 83, 85; Liddiard 2000b, 182–3; Dyer 1994, 110–11; Coss 1991, 157–8). It has even been suggested that royal permission to make a park, encapsulated in permanent and tangible form in a charter or letter patent, was a sought-after recognition of status, something which might in turn imply a parallel with the supposed cachet of receiving licence to fortify a residence (Cantor and Hatherly 1979, 79; Coulson 1982, 70–1).

The perceived connection between status concerns and park-making has been given added depth and sophistication where it has been fed into larger analyses of the nature, formation and growing stratification of the medieval aristocracy. For instance, certain key periods have been suggested in which the role of parks as status symbols was likely to have been particularly important, especially to groups or individuals newly self-conscious about their social status. Some historians have linked the apparent emergence of more complex 'designed landscapes' around the residences of great lords, often incorporating parks, in the second quarter of the twelfth century with a competitive reaction engendered by the challenge of 'new men' to the more established aristocracy (Liddiard 2005, 67–8). On a broader level, it has been suggested that knights created parks as part of their assertion of aristocratic credentials in the later twelfth and thirteenth centuries, providing them with places to hunt in emulation of greater lords in their wide forests. This may be seen as part of the same process of 'social diffusion', illustrated by knights adopting heraldic devices and improving their residences in the same period (Crouch 1992, 309–10; Coss 2003, 34–8).

On the other hand, many accounts of the later Middle Ages would seem to indicate that the later fourteenth and fifteenth centuries were in fact the time when parks truly came into their own as markers of high standing (Britnell

1997, 192; Harriss 2005, 154, 225). The post-Black Death period has, after all, often been characterised as one of social flux, witnessing the emergence of a new social order as old barriers were broken down (Du Boulay 1970, 66–7; Bennett 1987, 19–39; Rigby 1995, 195–205; Harriss 2005, 240, 242). Such an atmosphere could well have created particular concerns about status. The gentry in particular may have felt themselves faced by the prospect of social competition from increasingly literate and self-confident landowning burgesses and yeomen, and within their own ranks there was ever-greater concern to distinguish between members, with the addition of a new bottom rung, the gentleman. As fourteenth- and fifteenth-century sumptuary laws demonstrate, those who sought to protect their social standing feared that others were using expensive possessions, clothes and food to assert greater distinction than was their due; at the same time, the very emergence of more complex hierarchies of dress and manners provided a tool for the sophisticated social climber (Lachaud 2002, 119–23). The legislation of 1390 which attempted to restrict participation in hunting appears as the same kind of attempted social 'closure' (Rigby 1995); guides to proper manners, dress and hunting etiquette show a keenness to emulate accepted modes of gentle behaviour. The fact that rising labour costs and reduced agricultural profits made parks more costly to construct and maintain may only have served to attach greater prestige to their possession.

Looking for status

The perception of a strong and developing relationship between the act of park-making and the desire to proclaim high social standing does seem to be supported by some of the features of parks themselves. It is notable, for instance, that the park could be an impressive physical presence in the landscape. The sheer length of many park banks struck some contemporaries: the fifteenth-century antiquary John Rous seems to have been impressed by the length of the park wall at Woodstock (Oxon), which he believed was already seven miles in circuit in Henry I's time (Hearne 1745, 138). In the mid-thirteenth century, one of Earl Warenne's Yorkshire parks was said to have a circuit of five leagues (Illingworth and Caley 1812 and 1818, vol. i, 113). The larger gentry parks might also have perimeters of several miles. Such an enclosure would have demonstrated a considerable degree of social control and authority, providing an instantly recognisable sign of the wealth and lifestyle priorities of the owner, evident not least to the locals who were tasked to build or maintain a reserve which effectively kept large areas of woodland and pasture beyond communal control (Bettey 2000, 37). Walled or fenced park boundaries were substantial and would probably have reminded the viewer of castle defences and the kind of control and organisation of space that these signified. Indeed, where the park surrounded a residence it effectively became its outer perimeter curtilage: in a well-known passage from the late fourteenth-century Gawain poem, the narrator speaks of the defensive ditches of Bertilak's admirable castle in almost the same breath as he mentions the surrounding park's palisade of close-set spikes (Barron 1988, 72–3). Parks often had several gates and the main one was likely to be large, like the 'great gate' described in 1250 at 'Rigge' park, King's Somborne (Hants) (MCO King's Somborne 76). Such entrances might be approached across bridges or have smaller wicker gates set inside, in this way further resembling castle entrances (Fowler 1937, 116–17; Slade and Lambrick 1990–2, vol. 1, 299–300). By the end of the Middle Ages park gates seem to have reached an apogee of formalisation, as with Henry VII's crenellated gates at Clarendon (Wilts.) or the still extant castellated stone 'Prior's Gate' at the abbey park at Peterborough (Northants), constructed *c*.1510 (Richardson 2005, 116; Bond 2004, 176).

Impressive boundaries, close internal ordering and physical and symbolic association with castles seem likely to have been evocative of power. It may perhaps be plausible, then, that medieval park creators thought in a somewhat similar way to the late seventeenth-century agriculturalist John Houghton, who, although he disliked parks as uneconomic, recognised that they brought their owners certain advantages, in that 'they make or preserve a grandeur, and cause them to be respected by their poorer neighbours' (Thomas 1983, 202) (Figure 4). But of all the characteristics of parks, it was hunting and attitudes towards hunting which seem likely to have been crucial in projecting status (Mileson 2005a). Hunting has never been a socially neutral pastime – if such a thing could ever exist – even when a wide cross-section of society has participated. Anthropological studies suggest a recurring pattern in which hunting is a means of integrating and ordering communities as well as gathering food (Lee 1997, 252–3; Dean 2001). The hunting of larger game is particularly significant, since it usually requires group participation. In more complex societies, hunting seems to have involved a range of status-reinforcing rituals, for instance those centring on the dismembering of the quarry (Sykes this volume). Leadership of the hunt and possession of hunt objects seem likely to have allowed individuals to assert authority and gain prestige. In medieval England great men sometimes presided over grand hunts, bringing out large numbers of tenants and others to assist (Orme 1992; Lapsley 1905). Such hunts helped to cement social relations within communities, and not just between lord and non-gentle tenants: men of knightly status might act as huntsmen for greater lords, and nobles for the king (Roberts 1988; Baillie-Grohman 1904). Regular involvement in hunting was a way of demonstrating the possession of extensive leisure time, a traditional aristocratic characteristic. This is brought home by an anonymous late thirteenth-century poem, 'Contempt of the World', where the narrative voice, apparently that of a non-aristocrat, sees the worldly lives of the elite, including their hunting and hawking, as the source of their damnation (Davies 1964, 56–9).

Medieval kings and aristocrats did not just take a leading role in hunting, they also tried to preserve and control it, in forests and other hunting reserves, and this linked the hunt more directly with the question of authority. From at least the Carolingian period kings had claimed particular powers over hunting and a subject's possession of a hunting reserve represented the

FIGURE 4.
Merdon Park, Hursley,
Hampshire (1588).
The park, first recorded
in the early thirteenth
century, spread out
from the twelfth-
century palace of the
bishop of Winchester.
The palace had been
created on the site of
an earlier motte and
bailey, itself raised over
an Iron Age hillfort.
HCCAHBR 25400,
25401, 25404; image
used with permission
of IBM UK Limited

sharing of some portion of what has been termed the royal 'charisma' (Wickham 1994, 160). Providing hunting opportunities and distributing game meat
strengthened social ties, both vertical and horizontal (Greenway and Sayers
1989, 26; Roberts 1988, 71; CCR 1302–7, 21; Cox 1905, 193–5; Watkins 1993,
23). Parks themselves could be temporarily loaned out, giving other aristocrats
the chance to hunt in fine style. Venison could not be readily purchased, but
could only be obtained through hunting (legitimately or illegitimately) or
as a gift from the owner of a forest or a park; it was much sought after, for
celebrations and special occasions, by those who did not have it (Rackham
1986, 135; Birrell 1992, 126; Stamper 1988, 143; Roberts 1988, 72; Woolgar 1999,
115). Being able to supply this meat from one's own preserves was likely to
have been a visible sign of social leadership; simply receiving it showed an
individual's connections.

Occasionally the sources give us a more direct insight into the way parks
and the hunting opportunities they could offer appear as sources of pride
for their owners. Several English kings seem, for instance, to have thought
of their parks as reflections of their power and splendour, as was also the
case with their finest architecture. For example, the context of Henry III's

17

permission for Gaucher de Châtillon to hunt in Elham park (Kent) shows that Henry wanted to show it off (Coulson 1979, 75). The proposed park visit was to follow on from a tour given by the constable of Dover to demonstrate the nobility ('nobilitas') of the castle, a few miles away. Henry clearly wanted to impress Gaucher and thought that his deer-filled park at Elham would help to do so. In the later fifteenth century Edward IV's hospitality for the visiting Flemish nobleman Louis de Bruges had a distinctly ostentatious edge and much of the focus was on the delights of hunting in his Little Park at New Windsor (Anon. 1836). Louis had played host to Edward during his recent exile in the Low Countries and the English king, besides being grateful, was no doubt keen to convey a more suitably regal image than would have been possible in his straitened circumstances abroad.

Troubling the status symbol paradigm

It seems entirely plausible, then, that parks played a part in concerns about familial and individual image – concerns which, after all, have been seen as influencing many aspects of medieval aristocratic life. There seems to be little doubt that display helped to reinforce power: a fairly ostentatious, open-handed lifestyle was seen as a necessary part of a lord's standing or 'worship' (Carpenter 1992, 198–211, 245). The desire to demonstrate a suitably aristocratic lifestyle was given a sharper edge, no doubt, by the fact that there was a degree of fluidity within, and on the fringes of, landed society throughout the period. The reality of who held power, land and wealth in particular localities was liable to shift (Crouch 1996), and individuals' changing fortunes made image and the projection and assertion of social leadership significant, especially for the ambitious parvenu, but also, presumably, for the more established aristocrat.

Nonetheless, as many historians have recognised, understandings of the medieval aristocracy which focus on social mobility and the significance of display have their problems and limitations; and in the same way the link between the desires for a park and for social recognition has to be kept in perspective. It must be remembered that possessions, pomp and circumstance were not the ultimate foundation of social standing. Kings, after all, did not rely on fine possessions to demonstrate their authority. Rather, they carried in their crown and person a power and prestige that stemmed from their acknowledged and divinely sanctioned role as leaders and representatives of their people (Watts 1996, 16ff.). If the king had many fine houses, wide forests and expensively enclosed parks this may have been more because he enjoyed a certain lifestyle than because he consciously acquired them to impress with his power (for all that he might like to show them off occasionally). The same might have been true among the nobility, whose standing and prestige was hardly open to question and came from their great landholdings and power to resolve disputes and provide leadership. Status concerns might seem more plausibly influential lower down, but they were not necessarily paramount.

It might also be suggested that, since high status was not a finite commodity, the degree of competition for recognition can be exaggerated.

Just as significantly, the contemporary evidence for parks as status symbols is generally sparse and rather intractable, and calls for cautious interpretation. Few medieval documentary sources make any kind of direct comment on parks in terms of what they might have suggested to contemporaries about their owners or how these individuals wanted to be seen by others. Romances and other literary texts provide a suggestive ambience, but one which requires careful interpretation. Similar caution is required when treating the landscape record, where much, necessarily, has to be reconstructed from very incomplete data. Although the work of the last twenty years has shown how parks seem to have been used to offset residences from a very early period, it still remains unclear quite how commonly parks were carefully integrated with houses and other features in any particular period or locality. Besides the issue of distinguishing organised planning from piecemeal development, a great deal of detailed fieldwork and mapping remains to be done before this discussion can be put on a quantitative footing. But, more fundamentally, even where parks and houses were in close proximity, we must question whether this was primarily intended to make a visual statement, or whether other factors were at play, such as the use of marginal farming land, as at Castle Rising (Norfolk), or the creation of a space for retreat and privacy as much as ostentation, as appears to have been part of Henry I's intention at Woodstock.

The part that status concerns may have played in park-making also has to be set alongside the popularity of hunting as a leisure activity. It might be argued that a good deal of the motivation for park creation was often about the pleasure derived from having hunting facilities on hand; if this showed the owner's power over the use of the landscape and helped him to entertain in a more impressive manner, then that was all the better. Particular features of parks can be interpreted rather differently too, such as their boundaries. Their main purpose – keeping deer inside the park – actually ensured that park banks would often have been less impressive from the *outside* than some larger wood banks, since their ditches were usually internal rather than external. And if parks were such status symbols, it is perhaps rather odd that at any one time quite a number were likely to be in a poor state of repair, with faulty perimeters, depleted deer herds and ill-tended woods and pastures. As estate accounts and inquisitions *post mortem* demonstrate, where lords' fortunes or residential patterns shifted, they were as willing to allow some of their parks to fall into decay as certain of their manor houses and castles, or to see their purpose shift towards stock-raising or wood production.

These kinds of objections and apparent limitations to the status symbol approach clearly cannot be simply brushed aside. The question is how they can be reconciled with the case for status assertion outlined above. As suggested at the outset, one way forward seems to be through an examination of the individuals who actually owned parks and, more especially, those responsible for their creation.

Park ownership

Park ownership was focused at the top of the aristocratic scale and was extremely limited towards its lower end. Certainly no individual below the rank of manorial lord would have had the resources to create a park, but, equally, many manorial lords did *not* possess one. The king was by far the greatest single owner of parks, having many scores of them at any one time; some were ancestral creations, others acquired as part of estates escheated through failure of heirs or forfeited for treason. By the thirteenth century the greatest earldom, Lancaster, had several dozen parks and others, like Arundel and Norfolk, had fifteen to twenty; richer bishoprics like Winchester, Canterbury and Durham had approximately twenty and lesser ones at least a small number; greater monastic houses, like Bury St Edmunds (Suffolk) had several (Cantor and Hatherly 1979, 77–8; Roberts 1988, 67; Cantor 1983). Presumably most of the approximately 200 members of the greater baronage in the thirteenth century had at least one park, and similarly most of the 100 or fewer parliamentary peers of the later fourteenth and fifteenth century. Below this high level things are less certain, but there was a clear disparity between the number of parks and the number of honourable landowners.

The situation in the early fourteenth century gives an idea of this gap, even in the period when parks had probably reached their maximum numbers. At this time there were around 11,000 lay landowners, of whom some 3,000, the nobility and greater gentry, had property worth £20 or more a year. In addition, there were 843 ecclesiastical lords: archbishops, bishops and heads of religious houses (Given-Wilson 1987, 55, 69–72; Campbell 2005, 12–13). According to one estimate, which may be rather high, there could have been as many as 3,200 parks in existence at this time (Rackham 1986, 123). These raw figures suggest that only one in three or four landowners could have had parks, but the situation was in fact considerably more closely restricted. As explained above, many of these parks belonged to the king and greater lay and ecclesiastical lords: one estimate suggests that they owned at least 50 per cent of the total, although this figure is derived from a national total that underestimates overall numbers, perhaps slightly to the detriment of lesser-known parks belonging to more obscure individuals (Cantor and Hatherly 1979, 78). Nonetheless, in *c.*1300, leaving aside the king, great lords, bishops and the heads of the greater monasteries, there may have been something like 1,500 parks between over 11,000 landowners. The majority of these parks would have been owned by the greater or 'county' gentry and, to a lesser extent, religious houses, with far fewer parks in the hands of lesser gentry. But even among the greater gentry, park owners would have been a minority: perhaps no more than one in five. In other periods there would have been fewer parks to go round, especially in the twelfth century, when the substantial growth in park numbers was only at its beginning.

Although it is often said that park ownership extended down the landowning scale in the later medieval period, the situation did not actually change that drastically in the fourteenth or fifteenth centuries (Dyer 1991, 236; Harriss 2005, 154, 225). Great lords continued to own a disproportionate number of parks. Correspondence from John of Gaunt, duke of Lancaster, by far the greatest lay landowner in the late fourteenth century after the king, reveals that in the 1370s he possessed at least forty-six parks (Armitage-Smith 1911). At lower levels, park ownership remained much less common: as before, only the wealthier gentry could generally hope to afford the costs of creation and maintenance. In Staffordshire, for example, at least seventy parks are known by 1350, but 43 per cent belonged to a mere five leading landowners (Birrell 1990–1, 35). Over the next 150 years the overall number of parks in England dropped somewhat, perhaps by around 30 per cent. The circle of park owners must have been reduced as a result, and perhaps disproportionately so among the lesser landowners, since greater lords probably tended to have the resources to maintain their parks. Nor, in this period as in any other, was it easy to acquire full possession of a park via a lease. Although lords might farm out the profit of parks or appoint gentry or yeomen officials who had some control over them, it was rare for lords to rent out active parks in their entirety. In the later Middle Ages, although many lords leased out the great majority of their demesnes, they often still retained their parks (Roberts 1988, 81; Lomas 1978, 345; MCO Otterbourne 72).

This continued exclusivity was the result of the cost of creating and maintaining a park, which set certain limits on the use of these enclosures as an assertion of status by the parvenu. But, at the same time, this may have been part of what attracted the wealthier among the socially ambitious to try to acquire their own parks. While few parks were available for rent or purchase and only the better-established man was likely to attract an heiress with a park, there was little to stop anyone creating their own once they had sufficient control over the land on which they wished to do so and enough funds or labour services to carry out construction. For the man who wished to assert his high standing and wealth these expenses were perhaps worth meeting. We might assume that park-making would be particularly attractive for individuals who had newly risen up the ranks of the aristocracy, or those of a mercantile background who used their wealth to buy into country landowning and manorial lordship.

The identity and careers of park-makers

Many hundreds of individuals were involved in establishing, extending and redesigning parks throughout the Middle Ages. Unfortunately, in the majority of cases very little is known about their activities and in many instances even the identity of these individuals may be a matter of speculation. Detailed research can sometimes reveal more, but all too often the documentary sources required for precise information are lacking, especially outside some of the more richly documented royal and ecclesiastical estates. This necessarily means that it is only possible to discuss a relatively small proportion of park-makers, with the sample being biased towards those who obtained royal licences and those whose parks attracted particular contemporary comment or opposition. Both groups, however, we may suspect of being somewhat atypical.

Park licensees perhaps call for particular comment, since they are often the individuals who can be most easily identified as probable park-makers (Mileson 2005a). There is the potential problem that park licences do not always coincide with actual park creation, but sometimes represent the legitimisation of existing parks or merely mark the intention to impark. In fact, however, the majority of park licences do seem to relate fairly closely to actual park-making or at least refurbishment and restocking with deer. The motivation for obtaining a licence is also an issue worthy of comment, given that complying with legal formalities was scarcely automatic for medieval landowners. In other words, it might be thought that park licensees were those who felt more need for recognition or, perhaps, protection from the jealousy of their neighbours, like the parvenus who were supposedly keenest to acquire crenellation licences. However, leaving aside this interpretation of crenellation licensing, with which not everyone would agree, it seems safe to say that park licensing revolved around compliance with royal franchisal rights over forests, which were enforced, albeit variously (*TLS* 13 June 1997, 21). This creates a straightforwardly pragmatic motivation for licensing, with other factors being secondary.

It can be said at once that the link between park-making and social ambition was not always clear-cut. Not all those who rose in wealth and social position made parks: many of the gentry did very well from some combination of royal service, the law, marriage, the profits of landholding, even trade, without ever making or acquiring a park. More significantly, not all of those who did make parks were parvenus. Some lesser park-makers seem to have been fairly typical members of families of longstanding and relatively stable wealth and position in landed society. Of course, these men may have wished to augment their individual and family image by making a park, but this is difficult to prove.

Nonetheless, there are clear common themes in the careers of substantial numbers of known park-makers: rising social standing; wider improvements to and expansion of family estates; and emulation. Rising wealth and social standing is a frequently recurring part of the background of park creators, and this is evident even in very early periods. Early twelfth-century Warwickshire provides an interesting example: here the arch 'new man' Geoffrey de Clinton, who owed his position entirely to royal favour, had established a castle, priory and park at Kenilworth by *c.*1125, only three or four years after Henry I had made him sheriff of the county and installed him as a great lord there, more or less in opposition to the earl of Warwick (Crouch 1982, 114–17, n.25).

Succeeding centuries and other areas demonstrate similar trends. In the thirteenth, fourteenth and fifteenth centuries a substantial number of park licensees were royal servants from families of relatively minor backgrounds, making a name and wealth for themselves. They included men like William Brewer, Hubert de Burgh (newly earl of Kent) and Stephen de Segrave in the thirteenth century; William Montagu, William Clinton (both of whom were ennobled) and John Molyns in the fourteenth; and John Norbury, Sir Andrew Ogard (a naturalised Dane) and William, lord Hastings, in the fifteenth. Prominent among identifiable thirteenth-century park creators in Bedfordshire was Paulinus Pever, who rose from obscure origins to become a steward of the royal household. In the fourteenth century, many park licensees were knights who had served with Edward III, some of whom, like Sir Thomas Breadstone, had made large profits in France. In the next century, royal household knights and esquires were particularly prominent, above all those who were greatly enriched by the free-flowing royal patronage of the 1440s. Across the period there were also a number of clerks of fairly humble origins come good through royal service, most obviously men like Robert Burnell, John Droxford and Adam Moleyns. Still other park creators were men who had increased their family wealth through advantageous marriages, like John de la Mare or William Dives. Another notable feature was the creation of parks or the acquisition of park licences by individuals at times when their careers were reaching new heights, like Hugh de Courtenay, who seems to have created his park at Okehampton (Devon) around the time he was made earl of the county in 1297, or Michael de la Pole, who, while Lord Chancellor, received a licence to impark at Wingfield and elsewhere in Suffolk just a few months before being made earl of Suffolk in August 1385 (Austin 1978, 196; Fryde 1988). A particular feature of the fifteenth century was the new prominence of the merchant park-maker who had recently bought into landed society, especially in south-east England. Of course, some aristocrats had had trading interests in earlier centuries, but it was only in this period that those whose background was primarily grounded in commerce seem to have been actually creating parks in sizeable numbers (Mileson 2005b, 32).

A closer look at individual localities in the late fifteenth century seems to do much to confirm this link between social rising and park-making. Warwickshire provides an especially interesting case study, suggesting that here at least there was an ever-closer correlation between social ambition and park construction (Mileson 2005b, 32–3). Many of the imparkers in this county were men who were increasing or had already dramatically raised their personal and family status. Further detailed studies of other counties are required, but it is notable that in Yorkshire, although more established lords and gentry made many of the new parks, the park-makers included social risers like Sir Guy Fairfax, justice of the king's bench and lawyer come good (or perhaps his son), and William, lord Conyers, who moved from one of the top knightly families of Yorkshire to the threshold of the peerage. In late fifteenth-century Norfolk, too, several new men made parks (Beresford 1954, 59–60; Pollard 1990, 90–1; Liddiard 2000a, 110).

As suggested already, the second pronounced feature of park-makers was their tendency to be individuals who were carrying out substantial improvements to their estates, above all major building works on their residences and remodelling of their local churches. This link between parks and building or rebuilding projects can be seen on the grandest scale in the activities of the Crown. In and around Windsor royal residential building coincided with the development and extension of parkland from a very early date. This included Henry III's creation of a manor house in the Great Park in the 1240s; Edward II's construction of new manor houses and extension of the parkland; and Edward III's massive rebuilding of 1357–68, accompanied by substantial imparkment and the establishment and renovation of further park lodges (Astill 2002, 10–11; Harwood 1929, 124; CPR 1364–7, 95–6; CPR 1367–70, 136). The link between building and imparking was close at Clarendon and other royal estates (Richardson this volume).

But the same feature is just as visible with non-royal park-makers. Geoffrey de Clinton's park seems to have been set up along with his castle and priory as part of a package (Liddiard 2000b, 183), and the same pattern was repeated time and again. Richard of Cornwall built the castle at Oakham (Rutland), where he extended the park; Hugh de Courtenay built a stunning new domestic range at Okehampton; the Sir John Stonor who probably created the park at Stonor in the earlier fourteenth century was also responsible for major building works; Sir John Foxley set up a manor house at his new manor–park complex at Puckmere (Berks.) in the same period. The list could be greatly extended: William Cantilupe at Eaton Bray (Beds.) in the early thirteenth century; Pever at Toddington (Beds.) in the middle of the same century; John Wyard at Stanton Harcourt (Oxon) in the late 1320s; the Beches at La Beche, near Aldworth (Berks.) in the 1330s; and de la Pole at Wingfield, to name but a few. In the north-west of England in the fourteenth century a host of gentry were responsible for building tower houses and castles and providing them with parks.

In the fifteenth century, the connection between building (or rebuilding) and imparking was perhaps even stronger: John, duke of Bedford at Fulbrook (Warks.); Sir William Lovell at Minster Lovell, where he seems to have been responsible for the rebuilding of the church; William, lord Hastings, across Leicestershire, the county Edward IV had set him up to lead; William de la Pole and duchess Alice at Ewelme (site of the duchess's exceptionally fine tomb), to give a few examples. Indeed, most of the courtier park-makers of the mid to later fifteenth century were also setting up fine new houses in the same places: increasingly by the fifteenth century licences for parks were combined with licences to crenellate residences.

Finally we come to the third common feature, emulation or competition relating to parks and other hunting reserves. Emulation of others who owned or were making parks is seldom possible to prove, but circumstantial evidence suggests that it would often have been significant, just as with the building of many fine new castles and houses. Certainly by the fifteenth century the antiquarian John Rous believed that Henry I's imparking at Woodstock led directly to park-making by Henry, earl of Warwick and other lords, following his example (Hearne 1745, 138). Rous's view may well reflect fifteenth-century attitudes more than twelfth-century realities in this particular case, but there is no reason to suppose that such emulation was a new feature in the late Middle Ages (Stephens 1969, 467; Wallsgrove 2004/5, 239). It seems likely, for instance, that Abbot Samson of Bury St Edmunds' park-making in Suffolk in the late twelfth century was motivated by the desire to keep up with other lords who were able to offer their guests good hunting opportunities (Greenaway and Sayers 1989, 26).

In some cases emulation seems to have focused around contact at the centre. This perhaps partly explains the exceptional amount of park licensing among (mainly northern) knights in the 1330s and early 1340s, most of whom were prominently involved in Edward III's military campaigns; among yeomen of the royal household and king's sergeants more generally; and, most obviously, among Henry VI's intimates and ministers in the 1440s (mainly in the home counties). Elsewhere it was probably more local, as in Gloucestershire where several gentry parks seem to have been established following the Clare imparkments at Thornbury in the late thirteenth century (Franklin 1989, 154). A similar situation perhaps existed in north Yorkshire in the later fifteenth century, where Richard of Gloucester's park-making may have acted as a spur to others, and where Sir William Gascoigne received licence to impark within a few years of his fierce rival Sir William Plumpton. Very likely, a lord's leisure pursuits and possessions could inspire his fellows or retainers.

For all the caveats about established lords making parks, this brief study of park-makers does suggest a genuine correlation between park-making and the desire of 'new men' to assert their place within landed society. We need not, of course, be hugely surprised that rising men were more likely to be park-makers – since they were, necessarily, less likely to inherit parks, or even acquire them by marriage – but this, if anything, reinforces the significance of park possession to high status and gracious living. The frequent relationship between park-making and general programmes of building further strengthens the idea of a link with social assertiveness, especially where house and park were conceived as part of a package. Indeed, by the early sixteenth century, some, such as Sir Thomas Cokayne, whose tomb in Ashbourne church (Derbys.) explicitly refers to his house-building and park-making activities, self-consciously presented the establishment of parks as an important part of the furthering of their family names (Mileson 2005b, 33). In this light, we might wonder whether the creation of very large parks in the fifteenth century had a competitive element, as well as reflecting the availability of land in particular areas. The other side of this was that long-established aristocrats were perhaps particularly likely to have seen some new parks of the 1440s and 1450s as the vulgar acquisitions of disreputable upstarts. At any rate, we are not far here from Shakespeare's later idea, put in the mouth of Bolingbroke in *Richard II*, that parks and woods were signs of gentlemanly status; signs, moreover, which required defending, since their destruction could imply a loss of that status (*Richard II*, Act III, Scene I).

Conclusion

Any serious attempt to understand the cultural context of park creation clearly has to take into account considerable complexities. As has been seen, the range of those who created, inherited or acquired parks was wide; their numbers included kings, lay and ecclesiastical lords, gentry, young and old, men and women, well-established landowners and parvenus. If all shared in the same aristocratic cultural world, their priorities and perspectives must have varied considerably. Parks themselves varied too: some were fairly small, others very large; where parks were grouped together in the same area under one owner-ship they sometimes seem to have been used for different purposes. The use owners made of their parks might differ according to their location, size and internal arrangements, as well as being affected by the extent of the lord or lady's estates, their itinerary, leisure interests and estate management priorities (which could change over time). The degree to which parks were subject to agrarian exploitation, such as livestock grazing or wood production, or other complementary uses, such as breeding horses, differed widely between time and place. While some of the functions of parks, such as hunting or providing a landscape setting for a major residence, may seem to be compatible with a purported concern for projecting status and social power, others, like livestock grazing and wood production, appear less obviously related.

Nonetheless, for all this, the strongly distinctive features of parks – the combination of separation of land, deer-rearing and provision of facilities for hunting – suggest the possibility and relevance of a general analysis of social views and functions which incorporates the attempted expression of high standing. The status symbol idea has most to offer when approached through close attention to individual circumstances and particular local landscapes, economies and societies. It is the cumulative delineation of local case studies, informed by a greater awareness of the kind of larger context outlined here, which ought to offer a way forward to a fuller understanding of the social role of the park in the Middle Ages.

Note

1. CIM identifies John de Barham (*recte* Borham), a royal clerk, as the author of the report, but there are no clear grounds for this identification. I am very grateful to Dr John Watts for his helpful comments on a draft of this chapter.

CHAPTER TWO

'The King's Chief Delights': A Landscape Approach to the Royal Parks of Post-Conquest England

Amanda Richardson

> In the north part a grove of diverse trees should be planted [in]
> which wild creatures ... may ... hide. [In] the south ... let a handsome
> palace be built, to which the king or queen may resort ... to ...
> refresh themselves by these joys and solaces ... [H]ares, stags,
> roebucks, rabbits and the like harmless beasts may be put among the
> bushes ... Rows of trees close to the palace ... should run [towards] ...
> the grove ... so that one can see easily ... the animals ... In this
> fashion the palace would be made pleasant (Calkins 1986, 173).

This quote, from Piero de' Crescenzi's 'On the Gardens of Kings and Other
Illustrious and Rich Lords' (*c.*1304–1309), graphically articulates the ideal relationship between a high-status residence and its surroundings – the kind of
planned landscape usually associated, in historiographical terms, with the post-
medieval period (Whyte 2002, 20–1). Although deer parks are not explicitly
mentioned, the recommendations could easily be a blueprint for any number
of parks attached to medieval English royal residences. Crescenzi advised that
the perfect 'pleasure garden' (in any case a flexible term in the fourteenth century) should be 'twenty *jugers* [12.5 acres] or more' (Henisch 2002, 153; Calkins
1986, 173): the size of a small park. It should be surrounded by high walls or
fences, and, like many fourteenth-century and later parks at least, set out to
a compartmentalised scheme, here clearly prized as much for its aesthetic as
its functional properties.

Similar relationships between royal residences and their surroundings were
acknowledged in 1180 when, in the *Dialogue of the Exchequer*, Richard son of
Nigel noted that 'It is in the forests ... that kings' chambers are, and their
chief delights ... there ... they put from them the anxious turmoil [of] the
court, and take a little breath in the free air of nature' (Johnson 1950, 60).
Many royal parks were established, perhaps to underscore the exclusivity and

tranquillity afforded by those chambers, in the century in which Richard wrote his *Dialogue*. Accordingly, in this chapter some of the principal medieval English royal parks are discussed in order to establish how far they were intended as settings for the residences they served.

In the post-Conquest period, the Crown held at least 150 parks at some time or another; a figure that should be balanced against Rackham's well-known calculation of 3,200 in existence by 1300, especially since only around 70 remained in royal hands for any length of time (Bond 1998, 25). It is probably safe to assume that most parks larger than the average 100–300 acres (Bond 1994, 139), in which the elite paradises described above could most easily be sculpted, were royal. Thus, although Ludgershall, Wiltshire (*c*.250 acres), and Odiham, Hampshire (*c*.4 miles circumference), will be mentioned, Clarendon, Wiltshire (*c*.4,300 acres), Guildford, Surrey (*c*.1,670 acres), Windsor, Berkshire (*c*.5,000 acres today) and Woodstock, Oxfordshire (*c*.7 miles circumference), are the focus here. All were very large, and in royal hands from at least the twelfth to the sixteenth century.

The seigneurial deer park is certainly implicit in Crescenzi's layout. John Cummins notes that parks were sculpted according to the 'development of aristocratic preferences' born of the requirements of the hunt (Cummins 2002, 52), and the similarities are striking:

> All [medieval hunting] … required … areas of woodland … dense enough to harbour quarry, [with] denser areas in which the prime harts [might] linger. All … [needed] larger expanses of open terrain … sufficiently free of hindrance to enable pursuit by hunters … [alongside] smaller areas of … thicket (Cummins 2002, 42–3).

There is, here, the important issue of chronology. Crescenzi was writing in the fourteenth century, but he closely adhered to the writings of the German horticultural pioneer Albertus Magnus (1193–1280). As is so often the case with medieval didactic literature, neither suggested anything radically new, describing instead the customary layouts which they saw around them (Calkins 1986, 162–4). Yet nineteenth-century historians attempting to trace back into the Middle Ages the 'evolution of an interest in landscape grounded in art and literature' met with apparent failure (Cahn 1991, 11), perhaps because they tended to foreground administrative documents whose purpose was neither to communicate contemporary culture, nor to describe what was actually *there*. This writer, hoping to locate the sites of vanished park lodges, for example, soon found herself relying almost entirely on field evidence. More pertinently, few medieval park owners were involved in either the compilation or dissemination of documents. Most read and listened to Romance literature, however, and 'it is not outlandish to suppose that … an awareness of the literary … strongly conditioned the delight of the practical' (Cummins 1988, 9).

It is possible to bring a good deal of literary evidence to bear on the relationship between high-status residences and their parkscapes; an example

*'The King's
Chief Delights':
A Landscape
Approach
to the Royal Parks
of Post-Conquest
England*

might be the first sighting of Bertilak's castle in *Gawain and the Green Knight* (*c.*1375–1400):

> … On a promontory above a plateau, penned in by the boughs
> And tremendous trunks of trees, and trenches about;
> The comeliest castle that ever a knight owned,
> It was pitched on a plain, with a park all around,
> Impregnably palisaded with pointed stakes …
> The courteous knight contemplated the castle from one side
> As it shimmered and shone through the shining oaks (Creighton 2002, 68).

Gawain does not see Bertilak's castle alone; he appraises it within its landscape setting. What makes the building 'comely' is its lofty situation, the trees with 'tremendous trunks' (clearly parkland oaks) through which it is glimpsed and the 'impregnable' park pale 'all around'. The park is quite small, and may be compared to the 'little parks' (discussed below) invariably sited below, or adjacent to, seigneurial residences. The same scheme appears in Figure 5. A castle, shining white, occupies a promontory above a 'plateau' (many of *Gawain*'s translators prefer 'laund'). Here are ponds, if not trenches, and 'a park all

FIGURE 5.
Diana the Huntress.
Louise de Savoie Les
échecs amoureux MS
Fr. 143, f.116. French,
late fifteenth-century.
BIBLIOTHÈQUE
NATIONALE DE FRANCE

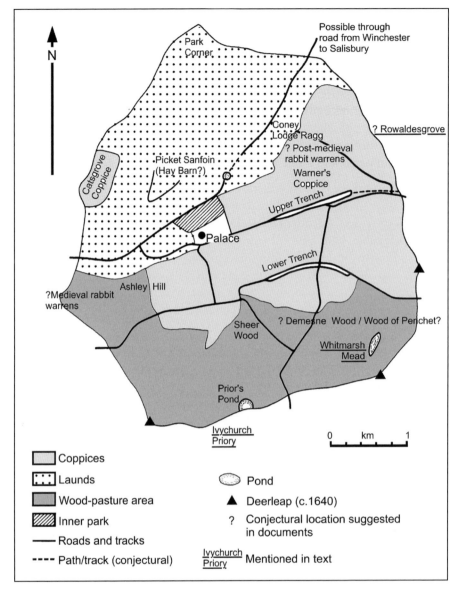

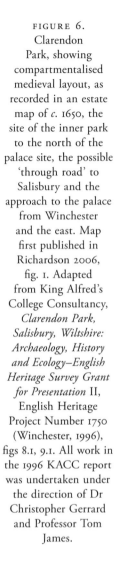

FIGURE 6.
Clarendon
Park, showing
compartmentalised
medieval layout, as
recorded in an estate
map of *c.* 1650, the
site of the inner park
to the north of the
palace site, the possible
'through road' to
Salisbury and the
approach to the palace
from Winchester
and the east. Map
first published in
Richardson 2006,
fig. 1. Adapted
from King Alfred's
College Consultancy,
*Clarendon Park,
Salisbury, Wiltshire:
Archaeology, History
and Ecology–English
Heritage Survey Grant
for Presentation* II,
English Heritage
Project Number 1750
(Winchester, 1996),
figs 8.1, 9.1. All work in
the 1996 KACC report
was undertaken under
the direction of Dr
Christopher Gerrard
and Professor Tom
James.

around' – complete with reclining stag – while bosky scenes form the back-drop. One might also point to images from the *Très Riches Heures du Duc de Berry* to argue for a preference for residences occupying elevated positions and framed by woodland suggestive of wilderness stretching into infinity.

The ideals discussed above can be traced in medieval royal parks. That at Clarendon is a case in point. The park was compartmentalised (Figure 6) with the launds (lawns/grazing) to the north. On the slopes opposite the palace, at least from the early fourteenth century, was a barn from which the deer would be fed hay. The palace, on a scarp, whitewashed and set in woodland, may in the thirteenth century have been on the edge of a smaller, still size-able, park (see below). Ludgershall and Windsor castles also occupied high

*'The King's
Chief Delights':
A Landscape
Approach
to the Royal Parks
of Post-Conquest
England*

ground, viewed against the skyline from their parks, and Woodstock Palace was first glimpsed, from the park's main gate, on a rise surrounded by woodland, just as Clarendon Palace appeared to those entering the park from the west. From the latter two palaces, the wider landscape, comprising launds, stretched northwards into the distance.

Art and literature thus reveal the ideal appearance of high-status medieval landscapes, and it is possible to identify parkscapes in which such principles were apparently reflected. Such sources, however, are now playing an increasing role in the reconstruction of past landscapes, and perhaps we too readily assume that the ideal invariably became reality, consequently reading too much into relict landscape features. Colin Platt (pers. comm.) has recently said as much concerning what he regards as the impulse to claim 'status' as the overriding principle behind both castles and the landscapes in which they sit, with particular reference to the difficulty in ascertaining firm chronological relationships between these various elements. Robert Liddiard, too, has questioned whether parks were actually '"designed" in the modern sense – that is, representing the deliberate intentions of ... a particular lord at a specific point in time' (Liddiard 2005, 119). Stephen Mileson (2005a, 117–23) has cast a critical eye over a range of the more subjective methodologies underpinning many landscape studies, and Matthew Johnson (2002, 44) has highlighted the urge to 'assemble ... evidence to affirm the symbolic aspects of ... landscapes', pointing out that this reinforces anachronistic divisions between the functional and the symbolic. The consensus of these disparate voices is that we should treat more subjective sources with a degree of caution. Accordingly, questions addressed here will be those recently advocated for the study of late medieval parks generally (Mileson 2005a, 122). How many actually surrounded (or were adjacent to) royal buildings? Do they appear to have been deliberately laid out in order to offset those residences, and can chronological relationships between parkscapes and royal houses be discerned?

The landscape approach, in which a monument's surrounding topography is incorporated into its analysis (in preference to single-site-orientated research), is now common practice in archaeology, and increasingly influences the interpretation of historic buildings. Since the late 1990s English Heritage has sought to 'widen the traditional curtilage around its sites and monuments' so that they are seen in a social, artistic or economic context rather than as 'isolated survivors' (Campbell 1999, 128). Accordingly, at Clarendon new English Heritage-funded storyboards on the palace site include an impressionistic spire, conveying spatial relationships between the palace and the city of Salisbury, visible a few miles to the west (Figure 7). Historians of medieval palaces have not, however, tended to see their subject matter in such terms – even where landscape manipulation is the main academic focus. In an otherwise forward-thinking survey of royal gardens, Howard Colvin saw parks as 'primarily for the benefit of the deer ... the park as an extension of a garden, of course [being] far in the future'. This seems an odd statement following, as it does, an account of the balcony constructed in 1354 in order to provide

Edward III's daughter Isabella with a better view over Woodstock Park. 'The record', Colvin tells us, 'is explicit that [the balcony] was built for that purpose' (Colvin 1986, 11).

This emphasis on the building (or precinct) has been typical of writing on medieval palaces. There is one reference to 'deerparks' in Tom James's index (1990), but ten to 'gardens', while three years later John Steane (1993, 117–22) devoted a whole chapter to 'Palace and Castle Gardens' but again neglected wider landscapes – although his *Archaeology of Power* (2001, 272–5) does include four pages on parks and lodges. Most surprisingly, Graham Keevil's archaeological publication on palaces (2000) carries just one paragraph on 'palaces and landscapes'. To be fair, most of these authors, whose foci were the buildings, were working from old excavations which took little or no account of the landscape context. Nevertheless, the idea that the medieval period lacked any landscapes in which 'certain social strata emphasised and transmitted their own social role …' (Cosgrove quoted in Whyte 2002, 20–1) has been both influential and tenacious.

Despite this, the influence of Romance literature in the worldview of medieval royalty is frequently put forward regarding 'Rosamund's Bower'

*'The King's
Chief Delights':
A Landscape
Approach
to the Royal Parks
of Post-Conquest
England*

at Woodstock (e.g. Colvin 1986, 19) and the Park of Hesdin, France, begun by Count Robert II of Artois and completed by 1306. This park fanned out northwards over 2.5 miles from its castle, and comprised three sections: gardens beneath the residence; woods and hills at its centre; and in its north, from 1293, *Li mares* ('the marsh'), encompassing valleys, rivers and fountains, with a substantial pavilion, reached by a bridge, at its epicentre (van Buren 1986, 129, 117–9). Hesdin has been convincingly interpreted as a deliberate manifestation of the settings of the medieval Romance, and is cited as 'proof' that parks were consciously sculpted (Cummins 2002, 46). Yet palace historiography generally gives the impression that it, and Rosamund's Bower, were exceptions, rather than the rule.

Parks as settings for royal residences: some observations

FIGURE 7.
Clarendon
reconstruction drawing
from the garden
terrace storyboard,
looking west. The royal
apartments (queen's
left; king's centre)
and the Great Hall
overlook the garden
terrace seen here,
below which is a steep
scarp down to the
valley from which the
northern launds rise.
Visitors would see the
palace above scarp and
terrace dominating
the skyline, backed by
trees, and would have
to climb the hill to
the western entrance
having traversed the
park below. The Inner
Park, including the
palace footprint, is
c. 26 acres compared
with Crescenzi's 12.5.
Note Salisbury
Cathedral spire to
the west (see Figure
6 and 13, and James
and Gerrard 2007,
49–54). Drawing
and copyright Philip
Marter, reproduced by
kind permission.

It has been suggested that some pre-Conquest deer enclosures survived as parks in the Anglo-Norman landscape, and that such continuity may have been widespread. For example, Edward the Confessor held estates rendering the farm of one night at Broughton (Hants) and at Wilton (Wilts.), near Clarendon, and a close connection existed between night's farm central manors and post-Conquest royal forests (Lavelle 2001, 114, 173). Close to the southern boundary of Clarendon Park a track linked two further royal estates, Amesbury (Wilts.) and Lyndhurst (Hants), and, as Tim Tatton-Brown has suggested (pers. comm.), Clarendon Park could have been connected to the 'Old Borough' at Alderbury, and its minster. Thus it was an ideal place for a hunting lodge – and indeed it has been claimed that pre-Conquest structures await discovery beneath the later palace (James and Gerrard 2007, 44 and figure 19). Tellingly, those manors closest to the later park were held by royal hunt officials at the time of Domesday (Richardson 2005, 7).

Evidence for other parks is firmer. King Alfred held a royal manor near Guildford in 880, and Stoke by Guildford is recorded as 'within the king's park' (*in parco Regis*) in Domesday Book (Poulton 2005, 5, 149). The West Saxon kings kept a hunting lodge at Old Windsor, adjacent to the later Great Park, and Domesday mentions woodland in 'the king's enclosure' (Roberts 1997, 249). A park may also have existed at Woodstock by 1086, since woodland attached to a nearby royal manor was described as 'in the king's defence' (*in defensione regis*), usually taken to imply enclosure – or at least restricted access (Crossley 1990). Thus the parks discussed here all have early origins and longevity: Clarendon, Windsor, Woodstock and Guildford remained in royal ownership into the early modern period, but they did not remain static: many were enhanced throughout the later Middle Ages. Windsor and Clarendon, for example, were embellished and greatly enlarged in the early fourteenth century against a backdrop of famine and murrain, and I have argued elsewhere that such major works on park pales and earthworks may have led to contemporary criticism of Edward II (1307–1327) as a 'hedger and ditcher' (Richardson 2006).

Palace	Size of park in acres	Position in relation to park	Inner park? (plus position)	Nearest major settlement
Clarendon	4292	At centre (at its south, 13thC?)	Yes; immediately below to north	Salisbury to W (from c.1220); village of Pitton to E
Windsor	Great Park 1364 under Henry III, 3650 in 16thC; Little Park c.250 by 1465	Inside Little Park; 5 miles from Great Park	Yes; immediately below to north	New Windsor
Woodstock	7 miles in circumference in 15thC. Today 9 miles circumference	Inside	No	Woodstock
Gillingham	c.4 miles circumference	Inside	No	Gillingham
Ludgershall	North Park 248; South Park 228	Adjacent (protruding) at south of North Park	Yes	Ludgershall
Guildford	1668	Adjacent (outside), across river (lodge at centre of park)	No	Guildford
Eltham	595 (Great Park), 333 (Little Park); 336 (Home Park) in 17thC	Inside	Yes	Village of Eltham

Table 1. Relationships between some medieval royal palaces and their parks

Proximity and position

Table 1 shows that the majority of royal parks discussed here had close spatial relationships with their accompanying residences. The palaces at Clarendon, Eltham (Surrey), Woodstock and Gillingham (Dorset) were all inside their parks. Other palaces, including Ludgershall and Windsor (in relation to the Little Park), were adjacent. This may once have been the case at Clarendon, whose launds, north of the palace, were perhaps the extent of the park under Henry III (1216–1272) and earlier (Paul Everson and David Stocker, pers. comm.). The palace was clearly intended to be viewed from this direction – that is, from the launds and inner park – rather than the approach from the south, from which it is hidden until one is almost upon it.

Of the larger parks under discussion, only Guildford and Windsor Great Park (Figures 8 and 9) were any distance from their residences, possibly due to their pre-Conquest origins. A distinction between castles and palaces is also valid; for example, the 'attention of [Guildford Castle's] Norman builders ... [was not] directed ... to the higher ground but the opposite way', towards the town (Poulton 2005, 134–5). Yet the palace built in the castle's shadow in the early thirteenth century tellingly faced *towards* the park, which was less than a mile away across the river Wey (Poulton 2005, 141). This spatial separation may have been thought unsatisfactory, as the moated lodge inside the park, first recorded in 1318, is clearly one of Mileson's (2005a, 124) 'new homes [erected

*'The King's
Chief Delights':
A Landscape
Approach
to the Royal Parks
of Post-Conquest
England*

in the thirteenth and fourteenth centuries] inside already established parks'
(Figure 8). The lodge was anyway the principal residence after Guildford Castle and Palace went out of use in the late 1390s. In 1369, it had been rebuilt
with a hall, four chambers and a chapel (Poulton 2005, 150; Underwood 2002,
216–17). Edward III had a similar lodge constructed between 1368 and 1375
inside Odiham Park, itself half a mile from the castle, replacing earlier structures documented in 1291–2 and 1332–3 (Roberts 1995, 92). As was the case at
Guildford, it stood near a river, but in this instance was accompanied by a
bridge. Attention had been given to its predecessor's setting in 1332–3, when
the garden was enclosed and furnished with turf benches, demonstrating that
this location was more than functional (Roberts 1995, 100).

Some lodges, like that at Odiham, and another in the park at King's
Langley (Hertfordshire), comprising a hall and one chamber, were fairly modest (Page 1908). Others were not. At Clarendon, where a lodge seems to
have existed under Henry III and whose palace was already at the centre of
the – admittedly enormous – park, the romantically named 'Lodge on the
Laund' was either constructed or substantially rebuilt from 1341 to 1344. Its
name reveals the significance of its landscape surroundings: it almost certainly occupied a high point on the launds opposite the palace, with which
it would have been intervisible (Richardson 2005, 69). References to 'la logge'
in 1354 suggest that Edward III's lodge remained the only such structure in
Clarendon Park, and it may have remained so into the fourteenth century
(Richardson 2005, 70–1). It was ostentatious, faced with the same Tisbury
stone used on the palace, and cost £46 15s in 1342–3. It comprised a hall,
two chambers, a cellar, pantry, buttery, kitchen, larder and stable (TNA:PRO
E 101/593/20). A similarly impressive lodge stood in Windsor Great Park 5
miles south of the castle from at least the 1240s (Mileson 2005a, 124). Here
there was a hall, one chamber and two chapels, and from the time it was
built until Edward III's improvements at the castle a century later it was the
main royal residence at Windsor (Roberts 1997, 409).

All these lodges are documented early: Guildford Lodge *c.*1220, Windsor
*c.*1240, Clarendon in 1251, and Odiham in 1291. Presuming that these were
more than 'working' lodges, given the special interest of the kings concerned,
it seems that from at least the early thirteenth century English kings, like
Bertilak, preferred their residences to be fully encompassed by parkland. This
predilection gained ground especially in the fourteenth century, facilitated in
part by changes to the shape and size of parks.

Park enlargement

Around the same time as the Windsor lodge was built in the 1240s, Henry
III enlarged and consolidated the Great Park, an undertaking which lasted
around thirty years. Its northern perimeter was still visible in 1607, labelled
as 'the olde ditch and banck' by Norden (Roberts 1997, fig. 255, 246–7). The
*c.*5-mile circumference (364 acres) of Henry's original park is traceable in the
south of the Great Park ('Manor Walk') in Norden's *Survey* (Figure 9), but it

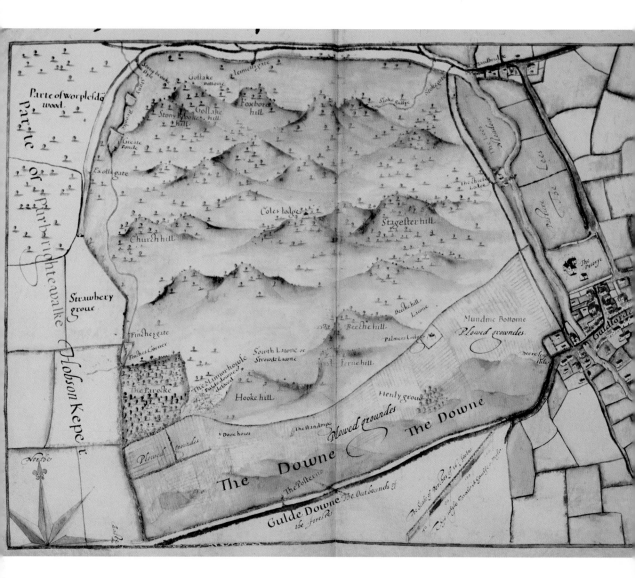

FIGURE 8.
John Norden's
1607 plan of
Guildford Park.
© British Library
Board. All rights
reserved, Harley 3749,
ff.13v–13

more than doubled in size through the fourteenth century. The central section ('Middle Walk') probably equates with the area imparked by Edward II in 1308, and the northern part ('Lower Walk') with land added in 1313 and 1359 (Roberts 1997, 251).

Under Edward II and Edward III particularly, money was poured into the enlargement and embellishment of royal parks; Edward III's imparkment of the manor of Wychemere (Windsor) from 1359–63 cost a highly significant £400 (Roberts 1997, 251). The emphasis on parks may have been occasioned by the reduction of land under forest law (Richardson 2005), while reduced royal itinerary doubtless resulted in heightened expenditure on the surroundings of fewer residences. This focus on landscapes probably fostered the marked increase in (or at least concern about) parkbreak and poaching under Edward III (Richardson 2005, 126–7).

FIGURE II.
View from Clarendon Palace, looking north-east from the eastern wall of the Great Hall across the gardens and park towards Figsbury Ring beyond. The royal apartments lay immediately to the east, and the inner park pale is visible just beyond the trees on the scarp. The (?post-medieval) deer course ran from left to right in the middle distance.

T. B. JAMES

FIGURE 12.
View south-west into Clarendon Park from Figsbury Ring, 2006. The eastern wall of the great hall has been visible among the trees since vegetation was cleared in 2002–3. It can be seen to the right of the ploughed field at centre.

T. B. JAMES

[It] is remarkable for its intimate integration with the thirteenth-century and later castle and its manipulation of the landscape in achieving that relationship … The image created looking out northwards is of a park going on for an unknown, but in imagination large, distance. (Everson *et al.* 2000, 105)

Figure 11 shows that there was a similarly multi-layered view northwards from Clarendon's royal apartments, across gardens, inner park pale and launds, towards the horizon (*cf.* Figure 7 looking south-east). The universal appreciation

of such landscapes, which contrast prospect and refuge, has been noted, and it has been argued that 'prospect' appeals to imagination and a 'spirit of quest', while clumps of trees or fenced-off enclosures suggest security from the hazards beyond (Cummins 2002, 37). This may particularly be manifest in the contrast between cultivated gardens and inner parks, and the views over the wider landscape. Some writers suggest that these were 'chivalric' landscapes, since in progressing through them hunting parties '[mimicked] the Romance movement of leaving the routine social space … for the wilderness … which was potentially magical in its associations, before returning to the original social space' (Howes 2002, 204).

There is no reason to think that medieval lords and ladies did not read landscapes in this way, and the presence of such apparently manipulated views across parkland in some of the palaces discussed is noteworthy. Views such as that at Clarendon may even have been set out in order to contrast cultured, recreational spaces (inner parks and gardens) with areas of relative productivity such as the launds (*cf.* Johnson 2002, 43). A surer way, however, of testing the role of landscapes in exhibiting residences is to ascertain the extent to which approaches and routeways were manipulated.

Manipulation of routeways

Inner parks often formed an element in the approach to royal residences, as at Clarendon, where the inner park was skirted to the north by the approach road to the palace's main gate from the east, and would have been visible from certain vantage points outside the wider park. Since the palace precinct was cleared in the early 1990s, and vegetation removed from its ruins ten years later, the palace has once again become visible from the high ground at Figsbury Ring, outside the park (Figure 12). Viewed from this point when originally complete, it would have given the impression of a palace overlooking a pleasant valley.

At Ludgershall, the primary route to the castle from at least the fourteenth century ran from the north-west, following the boundary of the North Park until the castle suddenly came into view as 'a striking image … sitting prominently [in] … a clearing created by its park within a wider landscape … densely wooded to the … horizon' (Everson *et al.* 2000, 109, 112). There are echoes here of Gawain's first sight of Bertilak's castle, and of the way travellers would have first viewed Clarendon Park and Palace. Indeed, the location of Clarendon Palace may have been a consideration, from 1220, when Salisbury was founded, in the approach to the city when travelling from London and the east. As Colt Hoare commented (Colt Hoare and Nichols 1837, 112), the path leaving Clarendon Park westwards towards Salisbury is 'plainly [a portion] of an antient road'. It has been claimed that this was the main road from Winchester running towards Salisbury and Wilton (Dale 1962, 79). If so, when approaching Salisbury from the east, travellers would have entered the main park through the so-called Winchester Gate, and proceeded under the palace's shadow along the northern limits of the inner park. It has been suggested that

*'The King's
Chief Delights':
A Landscape
Approach
to the Royal Parks
of Post-Conquest
England*

this through road was abandoned 'probably in the later Middle Ages' (Dale 1962, 79) – perhaps following Edward II's imparkment of *c*.1317.

Even if the route westwards through the park was never intended as a through road, visitors to the palace would have taken the same path, before turning back on themselves at the north-western corner of the inner park and mounting the hollow-way towards Clarendon Palace, whose main gateway would suddenly have appeared before them at the hill's summit (Figure 13). In other words, the north range, as seen in Figure 7, would have loomed over them to their left above the inner park and then disappeared from view, to be revealed once more as they were almost upon it. Looking over their shoulders before entering the palace precinct, visitors would have taken in impressive views across to Salisbury and its cathedral (Figure 14). (See James and Gerrard (2007, 49–54) for a more detailed discussion of routeways through Clarendon Park.)

Such circuitous routes through parks which displayed, hid and subsequently revealed the residences within them to travellers, are redolent of landscape manipulation with the aim of offsetting palatial buildings. Laura L. Howes suggests that medieval landscapes may habitually have been experienced in this way; that is 'processionally, sequentially, rather than all at once and from a particular vantage point', echoing the thoughts of Arnold Hauser, who imagined the act of perceiving a 'Gothic' building as one of active involvement:

> From no quarter does it present a complete ... view, disclosing the structure of the whole ... it compels the spectator to be constantly changing his viewpoint and permits him to gain a picture of the whole only through his own ... action and power of reconstruction (Howes 2002, 193, quoting Hauser).

This uniquely medieval way of experiencing landscape may have been responsible for the preference for gardens like 'small, outdoors enclosed rooms', designed to reveal themselves only as the visitor proceeded through them (Howes 2002, 193–4).

A recent study has estimated that around half of all parks contained internal compartments (Mileson 2005a, 18) and, although this layout was partly functional, it may be that preferred ways of experiencing the landscape were also responsible for the compartmentation of parks, which were divided into units including coppices, launds, rabbit warrens and even arable. Not surprisingly, this type of arrangement was viewed, until recently, in primarily economic/functional terms, many writers arguing that after the Black Death land managed exclusively (and extravagantly) for deer was seen as inappropriate (James Bond, pers. comm.). Compartmentation is one way to manage deer alongside trees, but, as Rackham has pointed out, the owners of parks had a choice (Rackham 1990, 157). They could either compartmentalise – for example, fence coppices off from deer (as at Clarendon, Figure 6) – or abandon underwood entirely, replacing it with pollards (as at Woodstock, which seems never to have been compartmentised). Yet Rackham implies that medieval social relations were embedded in the landscape when he states that 'compartmentalisation favours the owner of … trees [implying] … strong landowners and weak commoners' (Rackham 1993, 91).

The main approaches to Clarendon (after *c.*1220, through Salisbury), Guildford, Ludgershall and Woodstock parks each wound through their respective towns. All these urban areas can be seen as 'towns that grew up at park gates', comparable to Platt's (1976) 'castle towns' and 'abbey towns' like Bury St Edmunds. The principal gate into Woodstock Park, from which the palace would have appeared, once more, occupying a high position flanked by woodland, was approached from the town of Woodstock (Bond and Tiller 1997, 28). This park was entirely encircled, from at least the thirteenth century, with a

FIGURE 13.
Aerial view of Clarendon, looking eastwards across the inner park towards Winchester Gate, the main entrance into Clarendon Park from the east (*cf.* Figure 6, above). The tortuous route to the palace (right of centre on the scarp) is clearly visible.

D. ELISABETH BARTON

44

7-mile stone wall, and documentary sources single out for mention the section facing the town in 1250 (Bond and Tiller 1997, 27–8). Although physical and visual relationships between royal palaces/parks and their neighbouring towns have been neglected until recently, mention has been made of park pales as statements of power in the wider landscape.

Clarendon Park pale: the park as a symbol of royal authority and power

Parks were a reflection in the landscape of medieval social relations, in that they represented 'an extreme example of the ability of lords to take over land for their exclusive use' (Dyer 1988, 24). The most visible element of this was the boundary pale, whose significance would not have been lost on contemporaries. Enclosure, whether of gardens or larger areas, was heavily emphasised in late medieval illustrations, and it must have figured large in worldviews (Henisch 2002, 156). Indeed, park pales were arguably as redolent of the crown's power as were royal palaces themselves, since they enclosed areas which were then endowed with economic, functional, social and symbolic meaning.

At Clarendon there seems to have been a direct relationship between attaining the throne or gaining majority and re-establishing the park's boundaries (Richardson 2005, 113–21). This is evident in Figure 15, particularly with regard to Henry III's majority (*c.*1227), the Lancastrian accession (1399), those

45

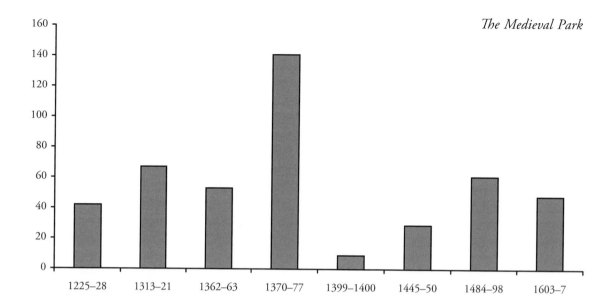

of Richard III and Henry VII (between 1484 and 1496), and James I (1603). The sum of £387 10s was also spent on the manor and pale together in the decade following the accession of Henry VI in 1422, but this has not been added to the chart because the outlay on each is not specified. Even in the second quarter of the seventeenth century, attention was lavished on the park. Six months after Charles I acceded to the throne in 1625, £331 16s 6d was set aside for its lodges and pales. As far as is known none of those kings, apart from Henry VI, actually visited the palace (and after 1500 it was uninhabitable), although James I did hunt in the park. One might argue that, even in the later medieval period, the aim of successive monarchs was not to visit Clarendon Palace, but its park. Indeed, in contrast to his other residences, visits in Edward III's *Itinerary* are listed as to 'Clarendon Park' (TNA:PRO 942.037, *Itinerary of Edward III and his Household: Regnal Years 1–7*).

Perhaps not surprisingly, Figure 15 reveals considerable expenditure in Edward III's reign (Richardson 2005, 113–21). Much of this went on repairs carried out after the 'great wind' of 1362. Gales also preceded the 1370–7 campaigns, which involved the large sum of nearly £140. Outlay was also considerably lower in 1225–8 than in 1313–21, suggesting that this latter period was when the park reached its optimum size. It may not be a coincidence that during the fourteenth century Salisbury's prosperity was growing rapidly. Repairs to the park pale, particularly by new monarchs, may thus have functioned as a visible reminder of royal power, directed both at the city and the cathedral close.

The enlarged and embellished parks of the fourteenth century served to advertise royal and seigneurial power to their surrounding communities. That the social order became inscribed in park landscapes is perhaps unsurprising in a century when that same social order frequently seemed about to be over-

FIGURE 15. Chart showing expenditure on Clarendon Park pale from the early thirteenth to the early seventeenth century. Reproduced from Richardson 2005, fig. 75

turned. Although kings' first concern was doubtless to impress foreign princes, nobles and senior churchmen, the manipulated hunting landscape inside such parks would have been read as an expression of status by the multifarious sections of society gaining access to them – including foresters and their staff, huntsmen, paupers gathering sticks, and even the occasional poacher.

Conclusions

It is possible to posit the fourteenth century as the great age of the medieval park, at least from the perspective of the English crown, and to see similarities between parkland landscapes and the literary and prescriptive tracts alluded to above. Like Bertilak, English kings clearly preferred their residences at the centre of their parkscapes, in the fourteenth as much as the fifteenth century. If parks were some distance from a residence, new parks were created nearby, as at Windsor, or lodges might be set up within them, as at Guildford. As to whether parks were designed in tandem with buildings at the instigation of particular lords, it is arguable that Edward II's visit to Hesdin influenced royal park design through the remainder of the Middle Ages. Moreover, he was almost certainly behind the expansion of Clarendon Park to its greatest extent (4,292 acres), at the same time as the palace was improved to provide a fitting venue for a parliament. Similarly, the hand of Edward III is apparent in the foundation of Windsor Little Park as a setting for his redeveloped castle, as is that of Edward IV in its enlargement and embellishment a century later.

It has been suggested here that the embeddedness of royal residences in their landscapes is discernible particularly from the beginning of the fourteenth century. However, there are caveats: cartographic evidence is lacking before the surveys of the early seventeenth century, and most of the medieval landscapes themselves have not survived. Moreover, many of these parks, and their residences, existed before the thirteenth century and an absence of written sources surviving in any number preclude a detailed discussion of their earliest forms. Certainly, higher clerics, such as the bishops of Winchester, had set up apparently aesthetically pleasing parks as early as the twelfth century. And only from the fourteenth century can a greater variety of evidence, including standing lodges (as at Odiham), be brought to bear.

Nevertheless, recent multi-disciplinary work on Clarendon has contributed substantially to our understanding, with implications for royal residences and parks elsewhere (see Richardson 2005; James and Gerrard 2007, 49–54). The chronology of attention to the park pale, discussed above, should be calibrated by similar studies and compared to perambulations of royal forests when new kings ascended the throne. As royal visits to the palace decreased from the reign of Edward III, expenditure on pales, gates and park lodges increased, although there were also significant correlations between the timing of the forest courts and construction and repair work on both the palace and the park's lodges. The way in which these buildings were *used* is also significant. At Clarendon, royal visits largely switched, from the reign of Edward I onwards, from winter to summer, the season for hunting bucks, in tandem with greater ceremony in hunting itself and attendant sculpting of the landscape. Comparable work should be done on other royal parks so that less localised conclusions can be drawn.

There is no doubt that parks were of key importance to the crown, in the medieval period and beyond. They were enduring symbols of royal power in the landscape, and often occasioned vast expenditure long after the residences within them were ruinous. The lodge at Guildford – and the park itself – helped to prolong royal interest for nearly two centuries after the palace was dismantled (Poulton 2005, 150), and monarchs continued to hunt in Clarendon Park for two centuries after the last recorded royal visit to its palace in the 1450s. Woodstock became Blenheim, the epitome of the eighteenth-century landscape park, and Windsor endured, both its castle and landscape sculpted by monarchs like Charles II who understood – albeit in a slightly different context – the value of planning parkscapes and residences together in order to symbolise most forcefully the power and authority of the crown.

CHAPTER THREE

Animal Bones and Animal Parks

Naomi Sykes

Animals have always been central to the creation, use and perception of cultural landscapes. The location and form of settlements, roads and enclosures reflect human–animal interactions. In other cases, animals may play a more psychological role in the construction of landscapes, their visual, audio and physical qualities providing media through which humans might experience and understand the world around them. Indeed, the meaning of a space is often defined, or at least evoked, by the human–animal interactions performed within it: maintaining domestic cattle within a field, chasing red deer across hunting grounds, or simply hearing the shrieks of seagulls at the coast. Despite this, landscape studies have all too often removed animals from the equation, seeing humans as the only significant agents in landscape construction.

Medieval park studies are prime examples of this oversight; landscape historians and archaeologists have traditionally placed more emphasis on park boundaries than on the animals and activities that occurred within the pale (Crawford 1953; Cantor and Wilson 1961). More recently, the economic and social functions of parks have started to be recognised, with enclosures described variously as game larders (Birrell 1992), masculine hunting spaces (Gilchrist 1999, 145), signifiers of Norman identity (Sykes 2005a), and socially divisive symbols of power (Liddiard 2000a; Herring 2003). Without giving detailed consideration to the meaning of, and human interaction with, the animals which these enclosures contained, however, it seems difficult to elucidate their function and social significance. In the absence of this information it is not possible to know if or how the meaning of wild-animal enclosures changed through time – whether, for example, Anglo-Saxon hunting reserves should be viewed in the same way as post-Conquest menageries or later medieval parks.

This chapter seeks to put animals back into the landscape. By combining a large zooarchaeological dataset (derived from Sykes in prep.) with evidence from animal behaviour, history, iconography and anthropology, it is hoped that the shifting function and meaning of wild-animal enclosures can be clarified. Furthermore, it will be demonstrated that, through scientific analysis of animal remains, imparkment can be detected even where physical evidence of enclosure is archaeologically invisible. This opens a new avenue for considering

Park function

Whilst the function of medieval parks was clearly multifaceted (see Liddiard 2005) they are, today, most frequently perceived as private spaces for deer hunting. The importance of hunting to medieval society cannot be overstated and is evidenced by the large corpus of contemporary literature, both practical and literary, detailing the methods and associated rituals attached to the acquisition, butchery and redistribution of different quarry (Cummins 1988; Rooney 1993; Almond 2003). By the later medieval period, parks were amongst a suite of 'hunting landscapes' – forests, chases and warrens – where such activities could take place. The definitions and characteristics of each space are well known (for instance, see Bond 1994) and need not be rehearsed here. Suffice to say that, in contrast to the other hunting spaces, parks were bounded, were typically of 100–300 acres and were deliberately stocked with particular animals: fallow deer (*Dama dama*), rabbits (*Oryctolagus cunniculus*), pheasants (*Phasianus colchius*), peafowl (*Pavo cristatus*), partridges (*Perdix perdix*), swans (*Cygnus* sp.), herons (*Ardea cinerea*) and freshwater fish were the most common by the later medieval period. It is noteworthy that the first four species are non-native animals and it is hardly surprising that these prized exotica were the principal park inmates.

In terms of their ecology, parks were different in species composition and animal density from the surrounding landscape (Pluskowski this volume). Their stock and design offered opportunities for a bountiful hunting experience that could not be achieved in the wider landscape; but they also imposed limitations, requiring the park to be engaged with and traversed in very particular ways. With this in mind, it is surprising that few scholars have examined how parks could have operated as hunting spaces (*cf.* Cummins 2002). Indeed, different hunting techniques are regularly considered as though they had a homogenous meaning and might be employed in any landscape to catch any animal, but this is unlikely to have been the case. For instance, a deer hunt must have met very specific physical and emotional criteria if it were to qualify as hunting *par force de chiens*. In this, the most ritualised form of medieval hunting, a single deer, the strongest of the group, would be selected as the quarry with the intention that it would provide sport for the whole day. It would be pursued by hounds, hunt servants and the mounted aristocratic hunters. Chased to exhaustion, it would then, if the hunt was successful, be killed by a sword to the heart. The strategic organisation of the hunt and the close physical relationship of the hunter to the deer, especially at the point of death, bears a resemblance to warfare and it is these elements which have seen the hunt *par force de chiens* linked repeatedly to masculine identity. But could such a hunt take place within a park? The answer must surely be no. Hunting *par force* was suited to the unbounded landscape of the forest and in

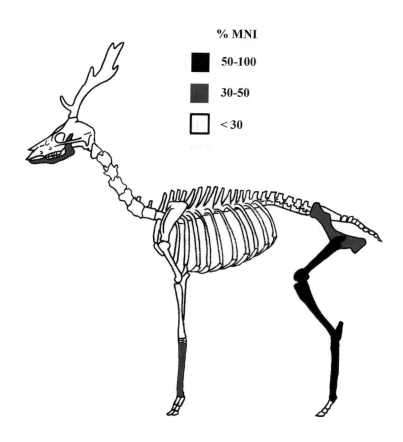

% MNI

50-100

30-50

< 30

FIGURE 16.
Anatomical
representation of deer
from elite sites.

particular to the behaviour of the red deer (*Cervus elaphus*), a species that has the capacity to run long distances: data from modern hunts show that pursuits may cover up to 22 miles (Bateson and Bradshaw 1997; Harris *et al.* 1999). Not even the largest of parks could provide a suitable level of movement and unpredictability for a satisfactory *par force* hunt. Furthermore, the physiology and behaviour of the principal park deer, the fallow deer, is not conducive to *par force* hunting because they have poor stamina and tend to maintain a herd structure during flight (Recarte *et al.* 1998). Within a park stocked with fallow deer, hunting methods must have been limited to the drive, or 'bow and stable', whereby deer were chased into nets or towards archers who were positioned on a platform, or 'stand'. This is indicated not only by historical records but also by the zooarchaeological evidence: arrow fragments have been found embedded in fallow deer remains (Sadler 1990, 487).

Anatomical representation data for medieval deer assemblages demonstrate that carcasses were treated similarly regardless of hunting technique. Ritual-ised 'unmaking' (skinning and butchery) methods were employed at the kill-site, with hindquarters being taken to the lord's residence (Figure 16), whilst forelimbs were distributed amongst hunters, foresters and parkers (Figure 17). However, this need not suggest that the two hunting methods and their respec-tive landscapes had identical social meanings. Indeed, it might be questioned

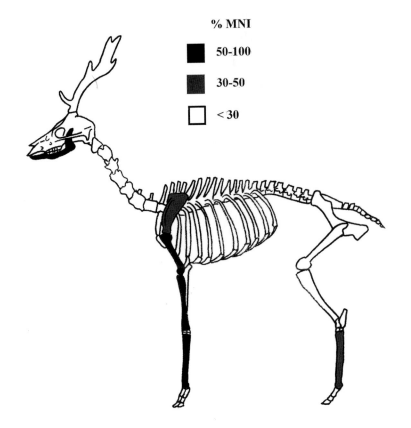

% MNI

■ 50-100

■ 30-50

□ < 30

FIGURE 17.
Anatomical
representation of
deer from parkers'
residences.

whether deer killing within parks was actually hunting at all. Cartmill (1993, 30) has argued that to constitute hunting, animal killing must meet four criteria: that the quarry is *wild*, not docile; that the quarry must be *free*, and that the kill must be *premeditated* and involve *direct* physical violence. It is debatable whether park-based bow and stable fulfilled all these criteria and it is certainly possible to take issue with concepts of wildness, freedom, and direct violence in a situation where, although known as 'wild animals' (*ferae*), fallow deer were in effect farmed, restricted and killed from a respectable distance (Birrell 1992, 115). Park 'hunting' can have done little to stir the warrior-like emotions invoked by forest hunting and the general dearth of historical evidence for seigneurial hunting within these landscapes suggests that it occurred infrequently as a lordly activity (Birrell 1992, 122).

Easier to reconcile with the evidence is the idea that most park 'hunting' was undertaken by professional servants – hunters and parkers – who employed no-nonsense drive methods to harvest venison in the most efficient way (Birrell 2006). To these individuals the park was a workplace and even, for some parkers, their home. It is important to recognise this quotidian function of parks and the lives of those who worked in them, as they are so often overlooked during the search for evidence pertaining to the aristocracy. Few parkers' residences have been excavated, but the animal bone assemblages from Lodge Farm in Dorset (Locker 1994), Donnington Park lodge in Leicestershire (Bent 1977–8) and Stansted Lodge in Essex (Bates n.d.) provide an interesting insight into the lives of the occupants (Sykes in press). Deer bones are exceptionally well represented (Figure 18), indicating that venison made a substantial contribution to the meat diet of parker households. Parkers also appear to have consumed the other animals they maintained: from the three park lodge assemblages alone come the remains of swan (Bent 1977–8), pheasant and heron (Bates n.d.), and peafowl, hare and rabbits (Locker 1994). The polecat (*Mustela putorius*) and ferret (*Mustela putorius furo*) remains identified in the last assemblage suggests that, where warrens were within the park boundary, the parker might have acted as rabbit catcher (Locker 1994, 108). Presumably, for parkers, this day-to-day management, culling and consumption of game animals diminished their luxury status: parks and park animals represented a mundane profession rather than an elite pastime.

It is perhaps unsurprising that parkers were responsible for catching rabbits; Middle English hunting manuals, in particular the *Master of the Game*, depict rabbiting as a distinctly low activity, unsuitable for respectable lords (Cummins 1988, 236–7). Whilst it may not have been fitting for a nobleman to participate, medieval illuminations suggest that ferreting was an appropriate pursuit for a lady: see, for instance, Queen Mary's Psalter (BL MS Royal 2B VIII, f.155). Its suitability may have derived from the fact that it required minimal physical exertion and that, even in the medieval mind, rabbiting was not classed as true hunting – the quarry being restricted by nets, with death usually inflicted by the ferret underground and out of sight of its handler. Similar reasons have been put forward to explain the association between falconry and medieval women: ladies were able to maintain their femininity as they were not responsible for the kill, which was mediated by the hawk or falcon (Almond 2003, 160).

Considering that falconry was a well-known part of a young woman's education, little thought has been given to establishing where in the medieval

FIGURE 18.
Inter-site variation in
the representation of
deer remains, shown
as a percentage of the
total count of mammal
bone fragments.

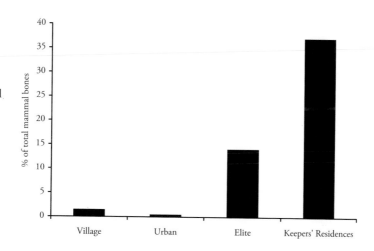

53

landscape such activities might have taken place. Roberta Gilchrist (1999) has argued cogently that medieval courtly society placed great emphasis on the seclusion and enclosure of young aristocratic women, seeing this as a way of ensuring the female chastity and purity so essential to patrimony. With their mobility and visibility restricted in public arenas – parish churches, banquets and even travel between households – it seems highly unlikely that young women would have been encouraged to practise falconry openly in the wider landscape. More probable is that it was within the confines of the park that ladies, such as the unaccompanied female shown in the Taymouth book of hours (BL MS *Yates Thompson* 13 f.73), engaged in falconry without fear of observation. It makes sense that parks were arenas for falconry, being stocked as they were with the very species – the heron, partridge and pheasant – that were amongst the sport's most prized quarry. It is notable that the zooarchaeological representation of these species increases dramatically on elite settlements dating to the mid-twelfth century (Figure 19 and see Sykes 2005b), a shift coincident with an upsurge in iconography, particularly ladies' seals, depicting females with hawks (Oggins 2004, 118). Perhaps it is not unfeasible that these prey species were managed in parks specifically with women's leisure in mind.

If it is accepted that parks were the setting of women's falconry, the natural step in the argument is to suggest that they may also have been the location for ladies' hunting. The level of female involvement in medieval hunting has been discussed by several authors (for example, Almond 2003, chapter 6; Cummins 1988). Whilst it is clear that mature married or widowed women were occasional active participants in forest hunting, and even poaching (Coss 1998, 67), there is little to suggest that young ladies were frequent members of boisterous wide-ranging chases. Controversy has stemmed from the numerous manuscripts that depict women hunting or unmaking animals: do these

FIGURE 19. Inter-period and inter-site variation in the archaeological representation of the grey partridge (*Perdix perdix*).

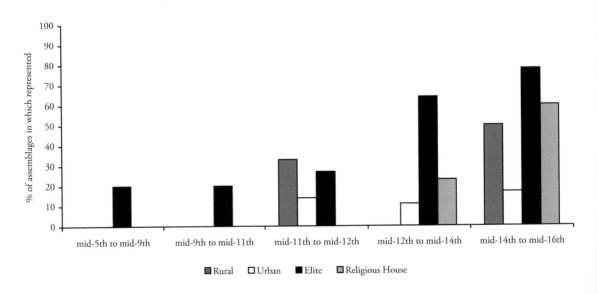

illuminations reflect real practice or are they simply part of the 'topsy-turvey world' artistic tradition? Some of the images are clearly comical, such as the unmaking scene in the Taymouth book of hours (BL MS *Yates Thompson* 13 f.83v), in which one female participant is shown blowing a horn upside down. Other illuminations appear more realistic, depicting women shooting arrows at rabbits and deer: significantly, where women are shown in association with deer it is often with the fallow deer, identifiable by their distinctive menil coat, palmate antlers and prominent penile sheath or 'brush' (see, for instance, BL Royal 10 E IV f.159v). It is tempting to see these illuminations, depicting as they do the principal park species, as accurate references to the activities of women within parks. Whilst it is unwise to read medieval images at such a superficial level, clear evidence that women hunted within parks can be found in the historical record. For instance, in John Coke's *Debate between the Her-alds* (cited in Cummins 1988, 7), the English herald states: 'we have also small parkes made onely for the pleasure of ladyes and gentylwomen, to shote with the longe bowe, and kyll the sayd beastes'.

To conclude that parks played a role as hunting spaces for women may seem to be at odds with my earlier argument: that deer-killing within parks is diffi-cult to classify as hunting *per se*. However, it is this very fact – that standing at a station and shooting at captive deer is little more than target practice – which made the activity a suitable one for women: it was the masculine arrow, rather than the holder of the feminine bow, which caused the death, and the kill was sanitised by physical distance. This is not to suggest that parks were solely female spaces; clearly they were not, as there are ample records of men culling deer or demonstrating their *skills* in hunting and falconry. Yet I would argue that they were also not the masculine domain that others have suggested (Gil-christ 1999, 145). When the evidence is viewed together, the impression given is that, for the aristocracy at least, parks functioned as extensions of the gar-den. Beyond landscapes of animal production they were social grounds where young ladies could engage unobserved in sporting activities and where, under the pretext of 'hunting and hawking', noble men and women could interact: as with the garden, the park was a contested space (Gilchrist 1999). Later medieval parks clearly had multiple functions and must have been viewed in equally diverse ways. It is now worth considering whether animal studies can shed light on the varied meaning of park landscapes and, in particular, the ways in which parks were perceived by different social groups.

Perception and meaning

Parks and the features they contained – warrens, dovecotes and ponds – are frequently described as symbols of social division: their boundaries a physi-cal reminder of the cultural partition between aristocracy and peasantry. To their owners, parks might have been viewed as landscapes of pleasure and plenty, but for others their connotations must have been very different. Her-ring (2003, 46) sums up popular ideas about peasants' perceptions of parks

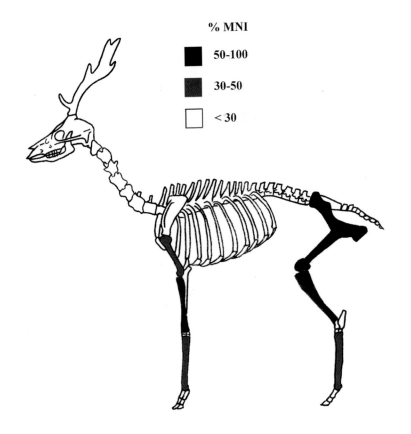

% MNI

■ 50-100

▨ 30-50

□ < 30

FIGURE 20.
Anatomical
representation of the
deer from urban sites.

with his suggestion that, to them, parks represented their 'powerlessness; low-liness of rank; and separateness or exclusion'. Certainly, the strict protocol of park management and game distribution was established to preserve ideals of exclusivity; park boundaries were maintained at great expense and the distri-bution of game meats was tightly controlled. But it was the creation of this very institution that provided excluded individuals with both an opportunity to subvert authority and a target for expressions of defiance, hence the spate of park breaking during the Peasants' Revolt of 1381 (Liddiard 2005, 118). Our image of the depressed and powerless lower classes is perhaps underestimating the spirit and agency of the average medieval peasant. That many of the lower classes viewed parks not so much as an oppression but rather as a challenge is clear from the level of poaching recorded in the documentary sources (Birrell 1982; 1996a; Manning 1993). Evidence can also be found in the zooarchaeo-logical record, urban deer assemblages being particularly informative. As can be seen in Figure 20, they do not demonstrate the structured anatomical pat-terning seen at elite and parkers' residences (Figures 16 and 17). Instead they show a skeletal distribution that indicates carcasses were brought to towns complete – they had not undergone the unmaking rituals and most probably reflect illegally obtained venison. I have argued elsewhere (Sykes in press, 158) that the zooarchaeological data support the historical evidence for organised poaching gangs, who are known to have worked out of urban taverns, where they also sold and consumed their bag (Manning 1993, chapter 6; Birrell 1982, 14). We should not see poaching as a peasant's last resort, something they did to avert starvation – there is very little evidence that peasants poached because they were hungry (Manning 1993, 20). Rather, parks were breached as a social statement. In many cases peasants and nobles poached together, particularly in cases of inter-household feuds, where aristocrats launched raids on the parks of their rivals (Manning 1993, chapter 2). Under these circumstances, far from being socially divisive, parks were places where the gap between the classes could actually be narrowed.

Poaching gangs negotiated a landscape that was very different to that experienced by authorised visitors: usually operating at night to avoid detection, they moved through parks that were dark, unknown and that probably felt more exciting and 'wild' than they did during daylight hours. With visibility and movement reduced by darkness, the park's size and shape may have appeared altered, allowing animals to evade capture more readily than in drive hunting. Its soundscape would also have changed, the activities and noise of nocturnal animals replacing their diurnal counterparts. In terms of the experience, poaching was probably closer to hunting than was the legitimate killing of park animals.

It should not be forgotten that park landscapes were in a constant state of change. Not only did their appearance shift by night and day, but it also changed more dramatically according to season. For nobles, parkers and poachers alike, cycles of animal behaviour – mating, birthing, antler-shedding – would have enhanced the temporality of the landscape. Parks could be understood as clocks, with different sights, sounds and activities occurring at different times: indeed, hunting and hawking manuals specify the various months in which different animals and birds might be taken. The temporal significance of parks was felt even beyond their boundaries, in the sense that they supplied meat for the feast days which structured the religious calendar: even peasant poachers were known to take game specifically for these special occasions (Birrell 1996a, 84; 2006).

Several authors (for instance, Liddiard 2005, 110) have highlighted the religious symbolism of park features, and it is not difficult to find the Christian imagery associated with park animals. Stocker and Stocker (1996) have argued that rabbits were maintained not simply for their socio-economic value but for metaphorical reasons: their fecundity, subterranean habitat and surface emergence was viewed as an allegory for human life, death and salvation, respectively. The same may be true of deer, which were repeatedly invoked as symbols of Christ, eternal life and resurrection (Cummins 1988, chapter 4). Within medieval culture the swan was also an icon of Christian virtue: Alexander Neckham saw the transformation of the grey cygnet into the white swan as symbolising the transformation of the repentant sinner; elsewhere the swan is equated with virginity and the Immaculate Conception (Rowland 1978, 172). Herons were similarly well regarded, being linked to Christ and piety (Rowland 1978, 80). It seems possible, therefore, that these park animals were chosen specifically for their Christian connotations. A further Biblical dimension was then added through the act of caring for them: stewardship of animals was seen as a sign of sanctity, fulfilling the duty of care (*dominion*) towards creatures set out in Genesis 1, 26 (Preece and Fraser 2000). In this way the meanings of parks went beyond mere expressions of socio-economic status; they represented spirituality, anchoring their owner at the highest position in the Chain of Being. Perception of parks as sacred landscapes may explain why so many were established and owned by members of the Church. The number of parks in archiepiscopal, episcopal or monastic hands has struck some as odd, especially given that hunting was forbidden by canon law (Coulton 1925, 508–12). However, the dichotomy seems less severe if it is accepted that parks were not true hunting spaces – animals may have been killed but only through passive methods. Indeed, it has even been suggested that the ritualised butchery of these holy creatures demonstrated respect for the natural world and became an emblem of the crucified Christ (Cartmill 1993, 69; Rooney 1993, 88).

At the other end of the moral scale, parks might contain animals that were the very essence of profanity. According to Rowland (1978), both the pheasant and the partridge had strong sexual connotations. The partridge was seen as particularly wanton and impure, a symbol of 'incontinent lust' (Rowland 1978, 124), an association which appears to have removed this species from the parks and tables of religious houses (Sykes 2005b, 96). Similarly, whilst the activities that took place within parks were seen as pure on the one hand, they could be eroticised on the other, unmaking scenes being classic devices for portrayals of courtly love (Almond 2003, 154). This interplay between the sacred and the sexual is similar to the conflicting imagery that has been identified for the castle garden: an enclosed feminine space that, like women, was seen as a symbol of both sanctity and lust (Gilchrist 1999). That we see the same type of ambiguous motifs represented within parks strengthens the argument that these enclosed spaces were also strongly feminised. But was this always the case? If the symbolism of a park was determined partly by the animals it contained, it seems possible that the meaning of an enclosure could shift, or even be consciously manipulated, according to its stock. The changing representation of species in the zooarchaeological record thus also provides an opportunity to chart the development of park landscapes.

Origins and development

There are now numerous animal bone assemblages from sites dating between the mid-fifth to mid-sixteenth centuries. Synthesis of these data reveals that most of the animals associated with the late medieval park were not managed throughout the entire period. Records for the partridge and swan suggest that the elite began to maintain them only from the mid-twelfth century, whereas the heron is poorly represented before the mid-fourteenth century, at which point it becomes a frequent component of assemblages from elite sites (Sykes 2005b). Exotic species demonstrate a similar pattern of representation: peacock and pheasant are rare prior to the mid-twelfth century (Poole in prep.); rabbits have been shown to be a late twelfth-century introduction (Callou 2003; Sykes in prep.); and the fallow deer was imported from Sicily shortly after the Norman Conquest (Sykes 2004). Since most of these species were either absent or unmanaged before the twelfth century it is difficult to argue that the meaning of earlier parks was in any way similar to their later medieval counterparts; the imagery must have been entirely different.

Many authors attribute the transformation of the medieval park to the Norman introduction of fallow deer (Rackham 1986, 123). Certainly, the post-Conquest rise in park numbers does parallel the zooarchaeological increase in the representation of fallow deer (Figure 21), and the timing of these shifts would appear to implicate the Normans as responsible. However, it is important to acknowledge just how long it would have taken fallow deer to become established as the premier park species. For the first few decades after their introduction, fallow deer would have been a great rarity, prized exotica to be observed and admired rather than chased and eaten. It is known that Henry I's park at Woodstock contained a suite of exotic animals – camels, lions, leopards and porcupines – and it seems likely that fallow deer originally formed part of similar collections. If associated with fallow deer, the small number of early Norman parks must have functioned as menageries, the ancestors of modern zoos. This lineage is exemplified by the Woodstock collection, which was moved to the Tower of London by King John and finally became London Zoo when it was transferred to Regent's Park in 1831. Despite its repeated movement, the meaning of this collection remained largely unchanged, the animals being maintained as heraldic symbols and metaphors for Empire (Ritvo 1987; O'Regan 2002).

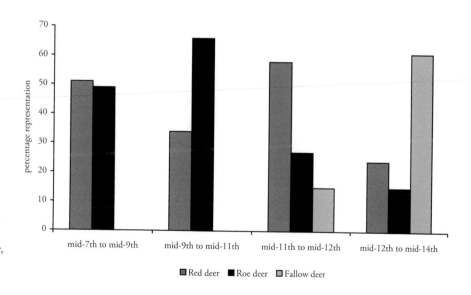

FIGURE 21.
Inter-period variation
in the relative
frequencies of red deer,
roe deer and fallow
deer.

It is problematic to view early Norman menageries as the progenitors of the later medieval park – their roles and meanings were simply too diverse. Instead, as Liddiard (2003) has suggested, the origins of the medieval park should perhaps be sought in the pre-Conquest landscape. It is well known that some English enclosures, most notably the *derhage* at Ongar, went on to become post-Conquest deer parks, and Liddiard has argued that English *haiae*, *hagan* and *deor-fald* were probably little different in role and physical form from later medieval parks. There are many reasons to suspect that this assessment is correct but, again, there is a need to consider what animals these structures actually contained if we are to understand their meaning. Literal translations of the Old English *der* or *deor* to mean 'deer' have misled, because these terms originally meant any animal, rather than deer specifically (Dalby 1965, 239). Indeed, John Hines (pers. comm.) has suggested that the classic pre-Conquest park at Ongar was, in fact, no more than a horse stud. In the absence of reliable documentary evidence it seems that the remains of the animals themselves may provide the key to understanding the identity of these pre-Conquest animal enclosures.

The zooarchaeological record provides little evidence for the presence of exotic animals in Anglo-Saxon England and the range of wild birds and mammals represented in most mid-ninth- to mid-eleventh-century assemblages is rather limited. Elite sites demonstrate the highest frequency of wild-animal remains and, as is shown in Figure 21, on these sites roe deer (*Capreolus capreolus*) are generally the most numerous: they dominate the wild mammal assemblages from Goltho in Lincolnshire (Jones and Ruben 1987), Ramsbury in Wiltshire (Coy 1980), Bishopstone in Sussex (Ingrem n.d.) and Faccombe Netherton in Hampshire (Sadler 1990). The abundance of roe deer at the last site is interesting given that a 'white haga' was recorded at Faccombe in AD 961 (Hooke 1989, 128). Documentary evidence also suggests an association between *haiae* and roe deer: in Aelfric's Colloqy the hunter drives roe deer into hays (Swanton 1993, 170) and the Domesday survey for Cheshire and Shropshire mentions *haiae capreolis*, hays specifically for roe deer (Thorn and Thorn 1986, 6.14, fo. 260b). Both Hooke (1989) and Liddiard (2003, 13) have suggested that *haiae* and *hagan* are related to woodland, an interpretation that supports the connection of these features with roe deer, which is predominantly a woodland species. If roe deer were the main quarry in these wooded landscapes, however, the interpretation of *haiae* and *hagan* as parks is problematic, because roe deer are notoriously unsuitable as park animals, the males in particular becoming dangerously territorial when confined. However, Liddiard (2003, 20) has pointed out that early English parks tended to be fairly large and this, coupled with the fact that the home range of roe deer is reduced within woodland (Tufto *et al.* 1996), may have alleviated the problem to some extent. Alternatively, roe deer may have been selected precisely because of their volatility when confined, giving the hunting ground a more dangerous feel. I would suggest that the *haiae* and *haga* associated with woodland were most probably intermittent boundary structures rather than continuous enclosures – thus enabling animals to enter and leave the woodland. This would explain why Domesday Book often records *haiae* in the plural, whereas parks are referred to in the singular (Liddiard 2003, 12). By allowing animals their freedom, they remained wild and unpredictable, and any attempt to catch and kill them could be classified legitimately as hunting. To hunt within woodland, an environment thought to be the residence of supernatural spirits as well as wolves and other dangerous animals, would have placed the hunter mentally alongside the warriors, heroes and saints of Old English literature (Neville 1999). Ecologically and psychologically, these wild, wooded and masculine landscapes were far divorced from the domesticated, feminised parks of the later medieval period. Even where there may have been continuity in physical space, it is my belief that the pre- to post-Conquest difference in human–animal interaction rules out any possibility of continuity in landscape meaning.

I have argued throughout this chapter that animals are central to landscape construction. Given the association between fallow deer and later medieval parks, it is worth noting the growing evidence for a short-lived presence of this species in Roman Britain. Recent analysis of first-century deposits from Fishbourne Roman Palace in Sussex has produced numerous remains belonging to the fallow deer, which can only have been an exotic animal at this time. Teeth from two mandibles were submitted for strontium isotope analysis, a geochemical provenancing technique, which revealed that one individual was imported to Fishbourne as a fawn whilst the other was born and raised at the site: both must have been imparked at the Palace. With this information it has been possible to tentatively identify a park, or *vivaria*, within the southern part of the Palace complex. The significance of this enclosed landscape is considered in Sykes *et al.* (2006), where we suggest that the park symbolised sanctity, social standing and Imperial membership and allegiance. In terms of landscape meaning, this is probably the closest to that of later medieval parks, perhaps validating their oft-cited classical origins (for example Rackham 1986, 122; Ladsun 1991, 1–4). Most importantly, this study demonstrates that even where physical evidence for parks may be difficult to detect archaeologically, their presence can be demonstrated through zooarchaeology.

Conclusion

My intention in this chapter has been to reconsider, through animal studies, several questions that have repeatedly been asked of medieval parks: what was their function? What was their meaning? And can the origins of the landscape features be traced? It has become clear that wild and semi-domestic animals have been managed in Britain since the Roman period at least: zooarchaeological evidence has provided evidence for the emparkment of fallow deer at first-century Fishbourne Palace; roe deer appear to have been enclosed, to some extent, in the woodland of Saxon England; the Normans brought exotic species – fallow deer, peafowl and pheasants – to exhibit in their menageries and, as the populations of these animals burgeoned, they were incorporated into the design of later medieval parks. In some cases it is possible to demonstrate inter-period continuity in the physical space that these enclosures occupied: for instance, the presence of Saxon *hagan* in the same location as later medieval parks. However, this does not necessarily reflect continuity in landscape function or meaning: the hunting of wild roe deer in a wooded space that was perceived as supernatural and dangerous, would have carried very different connotations to the culling of fallow deer in a manicured medieval park. For this reason, I would suggest that it is futile to attempt to trace the evolution of park landscapes. Because the significance of animal enclosures depends on the symbolism of the species they contain there can be no linear progression, each landscape having its own culturally specific meaning.

Whilst the human–animal interactions within, and the meaning of, these landscapes varied through time, the overarching significance of wild-animal enclosures is the same regardless of culture; they all reflect a society's perceptions of nature, and thus their own humanity. As such, the study of wild-animal enclosures is a unique opportunity to gain an insight into the ideology of the society and individuals who constructed or engaged with the spaces. For instance, I have argued in this chapter that later medieval parks were more than mere status symbols or providers of game meats; they were also an important structuring force that operated simultaneously to both amalgamate and segregate the different classes and genders of medieval England. While it could be contended that this chapter has taken a rather simplistic and broadbrush approach and is open to a number of criticisms, it is to be hoped that it has been able to demonstrate that animal studies, in particular zooarchaeology, can offer new insights into old questions and have the potential to play a central role in landscape interpretation.

CHAPTER FOUR

The Social Construction of Medieval Park Ecosystems: An Interdisciplinary Perspective

Aleksander Pluskowski

The emergence of a common aristocratic identity in western Europe in the latter centuries of the first millennium AD was closely associated with the development of an exclusive hunting culture. The degree of exclusivity varied from one region to the next, and changed over time, but by the mid-twelfth century a comparable language of seigneurial authority and identity, centred on the pursuit of deer and the practice of falconry, had emerged in a number of regions. The aristocracy emerged as a self-conscious 'predatory' class; skill in the art of hunting came to define the knight *par excellence*, whilst in contemporary courtly literature, where animals were used as metaphors for human society, different types of nobility were represented by powerful carnivores: lions, wolves and foxes (Salisbury 1994, 130–1). Such developments were paralleled within emerging heraldry by the popular adoption of lions and eagles as personal badges (Pastoureau 1993, 133–54).

In post-Conquest England, the construction of a unique aristocratic hunting culture, as part of the affirmation of a new political and ethnic identity, was enshrined in a new form of environmental management: a system reserving game, particularly deer, and its habitat within designated forests, chases and warrens (Sykes 2005a). At the same time foreign species – most importantly fallow deer and rabbits – were introduced over the course of the twelfth century, intended, it seems, specifically for containment in protected hunting grounds: parks (Sykes this volume). The proliferation of parks was accompanied by a diversification in their uses, but most recently it has been argued that the significance of deer in aristocratic culture remained the primary motivation for park construction into the fifteenth century (Mileson 2005b). If the park seems like the ideal aristocratic hunting ground – bounded, controllable, secure and visible – to what extent was this reflected in its physical design as well as in contemporary ideals of hunting spaces, and how should it be situated within the broader context of aristocratic hunting culture? This chapter aims to explore these questions, with the starting premise that some form of relationship existed between

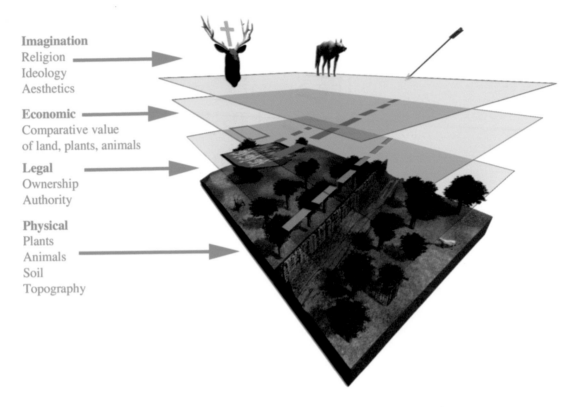

Imagination
Religion
Ideology
Aesthetics

Economic
Comparative value
of land, plants, animals

Legal
Ownership
Authority

Physical
Plants
Animals
Soil
Topography

how landscapes were conceptualised and how they were physically organised (Figure 22).

The relationship between physical and conceptual reality has been examined in the specific case of the park at Hesdin in Artois (van Buren 1986; Duceppe-Lamarre 2001) and, at the regional level, in the use of islands as hunting grounds by the Danish crown (Andrén 1997, 473–5). Both examples demonstrate how the ecology of seigneurial landscapes was tailored or appropriated in very different environments, and the construction of parks in medieval England can be readily situated within the context of hunting as practised and as imagined. Exploring the disjuncture between sources, between physical and conceptual reality, is the principal aim of this chapter.

FIGURE 22.
The medieval park landscape schematised as a multi-layered space; its fauna, flora and physical structure organised on legal, economic and imaginative levels.

Constructing park ecosystems

The construction of a park was extremely expensive at the outset, and so its geographic situation and layout necessitated careful planning. The majority of parks appear to have been designed with deer in mind (Birrell 1992; Rackham 1990, 152–3), and so the imparked landscape became tailored to facilitate both their breeding and hunting, taking advantage of existing woodland and topography (Richardson 2005, 27–8; Cummins 2002, 37). The basic requirements of the park included shelter, fodder and drinking water. Deer particularly required shelter during the fawning season and in winter, and

*The Social
Construction of
Medieval Park
Ecosystems: An
Interdisciplinary
Perspective*

whilst many parks contained some woodland pasture which fulfilled this requirement, in the fourteenth and fifteenth centuries artificial deer houses are also documented (Birrell 1992, 117). These could be quite elaborate: at Merdon Park in Hampshire they were timber-framed buildings with thatched roofs, whilst at the bishop of Durham's park at Stanhope the shelters for deer were described as 'hovells' (Roberts 1988, 78). The configuration of enclosed habitats was therefore the result of choices made at the time of initial imparkment, augmented by later modifications, which might include expansion across the landscape, the deliberate planting of trees and hedgerows, and the subdivision, as well as conversion, of land. In fact, only about half of all parks were compartmented, and smaller parks were less suitable for mixed use (Rackham 2000, 126). Moreover, there is good evidence that imparked woodland was infrequently managed to supply a local market, with the majority of timber and underwood used to provide shelter for deer and raw materials for fencing, as well as contributing a suitably 'sylvan ambience' (Mileson 2005b, 29). Although existing woodland was frequently enclosed, some park landscapes required vegetation to be established; in the early fourteenth century, for example, Abbot Chiriton of Evesham constructed oak and ash plantations in his park at Shrawnell (Bond 2004, 174). A purely wooded park would, however, have been difficult to sustain (Rackham 1990, 157), and it would have also reduced the efficiency of hunting deer, particularly from horseback, and so parks tended to include clearings within their wooded pasture, as well as more open, treeless 'launds' (Rackham 1980, 195).

Alongside shelter, it was important to maintain sources of drinking water for the imparked deer and other livestock. Rivers, streams and springs were deliberately incorporated into park bounds; in Wessex, for example, running water dissected at least half the parks (Bond 1994, fig. 6.10). Where no natural source of water was available, artificial ponds were provided for deer, and at Hambledon Park a water trough for game is noted in 1271–2 (Roberts 1988, 79). The provision of water within a park was not solely for the use of deer, but was fully integrated into the ways in which the site was managed economically and, as will be argued later, conceptually. Imparked streams, lakes and ponds were readily used for breeding stockfish and waterfowl, and could also be incorporated into moated complexes; for example, the majority of lodges and manor houses constructed within parks in Essex were moated (Ryan 2000, 190). The park at Bishop's Waltham was dissected by the river Hamble, which fed the complex of fishponds adjacent to the episcopal palace, which breached the eastern boundary of the park (Roberts 1988, 74, fig. 3). Rivers and marshes could also form convenient boundaries; the park at Closworth in Somerset was bounded on one side by a tributary of the Yeo river (Wilson and Cantor 1969).

Where parks were not wholly dedicated to the maintenance of deer herds, a variety of agricultural landscapes could also be found. Many episcopal parks in Hampshire were situated on productive soil suited to a broad range of agricultural activities alongside deer management; at Bishopstoke Park, for example, a field of oats is documented in 1246–7, and a vineyard in 1477–8 (Roberts 1988, 75–6). In Cambridgeshire, early thirteenth-century parks were situated on economically valuable land of a higher grade than was generally available in their parish, sometimes resulting in settlement disruption (Way 1997, 37–8). Parks could also be quarried: in 1400–1 gravel was extracted at Bishop's Waltham and potter's clay at Farnham (Roberts 1988, 75). The largest parks could therefore incorporate a very broad diversity of habitats for plants and animals. Not all parks were large enough to contain deer or livestock, or were intended for such a purpose (Way 1997, 3–4), but deer, more than any other animal, were the quintessential park species (Birrell 1992, 126).

The license to impark was often accompanied by a gift of deer from a royal forest to stock the park (Young 1979, 96). In all probability the initial distribution of forests mapped the biogeography of deer and ultimately represented a strong magnet for the location of parks. Where parks were constructed within or at the edges of forests, chases and warrens, they were probably integrated into a holistic system of game and land management (see below). This was not always the case, as an inherent tension is evident between the Crown and landed aristocracy over the extent of afforested land. During the thirteenth and fourteenth centuries, as royal control over the forest system waned, many parks were constructed at the shrinking edges of afforested land; following the relaxation of forest laws in the reign of Henry III, parks began to appear around Braydon Forest in Wiltshire (Watts 1998, 90), with similar trends evident in Berkshire (Hatherly and Cantor 1979–80, 67–8), Devon and Nottinghamshire following disafforestation (Crook 2002, 74), whilst in Staffordshire the proliferation of parks between 1200 and 1350 can be directly linked to the shrinkage of the afforested area and the rising political influence of local lords (Cantor 1962, 3).

Deer were managed skilfully during the Middle Ages; there is evidence of considerable understanding of the animal's habitat and needs (Birrell 1992, 113). The introduction and proliferation of fallow deer in England over the course of the twelfth century coincided with the popularisation of parks (Sykes this volume); this species' smaller size and herding tendencies may have made them more suitable animals to confine, and their popularity is demonstrated by their significantly increased representation at the expense of roe and red deer at high-status English sites from the thirteenth century (Thomas 2006). Fallow deer were exclusively taken from parks until the fourteenth century, when they are noted in a number of unbounded hunting spaces (Roberts 1988, 78; Birrell 1996b, 438–9). But alongside fallow deer, roe and even red deer were enclosed. Roe deer were not particularly suited to compartmented parks given their colonisation of hedgerows and small patches of woodland (Richardson 2005, 30), whilst the large size of red deer made them unsuitable for small parks. At Freemantle in Hampshire, from the latter half of the thirteenth century, roe and fallow deer were kept in separate parks; red and fallow deer could be found in the bishop's park at Waltham (Roberts 1988, 77, 81); and attempts were made to stock Plumpton

Park in Yorkshire with red deer in the late fifteenth century (Pollard 1990, 203). The healthy ratio for fallow deer was one animal per 5 acres of land, although some parks appear to have been overstocked. This would have ultimately been detrimental to the herd, as overcrowding promoted diseases such as murrain (Richardson 2005, 34).

Parkland could be seasonally leased as pasture for livestock, but the presence of varying animal species in the park was usually carefully controlled. During winter, livestock were often excluded from parks to preserve whatever meagre fodder was available for deer (Birrell 1992, 117). In fact, this practice could be perennial, indicating the overwhelming importance attached to the management of deer. However, in the fourteenth and fifteenth centuries, the economic focus of some parks shifted from deer to livestock. A clear example is Stanhope Park in Weardale, County Durham. This was initially reserved for deer, but from 1419, when its grazing was leased to the master forester, increasing subdivisions of space resulted in twenty farms and permanent settlement within the park by 1476, and by the end of the century deer were confined to a small enclosure – the New Park – within the pale of the old (Pollard 1990, 209). In the early fifteenth century, Alice de Bryan's park in Bures was used solely for raising livestock with no record of venison (Alston 1992, 3), whilst from the early fourteenth century Mere Park (Wiltshire) was mainly used by the Earl of Cornwall to enclose horses (Watts 1998, 98). Even occasional episodes of illegal livestock presence in parks are documented; in the mid-fourteenth century, Downham Park was 'invaded' by a large herd of pigs, almost certainly directed by owners intend on regaining pannage (Way 1997, 78). Yet the importance of livestock – at least in southern England – should not be overestimated; even in areas where profits could be made from cattle raising, some chose to focus their attention on deer (Mileson 2005b, 32).

While there is clear evidence for the siting and manipulating of the ecology of many parks in favour of deer, the enclosure of rabbits required a comparable attitude to the landscape. The earliest enclosures for rabbits were found on naturally bounded islands, and the shift to the mainland occurred during the thirteenth century (Yalden 1999, 159; Sykes in prep.), although the numbers listed in household accounts do not increase significantly until the late fourteenth century (Roberts 1988, 77–8). Rabbit 'warrens' or 'coneygarths' were artificial constructions ranging in size and shape from small oval mounds to immense lozenge-shaped structures supplied with ready-made tunnels (Williamson 2006). They were enclosed, although rabbits, like deer, could breach the bounds of their enclosures and there are occasional examples of entire crops being destroyed by escaped conies (Bond 2004, 181). Associated lodges housed wardens to combat the threat of poachers, and were also used as a base for the organisation of rabbit hunts. Rabbits warrens could also be found within parks, where they can be identified by field names or surviving earthworks, although the term 'warren' in place-names may have referred to hares, as 'coneyger' was more typically used for rabbits (Richardson 2005, 35).

Hares, unlike rabbits, live above ground, sheltering in shallow depressions, or 'forms' (Corbet and Harris 1991, 154), and were more typically encountered in the unbounded hunting landscape, but their occasional mention in park and warren records suggests they could be fully integrated into the imparked landscape; in 1301, the fence of Somersham Park was broken and burnt, and deer and hares carried away (Way 1997, 75), and in 1365 raiders took hares, conies, partridges and pheasants from the Earl of Arundel's warrens in Sussex (Ticehurst 1957, 18–19). Manorial stewards regularly accounted for the sale of rabbit and hare skins taken from estates, although the earliest evidence for the export of rabbit skins from England dates to 1305, and the industry would take off in subsequent centuries (Veale 2003, 58, 209). By the sixteenth century, rabbits had escaped their bounded warrens and proliferated to become truly indigenous (Williamson 2006; Dam 2002). Wild boar appears to have been stocked in some parks into the early modern period (Roberts 1988, 72; Richardson 2005, 39) and, although little is known about its management, the maintenance of wooded pasture within parks would have provided suitable habitats.

Parks also included habitats for a diversity of wild bird species, of which a few, such as partridges, swans, herons and pheasants, were actively maintained for consumption (Sykes this volume). Concentrated pheasant and swan breeding increased during the fourteenth century and, within the broad trend of increasing wild bird consumption during the late medieval period, zooarchaeological data suggests the consumption of swan increased most dramatically (Albarella and Thomas 2002, 33–4). This was paralleled by the increased regulation of swan breeding; a royal license was required to keep swans and the practice was regulated by the King's Swan Master and his regional deputies, with ownership recorded in elaborate swan rolls and from the fifteenth century enforced by a special court (Ticehurst 1957). Although swans were generally procured from common waters, they were also bred in parks, warrens and chases, with occasional mention of swan-houses and pits (Ticehurst 1957, 115). The dynamic ecology of a park – a shifting combination of the natural and artificial – would have attracted a host of other animals, such as squirrels and moles, and perhaps even foxes and otters, all of which could have been trapped for their fur.

While a diversity of resources facilitated by the imparked landscape could be exploited, the management of deer lay at the heart of medieval park culture. The hunting of deer required woods of different size, age and density separated by areas of open ground and water features; without the restrictions of the forest, all this was achievable in a park (Cummins 2002, 46). Given the importance of deer in aristocratic hunting ideology and the level of control that could be achieved over them and their environment within an enclosed space, is it possible that parks were perceived as idyllic hunting grounds – an aristocratic paradise on earth?

*The Social
Construction of
Medieval Park
Ecosystems: An
Interdisciplinary
Perspective*

Mirrored in romance? Imagining park ecosystems

The development of the forest as a literary landscape from the later twelfth century is rooted in Biblical and Classical traditions, but incorporated the economic reality of the seigneurial forest or *forestis* (Saunders 1993, 204–5). By the end of the twelfth century, as stated above, a common aristocratic hunting culture and semiotic system existed in western Europe, in part reflected by the widespread use, in French, German and, from the thirteenth century, Middle English Romance, of hunting narratives set in the forest. While enclosed parks are occasionally mentioned as recognisable features of the seigneurial landscape (for example, in Chrétien's *Lancelot*), actual hunting episodes in Middle English literature (as on the Continent) are primarily concerned with the pursuit of the hart, and are set within the unbounded landscape of the forest (Rooney 1993). In *Sir Gawain and the Green Knight*, which contains the most developed hunting narrative in Middle English literature, when Gawain comes across the castle close to the green chapel in the midst of a wood, he sees an impregnable palisade of pointed stakes on a plain with a park all around, containing many trees in its 2-mile circumference. This is the only mention of the park and the subsequent hunting episodes, targeting barren female red and fallow deer, a wild boar and fox, take place in the woods and hills beyond its boundaries. Referring to the forest in Chaucer's *Book of the Duchess*, Saunders (1993, 156) argues that the placement of trees at measured intervals and the use of a planned hunting route with relays indicate an enclosed hunting ground. But narrative action in parks is otherwise rare.

Yet if the park was not a popular setting for hunts (or much else) in the semi–imaginary worlds of medieval Romance, the control of wild resources was imaginatively incorporated into expressions of aristocratic authority. Rabbits scurrying in and out of burrows feature on the seal of John de Warenne, the eighth Earl of Surrey (Figure 23). The warren, which occupies a central position on the seal, is accompanied by other visual references to the control of animal resources (Heslop 1987, 117): below it, two swans glide on a river or lake; above it, two pairs of deer flank the Warenne arms, of which at least one is a fallow deer, as indicated by its distinctive antlers. Completing the composition are birds and a squirrel perching on pollarded trees in the background. A second seal shows the earl seated on a throne within a warren (Figure 24), his feet resting on rabbit burrows with a deer browsing to the side, the regal iconography referring to his attainment of a palatinate in 1333 through the acquisition of the earldom of Stratherne in Scotland (Hope 1914, 124–5). The reverse shows the armoured earl on horseback in full gallop, and underneath is a pool with a pair of swans and two cygnets, as well as a crane or stork on each bank.

The use of animals, particularly rabbits, on the two seals is more than simply a pun on the name Warenne, it is also a clear proclamation of access to (and control of) wild animal resources within the context of a hunting landscape, alluding to the hunting privilege of 'free warren', the meaning of

FIGURE 23.
Seal of John de
Warenne.

THE PRESIDENT AND
FELLOWS OF MAGDALEN
COLLEGE, OXFORD

FIGURE 24.
Palatinate Seal of John
de Warenne, 1346.

THE PRESIDENT AND
FELLOWS OF MAGDALEN
COLLEGE, OXFORD

*The Social
Construction of
Medieval Park
Ecosystems: An
Interdisciplinary
Perspective*

'warenne' as game park and *warren* as an interchangeable term with Middle English *coney-garth* (Nishimura and Nishimura forthcoming). John de Warenne, who possessed a number of parks and warrens in Norfolk and Sussex, was almost certainly the patron of the Gorleston Psalter, in the margins of which immense numbers of rabbits scurry around warrens as self-contained emblematic images. The earl was also likely to have commissioned the Macclesfield Psalter, which contains similar representations of rabbits on five of its pages; here they are acting out human roles, such as jousting, and there is only one example of a warren (Panayotova 2005, 56). The Psalter also contains other hunting references in its margins, such as the capture of a fallow buck (f193v), again alluding to the patron's control of, and access to, animal resources within the confines of his parks and bounded warrens. The park, then, could be actively deployed in the visual language of power. A very different visual construction of aristocratic control over wild animals can be found in a fifteenth-century manuscript of *The Master of Game*, a hunting manual adapted by Edward, Duke of York, from Gaston Phoebus's influential *Le Livre de la Chasse* (Figure 25). Here, a park is pictured as a crenellated walled enclosure with four towered buildings positioned at its corners. Within, a hummocky landscape dotted with pollards contains an unlikely combination of animals: a wild cat, wild boar, fallow, red and roe deer bucks, a wolf, fox, rabbit or hare and perhaps a beaver and otter. This is not the representation of an actual park, but one that employs park iconography as the quintessential expression of aristocratic hunting rights, which despite Richard II's game law (see below), continued to focus on particular spaces rather than animals. By the fifteenth century forests had lost their earlier economic function while the park had become established as an exclusive multi-functional economic, social and aesthetic enterprise. In the fifteenth and early sixteenth century, however, the visual enclosure of animals in book illustrations, tapestries and paintings has more often been interpreted in the symbolic and aesthetic language of gardens. Yet the distinction between park and garden was not as sharp as imagined by Bond and Iles (1991, 36–7) in their survey of medieval gardens in Avon and Somerset – enclosures for cultivating plants rather than grazing animals.

In Romance literature, the open and potentially dangerous forest contrasted with the enclosed garden, the typical setting for the most intimate and private encounters between lovers. But the hunt in the forest and the *liaison* in the garden were linked by the language of amorous predation, drawing on a common set of animal symbols. Representations of the walled garden in fourteenth- and fifteenth-century manuscripts of *Le Roman de la Rose* sometimes include elaborate details of its ecological composition. One example (from BL MS. Egerton 1069 f.1) contains a range of pollarded and shredded trees, rabbits scurrying in and out of burrows, and a stag. Superficially, its composition appears closer to that of a park. Yet this is what Piero de' Crescenzi described as a 'pleasure garden' in his *Liber ruralium commodorum* (1304x1309). His text became one of the most frequently published works on

FIGURE 25.
MS. Bodley 546 f.3v.
BODLEIAN LIBRARY,
OXFORD

gardening, and while largely reflecting contemporary agricultural practices in fourteenth-century Italy, it was widely recognised across western Europe as an instructional manual; in the fifteenth century it could be found in the most important royal and aristocratic households in England and France (Calkins 1986, 162). Whilst Crescenzi's descriptions of small and moderately sized gardens focus on arrangements of plants, his recommendation for a royal

*The Social
Construction of
Medieval Park
Ecosystems: An
Interdisciplinary
Perspective*

or seigneurial garden includes the construction of a palace with a view into the walled garden, which should contain a range of wild fauna: hares, stags, roebucks, rabbits, a fish pond, pheasants and partridges, as well as a range of songbirds. The carefully designed ecosystem, which contained animals representing edible game and sensual ornaments (Calkins 1986, 173), contrasts with the enclosed animals represented in *The Master of Game*, where the focus on aristocratic hunting is underlined by the noticeable absence of birds and fish. At the same time, the presence of four turreted buildings in the corners of the park suggests a shared interest with Crescenzi's emphasis on viewing animals within a carefully controlled environment. The importance of being able to see and access a park directly from a residence is evident from analyses of the spatial relationships between parks and manorial sites (see below and Richardson this volume). Furthermore, gardens were constructed within parks, with plants cultivated for alimentary, medicinal and aesthetic uses (Stannard 1986). These could be very noticeable features in the landscape; in 1332, a sizeable *herbarium* was constructed within the royal park at Odiham in Hampshire, surrounded by 2,000 feet of hedge, and with an inner enclosure protected by a boarded fence with five doors, and furnished with a garderobe and turf-covered benches (Colvin 1986, 11). Gardens and parks were designed to be viewed from a distance, as well as from inside, and where both were located next to a manorial site, they effectively represented extensions of the owner's living quarters (Stockstad 1986, 181). It is surely too simplistic to say that the composition of literary gardens and forests was an unrecognisable distortion of (privileged) contemporary experiences (Busby 1987, 85). Indeed, the fantasies of early Romance were ultimately given material form in courtly ritual, paintings, ornaments and tapestries which blurred the distinction between ideals and reality, and in turn inspired further idealised expressions (Barron 1987, 57). Artistic and literary sources which employed animals in recognisable yet simultaneously complex symbolic contexts, rather than being complete fiction divorced from any form of reality, appear to have had material resonance, particularly in late medieval society (Taylor 2000, 51). Even though the park was not a major literary *topos*, its symbolism – as expressed in animals, plants and a relationship with the landscape – seemed to bridge that of the garden and the forest.

Parks and forests: the social ecology of medieval hunting space

Parks seem to have been overwhelmingly geared towards the management of deer, even in the fifteenth century, when economic conditions in many parts of England were likely to promote rival uses for their spaces (Mileson 2005b, 29). What was the relationship between parks and imagined spaces populated with deer? Parks and fallow deer – alongside forests – are mentioned in the fifteenth-century ballads of Robin Hood, which, unlike Chrétien or Marie de France's literary landscapes (still popular in the late medieval period), were firmly grounded in the social and economic realities of contemporary England

(Pollard 2004, 63). Despite this, the aristocratic imagination clung onto the forest. Richard II's law of 1390 restricted the hunting of all designated game to those with a salary of 40 shillings or above, irrespective of the animal's location. This effectively targeted the liberty of rural labourers and artisans by suspending common hunting rights – the entire country became a hunting reserve (Marvin 1999, 228–9). During this time, the emphasis shifted from forests as fundamental economic assets back to hunting preserves (Young 1979, 171–2). Moreover, after centuries of developing a successful literary *topos*, it is perhaps unsurprising to find that the forest continued to be the landscape of choice for narrative action into the fifteenth century. Thomas Malory included hunting as a recurring theme in his *Morte D'Arthur*. For him, the chase in the open forest represented the quintessential knightly occupation, surviving untarnished from the golden age of chivalry (Saunders 1993, 173). Artistic sources are equally biased towards representing the forest in hunting scenes; however, their potential to contribute to an understanding of the prevalence of particular motifs is limited by poor preservation. For example, whilst the famous cycle of Devonshire hunting tapestries are set in idyllic woodland landscapes with no evidence of enclosure, they represent only a fraction of what once existed (Woolley 2002, 40). Literary and artistic sources hint at the continuing relevance of the forest, and yet the hunting and consumption of fallow deer in parks remained a fundamental component of late medieval aristocratic culture. The ways in which the two spaces compared remain open to debate, but the idea that the park was an ideal forest in miniature certainly deserves consideration (Cummins 2002, 47)

To some extent parks and forests were explicitly perceived as separate entities; physically, in literature (as indicated above), and in law: parks were not subject to the jurisdiction of forest law, although trespassing and poaching within parks were covered by royal legislation (Young 1979, 97). Deer populations within parks were maintained, in part, by animals driven or attracted in from the surrounding countryside, and so parks can be understood as one aspect of deer management within a wider context. Parks and forests privatised both space and the select animals and plants contained within. Indeed, Richardson's (2005, 153) study of Clarendon has demonstrated how the management of diverse resources in the royal forest and parks was co-ordinated, a strategy that may have been adopted in forests across the country; certainly, from the Crown's perspective, the forests were very different from one another (Rackham 1980, 184–5). This particular relationship did not, however, bring the ecology of the park closer to that of its surroundings. Unlike forest deer, park animals became wholly dependent on the additional care provided to them (Birrell 1992, 119–20). During episodes of political instability, social unrest or mismanagement, park species could be adversely affected (Richardson 2005, 34). Moreover, species composition and density varied on either side of the park pale. The ecology of forests and chases, both significantly larger than parks, was far more complex. Even if we only focus on the largest mammals there is evidence for very intricate and dynamic ecological relationships; wolves, foxes,

*The Social
Construction of
Medieval Park
Ecosystems: An
Interdisciplinary
Perspective*

wild cats, hares, more often than not red and roe deer (and ultimately fallow), and even feral cattle, roamed independently in the unbounded landscape. It needs to be emphasised that, despite the extensive attempts at habitat – particularly woodland – management, these relationships were very difficult to control. Nonetheless, for the literate aristocrat, hunting in the forest or chase must have retained something of the charm of Arthurian romance, with the possibility of the quarry escaping, of adventure (Cummins 2002, 46).

During the twelfth and thirteenth centuries, the majority of royal houses were located in, or close to, forests, a spatial association that persisted into the fourteenth century (Colvin 1963, fig. 85). As a result, hunting opportunities were readily available in the quintessential unbounded landscape of the chase, although the frequency of royal and aristocratic hunts varied dramatically (Birrell 1992). By the late medieval period hunting in forests was far more unpredictable; from the fourteenth century the office of ranger was responsible for driving deer back into forest bounds. It became significantly easier to organise hunts in parks: 400 deer were driven from the New Forest into the New Park in preparation for Richard III's hunting expedition (Pollard 2004, 87). But then parks had been designed for reliable access to game; keeping prized animals such as swans and deer in a controlled environment not only enhanced parks' symbolic and aesthetic content, but also facilitated ease of access for the purpose of gift-giving, as well as for commercial and alimentary uses (Ticehurst 1957, 11–15). The shift in reliance from forest to park venison is striking in the changing representation of deer species at high-status sites (Thomas 2006).

The reason for the shift was in part due to ecological transformation occurring on a regional, if not national scale. Parks were more strongly correlated with the distribution of woodland than were forests; around a sixth of English woods had been imparked by 1300, although, ironically, these were subsequently reduced as a result of severe grazing pressure, contributing significantly to the overall shrinkage of woodland in the country (Rackham 1980, 191, 195). Populations of wild deer across the country appear to have been in decline from the thirteenth century as their habitat was steadily reduced (Birrell 1992, 124). The war against the wolf in England, largely funded and driven by the Crown, succeeded in exterminating the main source of competition for wild ungulates, but was unable to prevent the decline in roe and red deer populations by the fourteenth century (Pluskowski 2006). By the thirteenth century, wild boar were confined to the Forests of Dean and Pickering, and the rest appear to have been maintained in parks (Yalden 1999, 157); in the north-west of England, the red deer population south of the Lake District was almost entirely enclosed (Higham 2004, 112). It has been suggested that deer populations recovered as a result of the reduction in hunting pressure following the Black Death (Almond 2003, 169) – a population of wild red deer existed in the Peak Forest into the seventeenth century (Jourdain 1905, 157) – but this appears to have been short-lived in some parts of the country. Over-hunting in the Forest of Pickering (Yorkshire) almost

destroyed the resident population of red deer in the latter decades of the
fifteenth century, prompting a royal moratorium on all hunting within its
bounds (Pollard 1990, 205). Whilst the maintenance of parks became increasingly expensive from the latter half of the fourteenth century, prompting
some diversification of land use, as well as abandonment (Bond 2004, 179),
Mileson (2005b, 22) has recently estimated that perhaps 70 per cent of the
3,200 parks existing in 1300 were still functioning by the mid- to late fifteenth century, in contrast to the difference in the extent of afforested land
between the twelfth and fifteenth centuries.

If medieval aristocratic hunting ideology revolved around the control of
game, then parks were clearly included; Rackham's (2002, 22) repeated assertion that 'parks and forests were not "hunting preserves"' cannot be sustained
(Mileson 2005b, 27). Hunting figured as a pre-eminent political factor in daily
life in medieval England (Marvin 1999, 235). Liddiard (2003, 20) has argued
that imparkment had become an issue of enclosure rather than deer management by the thirteenth century, and parks remained the source of tensions
over access to game throughout the fourteenth and fifteenth centuries. Such
stresses found expression in the demands of the rebels during the Peasants'
Revolt in 1381, in violent and bloody park breaks leading up to the 1390 law
(Marvin 1999), and subsequently in Henry VII's hunting legislation (Mileson
2005b, 37). Park breaks, particularly in the late medieval period, were not so
much about subsistence as social discontent and disorder, targeting the physical manifestations of the very identity of aristocratic culture (Way 1997, 77,
81). This manifest identity was underlined by the spatial relationship between
parks and manorial sites. The hunting narratives typified in *Gawain* reinforce
the notion of an idealised hunting landscape in close proximity to the aristocratic house. Manorial sites were occasionally located within parks from the
twelfth century, although lodges, designed mainly for the use of the keeper
as well as to accommodate visiting parties, were more common (Roberts 1995,
98). But during the fifteenth century there was a noticeable increase in the
construction of residences within parkland; sometimes licenses to crenellate
residences were accompanied by permission to create surrounding parkland
(Mileson 2005b, 24).

What developed was a visual relationship between late medieval manorial
sites and their adjacent parks; famously in 1354 a balcony was constructed
at Woodstock in order to facilitate a view of the park (Colvin 1986, 11). At
Harringworth in Northamptonshire, a fifteenth-century stone structure with
a first-floor viewing platform overlooked the centre of the park and an extensive lake, with a similar example at Kelsale in Suffolk (Hoppitt this volume;
Taylor 2000, 42). The exclusive resource of the aristocracy – deer – would be
perpetually visible, as would occasional hunting activities, which, as suggested
by representations of hunts in late medieval art, were meant to be observed.
Parks, much more than forests, would have facilitated the successful chore-
ography of the hunting performance (Marvin 1999, 239–40). It is therefore
useful to integrate the park into the spectrum of late medieval seigneurial

*The Social
Construction of
Medieval Park
Ecosystems: An
Interdisciplinary
Perspective*

culture, which stretched from the deer herds roaming outside to the hunting tapestries displayed within the aristocratic household. In some cases manorial buildings encroached into the park itself, so enabling direct entrance into an exclusive domain, as at Okehampton Park, where the bounds were funnelled into the gates of the castle, the whole complex set within a chase that covered much of the parish (Austin *et al.* 1980, 45). Privacy and exclusivity were clearly increasingly important motivations for park construction, although even from the twelfth century they would have provided secure and controllable environments for practising falconry, especially for young women, and it is not unfeasible that avian prey species were managed in parks specifically with women's leisure in mind (Sykes this volume). Medieval hunting reserves lent themselves to association with domestic sanctuaries by virtue of the level of social and ecological control that could be exerted over them, as well as their proximity to manorial hubs. This relationship featured in the late medieval literary imagination; the parallel use of the hunt and the bedroom features in works such as *Gawain* and *Sir Degrevant* (Marvin 1999, 243–4).

Conclusion: towards an environmental archaeology of parks

Commenting on deliberate attempts to recreate medieval landscapes in eighteenth-century parks, Phibbs (1991) emphasised the benefits of an archaeological approach to understanding the park as a dynamic space. Archaeology has certainly contributed to an expansion of our understanding of imparked landscapes in recent decades; however, applications of environmental archaeology to this field remain limited. Exceptions include the work of Naomi Sykes (this volume). This chapter has suggested how park ecosystems were tailored to specific purposes, and what is required now is more detailed temporal and spatial resolution of this process. The study of parks has been characterised by an obsession with *minutae* and with local case studies, and whilst some have called for national and inter-regional synthesis (for example, Mileson 2005b), others have demonstrated the continuing relevance of the micro-scale (for example, Way 1997). An environmental archaeological approach would encompass both, ranging from attempts to reconstruct the complexity of ecosystems within a single park, or a subdivision within, such as a moated complex, garden or wood (*cf.* Murphy and Scaife 1991, 93), through to the regional ecological context and the employment of a broad range of palaeoecological techniques. An interdisciplinary perspective is also required to give the ecology of parks a meaningful historical context. Again, this chapter has suggested that the construction and maintenance of some, perhaps many, imparked landscapes brought together physical and conceptual aspects of forests and gardens. The park was as much a product of the seigneurial imagination as it was of economic practicality, but it was not a fantasy world divorced from any sort of reality – on the contrary, the park was a social structure fully integrated into the seigneurial landscape. It provided multiple opportunities for, and challenges to, dynamic ecological manipulation, and, appropriately perhaps, the park lies at the centre of significant ecological transformations in England: the proliferation of imported exotics, the extinction of native fauna such as wolves and the depletion of indigenous wild ungulates. Its role in these transformations deserves further attention.

Acknowledgements

I would like to thank Robert Liddiard and Naomi Sykes for their help and support with the preparation of this paper.

CHAPTER FIVE

The Historical Ecology of Medieval Parks and the Implications for Conservation

Ian D. Rotherham

An introduction to parks and their ecology

Since Oliver Rackham's seminal works *Ancient Woodland* (1980) and *The History of the Countryside* (1986), it has been clear that wood pasture was once the most abundant type of wooded landscape in north-western Europe. In essence, wood pasture is a system of land management where trees are grown but grazing by large herbivores is also permitted, be they domesticated, semi-domesticated, wild, or a combination of these. Wood pasture is well documented in England for over 1,000 years, and Domesday Book (1086) probably records a landscape dominated by this type of land use. It has been suggested that wood pasture was an ancient system of management that developed in a multi-functional landscape where woodland was plentiful and where there was little need for formal coppice (a more intensive and rigorously managed system, intended to ensure vital supplies of wood and timber in a resource-limited landscape) (Fowler 2002; Hayman 2003; Perlin 1989). Wood pasture is an older and in many ways a more 'natural' system and, significantly, most livestock, wild or domesticated, will take leaf fodder or browse, if offered, in preference to grazing (Vera 2000).

It would appear that medieval parks are part of a suite of landscape types that mix trees and grazing or browsing mammals. These include wood pasture, wooded commons and forests: the relics of what was probably, in prehistory, a great wooded savannah across much of north-western Europe. In both origins and ecology, parks are essentially a form of 'pasture-woodland', related to forests, heaths, moors, and some commons, with grazing animals and variable tree cover. Aside from the obvious surrounding enclosure, these landscapes are often essentially unenclosed grazing lands. In considering their ecology it is important to establish origins and relationships to other wildlife habitats.

The idea and techniques of constructing and maintaining a park to keep animals such as deer long pre-date the Norman Conquest; parks are known from the first century BC in both Roman Italy and Gaul. Cummins (1988) notes a document of Charlemagne from AD 812 that clearly refers to the maintenance of a hunting park and its boundary. The dates of establishment and the numbers of parks in England remain a matter of debate. There is evidence at Conisbrough Castle Park, South Yorkshire, for example, of a possible lineage of enclosure from around AD 600–700 (Paul Buckland and Colin Merrony pers. comm.). However, the functions are not confirmed and the locations of earlier and medieval features differ. Liddiard (2003) presents an overview of parks in the context of Domesday Book, drawing attention to the possible similarity between parks and hays; the latter are rather enigmatic and perhaps represent a variety of hunting structures with differing degrees of permanence. In the two centuries following the Norman Conquest, the number of parks in England increased dramatically to perhaps 3,000, with possibly 50 in Wales and 80 in Scotland (Rackham 1986). From the early thirteenth century a royal licence was technically necessary to create a park in areas of royal forest, though Cummins (1988) notes that in both England and Scotland baronial parks were also created without licence. Where documents survive, they provide invaluable reference materials for a now vanished age, giving insights into landscape and ecology. The average medieval park in England was around 100 acres, although size could vary considerably. The date of establishment, the area enclosed, the functions of the park and the interplay between enclosed and unenclosed areas all influenced the ecology of these landscapes (Jones 1996; Jones *et al.* 1996).

In Britain, there are two broad distinctions in 'ancient woodland' landscapes. First, there are coppice woods, often managed since the medieval period as simple coppice or more frequently 'coppice-with-standards'. Such areas have relatively few large trees, but strikingly rich and sometimes diverse ground floras. Secondly, there are parklands, which may have historic links back to their use as medieval parks. These areas generally have poorer ground floras due to grazing livestock, and are characterised by massive and ancient trees, chiefly pollards. In terms of wildlife conservation, it has been assumed that coppice woods were an excellent habitat for woodland birds and flowers, and parks for rare lichens and fungi growing on the trees, together with insects or other invertebrates that depended on veteran tree deadwood habitat. The general assumption was that coppice woods had strong links to ancient landscapes and vaguely conceptualised 'wildwood' (Beswick and Rotherham 1993).

Research over the last twenty years has shown many of these assumptions to be incorrect or naïve in their interpretation. Researchers such as Paul Harding developed interest in British pasture-woodlands, and Frans Vera has challenged many accepted 'truths' of woodland history by placing park landscapes in their wider ecological context. There is currently much excitement about the landscape ecology of deer parks because they appear to represent the closest analogies to north-western European primeval forest landscapes. Juxtaposed

with, but different from, medieval coppice woods, parks are unique resources for conservation, and provide insights into ecological history (Rollins 2003). Research by scholars such as Keith Alexander (1998) and Roger Key has transformed the understanding of the importance of parks for invertebrates, and Ted Green has awakened interest in ancient tree fungi and the significance of the trees themselves. In northern Britain, Chris Smout (2003) and others have transformed our knowledge of Scottish woods and the Caledonian pine forests, and palaeoecologists such as Paul Buckland (1979) have closed gaps in information concerning these landscapes and their ecologies in prehistoric and more recent periods.

Recent studies are encapsulated by the seminal writings of authorities like Oliver Rackham (1976), George Peterken (1981 and 1996) and Donald Pigott (1993), and provide coherent visions of woodland landscape ecology, with parks representing an important component of this. From a broader 'woodland' perspective it is possible to assess the historical ecology of medieval parks. Parks have trees (usually but not always), and large (and sometimes smaller) grazing mammals, and to survive trees need protection. Some parkland trees are ornamental and others are managed 'working' trees; fundamental differences in species and structures are associated with these different functions. Taigel and Williamson (1993) and Bettey (1993) give useful introductions to the complexities of these landscapes. Such historical contributions are important since the ecologists must understand history, and the historian the ecosystem. The potential of cross-fertilisation is considerable: Rackham (2004) provides an eloquent exposition on the evolution of park landscapes and of their trees in particular, and Muir (2005) is a particularly accessible account of recent developments.

It is necessary to differentiate medieval parks from other imparked areas and from other associated grazing landscapes, a process than can often be difficult. Parks share features with other unenclosed grazed landscapes which contain trees and woods, such as chases, forests, moors, and heaths. A complicating factor is that many parks took in significant elements of earlier landscapes when they were enclosed, often from 'waste' or 'forest'. In some cases, park management has allowed parts of this ancient ecology to survive; in other cases, parks include features from periods of positive management with specific ends and outcomes, followed by abandonment or changed use. Each phase will necessarily preserve, modify, or remove the earlier ecology of working landscapes that have sometimes evolved over 1,000 years or more. To understand today's ecology requires awareness of changes through both management and neglect, and imparkment may have affected the original ecology in different ways:

Preservation: original features and species maintained within the enclosed area.

Modification: original features and species maintained but modified within the enclosed area.

Removal and replacement: original features and species removed by enclosure and subsequent management, to be replaced by new features and a new ecology.

Such processes may have occurred during the original establishment of a park or at each subsequent phase of 'improvement' or abandonment, generating both continuity and innovation. This process will have varied from site to site: in some cases all that remains today is a single veteran tree, but in other cases a significant parkland resource with substantial elements from earlier periods will be extant. Trelowarren Park, on the Lizard (Cornwall), retains an intact boundary with mature trees and an ancient woodland flora; yet the parkland core has long since gone, replaced by agricultural fields. Veteran trees on the park pale are not park trees, but hedgerow trees since grown out. Earthworks and differences in vegetation may be evidence of changed land-use and boundaries. At Calke Abbey in Derbyshire (Figure 26), for example, the present-day park includes large areas of former medieval open fields, with their characteristic sinuous ridges and furrows.

Much ecological research has failed to differentiate between different origins and histories. For many ecologists, a park is a park. The historical reality is very different and, consequently, the study of ecology in parks is often not placed within a reliable historical framework. There is also little hard information on the ecology of these landscapes in the period when they were 'functioning' parks, and assumptions about this matter are often made retrospectively based on modern observations, or gleaned from material such as household and estate accounts. However, it is essential for an understanding of the historical ecology of parks to appreciate their form and function, and how these have changed over time. In many cases only a fragment of the earlier landscape is visible today, and sometimes these fragments remain unrecognised; even where a park survives with proven continuity to earlier periods, the management today will differ from that in the past. While the former ecology or the management that maintained it may not be fully understood, it is known that the two were inextricably linked. It is not in doubt, however, that the management of a park, the wider landscape in which it is seated and specific features within it will have fluxed greatly over what is often a long history, and the ecology of today reflects this part continuum and part palimpsest. The complexity of park occurrence and presentation in the landscape, both today and in the past, is illustrated by Squires and Humphrey (1986), who have investigated and mapped in detail the parks of the former Charnwood Forest, Leicestershire. As they suggest, the appreciation of any particular park requires consideration of form and function, and an awareness of its historic development. Such thinking applies to a park's ecology as much as anything else.

The uses and functions of medieval parks

Cantor (in Squires and Humphrey 1986) notes that the medieval park was an important feature in the contemporary landscape. He emphasises, however, that the medieval park was different in character to its modern counterparts, the eighteenth- or nineteenth-century 'landscape' park and the nineteenth- or twentieth-century municipal park. As Cantor notes, medieval parks were often areas of rough, uncultivated landscape, were usually wooded, and were frequently located on the edge of manors, away from cultivation (Cantor and Hatherly 1979). It would appear that the working medieval park existed within a landscape of open fields, waste, woodland, and royal forest, with the ecologies of these various land-use types being inexorably linked.

Medieval parks were designed primarily as hunting parks, and to this end were stocked with deer (fallow (*Dama dama*) and red (*Cervus elaphus*)) and other game, which were utilised for the table and for the hunt. In the latter case, this sometimes involved release from the park and into the chase beyond (Whitehead 1964 and 1980), and there were links between hunting in parks and in the forest or chase beyond, and in these landscapes' ecologies: parks were imposed on the wider landscape, including its species and communities, and while the movement of some animals was restricted during some of the time, many species were able to come and go relatively freely. Alongside deer, other livestock exerted additional grazing pressures: wild boar, hares, rabbits (reintroduced to Britain by the Normans), and cattle and sheep. There might also be game birds and fish in fishponds. In the case of parks such as Bradgate, pannage (the feeding of pigs on acorns) from the oaks provided revenue in rents. There were generally large areas of heath or grassland (called launds or plains) dotted with trees, along with woodlands (called holts or coppices, and, if for holly (*Ilex aquifolium*), hollins). The launds and the coppices provided food for animals, and fodder might also be provided through the winter months by the hollins, from which holly was cut on rotation to feed the deer. Solitary trees in the launds were pollarded, and some were shredded (side branches were removed from the main stem). The only new tree growth outside the woods took place in the protection of thickets of hawthorn (*Crataegus monogyna*), holly, and bramble (*Rubus fruticosus* agg.).

The park was surrounded by a boundary fence, called the park pale: a cleft oak fence, or a bank with a cleft oak fence, or a wall. If there was a bank, it normally had an internal ditch in order to prevent the escape of the deer. Park pales often contained structures called deer leaps designed to entice wild deer into the park. Associated buildings included keepers' lodges, banqueting houses and, later, manor houses: the relationship between parks and great houses changed with time and fashion. Originally an enclosed area at a small distance from the main house, perhaps containing hunting lodges, later parks were increasingly the settings for houses and gardens. The house moved to the park, or the park was moved or modified to envelop the house.

Parks were also multi-functional, forming part of the wider economy of the manor. They provided foodstuffs, and wood and timber for building and fuel. Turf and stone were extracted, mineral coal too if it occurred. Squires and Humphrey (1986) noted that arable crops such as cereals were sometimes grown within the park pale. Deer were a priority but, as noted above, shared the landscape with other domestic stock, such as cattle, horses, and even goats. The park at Wharncliffe Chase, near Sheffield, even acquired North American Buffalo in the early twentieth century (Jones and Jones 2005).

The size of parks varied greatly, from smaller baronial parks with semi-domesticated animals to the much larger royal parks (Cummins 1988). Some extended over many miles: Woodstock (Oxon) had a perimeter of 7 miles, permitting hunting on a grand scale. Others were much smaller, perhaps little more than deer paddocks. It follows, therefore, that their ecology must have been similarly varied, larger parks being able to maintain more of the earlier wilderness and the associated ecology. The extent of landowners' influence over parkland landscapes could be substantial, and often went beyond the scale of the individual site: according to Cummins (1988) in 1512 the Earls of Northumberland had a total of 5,571 deer in twenty-one parks spread across Northumberland, Cumberland and Yorkshire.

With socio-economic changes the fashions for parks and the means for their upkeep fluctuated. Most were created from 1200 to 1350, and then declined following the Black Death (*cf.* Mileson 2005b). Consequently, boundaries moved and small parks were enlarged, or were replaced by new creations. As the rural economy changed so did the values and costs of a park. Expensive and difficult to maintain, many parks were abandoned and destroyed. Between the fifteenth and eighteenth centuries medieval deer parks were deliberately removed (disparkment), to become large, compartmented coppice woods, or farmland. Many were abandoned during the English Civil War, and few survived intact as the wave of agricultural improvement swept through the landscape from 1600 onwards. Some, such as Tinsley Park in Sheffield, and Tankersley Park in Barnsley, were lost to industrial development as landowners discovered coal and ironstone beneath their land. A small number retained their medieval character, and some of their functions, to the present day.

Park ecology

The ecology of working parks reflects the factors described above, and today's survivals mirror these events and pressures. Park landscapes had unimproved grassland across much of the grazed area, the species and communities of which varied with grazing intensity. Many grassland plants and associated invertebrates cannot cope with short swards and intensive grazing. If grazing levels were low or areas seasonally protected from livestock, however, the vegetation would have been able to grow tall, flower, and set seed, and would have been similar to modern unimproved pasture and hay meadow. Such areas would have been rich in wild flowers and in associated invertebrates such as butterflies, bees, and hoverflies, with a patchwork of shorter grass, bare ground, and in acidic locations, heath. Wet areas such as valley bottoms, or land with impeded drainage, had extensive moist grassland, marsh or bog. The typical plants of ancient woodlands (such as dog's mercury (*Mercurialis perennis*), wood anemone (*Anemone nemorosa*), primrose (*Primula vulgaris*) and bluebell (*Hyacinthoides non-scripta*)) would have been restricted and found only in enclosed woods, copses, lane sides, hedgerows or streamsides, and perhaps in areas of less intensive grazing.

Key species in the park were deer, with other grazing mammals of varying domestication; these were the main drivers in the park ecosystem. Other important ecological components were fungi associated with both the unimproved grasslands, and extensive animal dunging. There would have been a rich fungal flora of mycorrhizal associates of both trees (ectomycorrhizas), and of grasses and forbes in the sward (vesicular-arbuscular mycorrhizas). These would present as both individual groups of toadstool fruiting bodies, as can be seen today with the dung-associated species such as the shaggy ink caps (*Coprinus* sp.), and as spectacular 'fairy rings'. Associated with animal dunging would be rich faunas of coprophagous and predatory flies, and dung beetles. It can be assumed that high stocking densities would lead to carcases and faunas of species such as burying beetles, and with the mammals also came rich faunas of parasites such as mites, ticks, and biting or egg-laying flies.

Imparking sometimes included the deliberate or accidental preservation of domesticated, semi-domesticated, or wild grazing mammals within the enclosure. The white park cattle are a case in point, with the Chillingham Park herd in Northumberland perhaps the best example; aside from a small herd established some distance away as a precaution against foot-and-mouth disease, this unique breed of ancient cattle survives at only one location. In the late nineteenth century Whitaker described the park as 1,500 acres, well wooded, and with moor and wild grounds (Whitaker 1892). This ancient and extensive park thus enclosed and encapsulated an entire ecosystem that has been maintained ever since. Outside the park, wild species, including the cattle, have long since disappeared. The enclosure of large areas of semi-natural landscape was not the exclusive prerogative of the medieval parks, however. Ornamental parks of the seventeenth and eighteenth century often involved similar scales of enclosure, sometimes from common fields but often from the 'waste'. This may have included marshes, grasslands, heaths and extensive bogs. Hotham and North Cave Park in the East Riding is such an example (Neave and Turnbull 1992). Parkland management also impacted on other species both within and beyond the pale. In particular, predators were vigorously culled – the control of foxes, for example, being noted in estate accounts – and this would have impacts on ecology that were deep and long-lasting.

Trees and wood

The significance of ancient or old wood, living and dead or dying, standing or fallen, has been recognised over the previous two decades. Key publications (Read 1999; Speight 1989; Kirby and Drake 1993) have highlighted the importance of wood for saproxylic invertebrates, especially insects. Others (Rose 1974; 1976; Harding and Rose 1986) have noted the habitat value for epiphytic plants, lichens and fungi. A characteristic of most, but not all, parks was the presence of large, often very old, trees. In the best cases these provide good-quality saproxylic habitats and important continuity of resource over many centuries (Figure 27).

Park trees may have been a mixture of timber trees enclosed when the park was formed, and others planted deliberately as part of the park management. Many parks, such as Chatsworth in Derbyshire, include later additions through the imparkment of field systems and their hedgerow trees. These trees are now veterans in the parkland landscape, but originated in an agricultural environment. Most of the very old trees, often oak (*Quercus robur*), are specimens that have been actively managed for at least several centuries and then abandoned. Now ranging from youngsters of maybe 400 years, to real veterans of anything from 800 to 1,200 years, these specimen trees represent one of the most precious resources of former medieval parks. Early estate survey maps often record significant veteran trees which can be matched to the modern landscape, demonstrating long-term continuity. Indeed, there are many examples where the veteran trees have survived the park. Not all parks have old trees, however, and examples such as Prideaux Place Park in Cornwall are devoid of major veteran trees. It is possible that some parks never had them, or that they have been removed at some point in the park's long history; in some cases, removal is recorded in estate accounts. Younger veterans, potentially valuable timber trees, could be taken in time of financial pressure. When the Duke of Newcastle's Clumber Park estate in Nottinghamshire was sold in the 1940s, the main interest was from local timber merchants who planned to remove all the veteran trees of any commercial value. The National Trust acquired the site and developed it as a recreational park, recouping some of their outlay from the sale of large oaks from the park's ancient woods.

Large trees performed many functions in working parks. They provided shelter in winter and shade in summer for cattle and deer, and, importantly, they could also provide herbage, most deer and cattle preferring to browse on leaves and shoots than graze grass. To ensure a continuous supply of branches and leaves, the trees were pollarded (cut high, several metres above the ground), keeping regrowth out of the reach of the grazing animals until the parker cut it for fodder. Furthermore, the provision of special hollins and hags ensured that herbage was provided for livestock throughout the winter. During the winter months – and beyond, during colder periods – grass does not grow in Britain and stock consequently depend on stores of hay, a valuable and often scarce commodity, and cut branches of evergreen holly. Pollarding extended the lifespan of trees beyond that normally achieved and, in so doing, ensured a major supply and continuity of the deadwood component of the living tree, which is a highly important wildlife habitat.

Large oaks were also grown for timber. In some cases, the trunks and boughs were carefully nurtured to form particular shapes and sizes for specific functions. Careful planning and management over many decades are therefore key aspects of park historical ecology, and the records of great estates often give precise details of the removal of trees, their price and destination. Planting occurred as well as removal, however: around the park, as individuals or as small groups, trees of various native and exotic species were planted, the form and species varying with time and fashion. Now neglected, these younger veterans add to the resource of dead and dying wood in the contemporary park landscape.

Where air quality allows, the bark of these great trees provides habitat for rare lichens. However, oaks have acidic bark, are relatively poor in lichens, and gross air pollution for over a century has exterminated many species over large areas, especially in the English lowlands. With air pollution now falling, there has been a remarkable recovery in the lichen populations of many areas, including within former medieval parks. The importance of ancient pasture-woodlands for the survival of rare epiphytic lichens was highlighted by Francis Rose and his colleagues, and the recovery was well documented by Oliver Gilbert (Rose 1974; 1976; Rose and James 1974; James *et al.* 1977).

The importance of deadwood

Of all the ecological features of ancient parks, conservationists regard the veteran trees and their deadwood as the priority resource (Figure 28). EU regulations have targeted deadwood because of its associated unique and

FIGURE 27.
Rot pocket with
important deadwood
habitat and
invertebrates such as
rare arachnids.
IAN D. ROTHERHAM

diverse fauna and flora and because habitat loss and modification has resulted in critically low levels of this resource across Europe. Dead and dying wood provides unique opportunities for specialist fungi, invertebrates, slime moulds and birds such as woodpeckers, while hole-nesting species such as owls and bats benefit from veteran trees. Nesting birds are protected by law during the breeding season, and bats are specially protected under EU and UK legislation following dramatic declines over the last fifty years. Parkland, especially if it includes rivers and lakes, provides some of their best habitats.

The value of deadwood for wildlife varies with aspect, humidity, temperature, state of decay, continuity on site (as many associated species are highly immobile), and its location on either living or dead trees. If dead, then the tree's state – standing or fallen – also affects associated ecology. The careful analysis of associated fauna and flora provides insights into ecological history and former site management and has the potential to create an ecological archive, complementing other sources of historical information. In particular, many associated species require habitat continuity over time, the presence or absence of key species giving information on site management and on significant breaks in parkland regimes.

Relationships between ancient woodland, especially pasture-woods, and their saproxylic fauna are critical to understanding park historical ecology. Invertebrates vary dramatically in habitat requirements and, importantly here, in dispersal behaviour. Some species migrate, in many cases over considerable distances, and others disperse moderate distances from their breeding sites to new areas. A few species are very limited in their ability to move, and in a very few cases, at least under contemporary environmental conditions, this means only a few metres from the trees from which they emerged. In most cases

89

the larval stage lives in the deadwood or associated habitats, and the adult, perhaps a beetle or hoverfly, emerges to disperse, breed and lay eggs. The critical habitat is the dead and dying wood of ancient parkland trees, but other environments and communities in the park matrix are also important. Adult insects, such as hoverflies or beetles, may feed on the nectar and pollen of plants such as bramble (*Rubus fruticosus*) or hogweed (*Heracleum sphondylium*) and require suitably mature plants in abundance, along with the right light and temperature conditions. Some ancient woodland indicators, for example certain hoverflies, feed not on deadwood itself but on abundant aphids associated with old trees. However, the hoverflies still seem to be closely associated with the continuity of old trees on site. Of the deadwood specialists, some feed on the wood itself in varying degrees of decay, others on the fungi that cause rot. For high-grade invertebrate faunas in these ancient habitats, the keys are habitat continuity and quality. Some species are very specific, such as the black and yellow wasp mimic cranefly *Ctenophora flaveolata*, a Red Data Book species, which is dependent on the soft, decaying heartwood of massive veteran beeches (Figure 29).

It is important to differentiate between species requiring deadwood habitats and those that need continuity because, as indicators, they tell different stories. Interpretation depends on assumptions about behavioural changes associated with climate fluctuations; for example, many invertebrates disperse more effectively during periods of hot weather. Such dispersal may be infrequent, but one instance every fifty years, for example, could facilitate colonisation of a new site, provided the habitat is suitable. Entomologists have meticulously compiled species lists for contemporary sites, and have also generated lists for sites in the prehistoric landscape. These are powerful tools for the assessment of park landscapes, though palaeoecological information is limited by the preservation of suitable remains for analysis. Invertebrate taxa associated with veteran or over-mature trees in lowland England include beetles (Coleoptera), flies (Diptera), spiders (Aranaea), and pseudoscorpions (Pseudoscorpiones), with species dependant on specific stages of decaying wood or bark, and particular humidities and temperatures. Not all the taxa are specific to old trees; some, such as the furniture beetle (*Anobium*), the larvae of which are the woodworm, have adapted to old buildings and even seasoned timber in the open air. A few species, such as the highly synanthropic death-watch beetle (*Xestobium rufovillosum*), have their only records away from old buildings, in the timbers of ancient park trees (Buckland 1975, 1979). Harding and Rose (1986) provided a very useful overview and, although lists have since been updated, the principles remain very useful. They presented taxa in three categories:

Group 1: Species known to have occurred in recent times only in areas believed to be ancient woodland, mainly pasture-woodland.

Group 2: Species which occur mainly in areas believed to be ancient woodland with abundant deadwood habitats, but which have been recorded from areas that may not be ancient or for which the locality data are imprecise.

Group 3: Species which occur widely in wooded land, but which are collectively characteristic of ancient woodland with deadwood habitats.

Harding and Rose noted that reliable interpretation depended on understanding species' ecologies, and variation within species' range. Some invertebrates are very reliable indicators of habitat continuity at the periphery of their range, but occur more widely (in hedgerow trees or even gardens) at the core of their distribution. This suggests that with global climate change some species' distributions may vary markedly. The Lesser stag beetle (*Dorcus parallelopipedus*) is locally common in southern England, occurring widely in ash woods and hedgerows, but much more restricted further north. Another beetle species, *Hylecoetus dermestoides*, is widespread in woodlands and plantations in the north and midlands of England, but has a much more tightly defined range in the south, being restricted to a few ancient pasture-woodlands. The most dramatic clusters of records occur at famous sites such as Moccas Park, Sherwood Forest, and Windsor Park, but there are many records for a similar range of taxa outside known parkland sites (Harding and Wall 2000). This does, of course, raise the issue of whether some of these records relate to unrecognised remnants of medieval park landscapes, and thus highlights the need for further integrated studies.

The demise of the park and the impact of 'landscape' parks

Rackham (1986) states that parks were troublesome and precarious enterprises, the boundary in particular being expensive to maintain, especially for large parks. Owners were often absent for much or all of the year, a situation that could lead to mismanagement and neglect. Deer often died of starvation or of other rather vague causes, such as 'Garget', 'Wyppes' and 'Rot'. In Henry III's park at Havering, Essex, the bailiff was instructed in 1251 'to remove the bodies of dead beasts and swine which are rotting in the park' (Rackham 1978). Even well-run parks faced ongoing problems of maintenance. Rackham (1986) noted that many smaller parks were short-lived, and by the thirteenth century some were already out of use. Sometimes a park was retained but its location changed within the manor, with consequent impacts on the delicate ecologies of these landscapes.

During the sixteenth century, the primary function of the park shifted from game preserve and source of wood and timber, to country house setting. A disused park might revert to woodland through neglect or deliberate replanting, but many former parks became farmland, some, such as Trelowarren in Cornwall, retaining the park pale, which bounded the newly enclosed fields. The late seventeenth and early eighteenth centuries witnessed a fashion for formal design and rigid regularity in both existing and new parks. Landscapes were dominated by straight, tree-lined avenues, walks and canals. At the same time there came a renewed interest in planting trees, and, while wide vistas were cut through existing woodlands, new woods were designed in regular patterns within the overall vision. Nature was perceived to be under strict control, and the parks paralleled the great gardens and houses they accompanied (Lasdun 1992).

Changed fashions provided a new lease of life for some old landscapes, however, with the injection of capital necessary to maintain them against pressure to 'improve' in agricultural terms. If changes allowed habitat-continuity, then some original ecology such as rare deadwood insects might hang on. As Rackham (1986) has pointed out, new parklands were not created from a blank canvas; rather, designers of parks and gardens generally adapted and imposed on earlier landscapes. This could mean working with and maintaining elements of an original park. It might also lead to the creation of a new park that incorporated earlier features from a non-park landscape. Even when formality was very much in vogue it was still felt that venerable trees added dignity to the feel of a country residence. In a social landscape where lineage and continuity were highly valued, then a park that was new but looked and felt old made an important statement. The designer would therefore not only plant anew but would incorporate elements of ancient countryside into their new landscapes. Old pollards and other trees from ancient hedgerows, lanes, or other boundaries were retained and made significant in new settings. This ensured that ancient pollards and sometimes coppice stools can be found embedded in a landscape dominated by seventeenth- and eighteenth-century plantings.

Rackham describes these as 'pseudo-medieval' parks, suggesting that this phase of landscape history both preserved some ancient parks, and created these new sites. He notes the New Park at Long Melford Hall, Suffolk, which incorporated earlier field boundary trees. Similarly, in the eighteenth-century landscape park at Chatsworth, Derbyshire, trackways, boundaries, ridge and furrow and veteran trees survive from the old field systems. Oakes Park, in West Yorkshire, also uses old field-boundary trees to lend an air of elegance and antiquity to a park created in the eighteenth century. Such sites are identifiable from archives and records, from field archaeology (where early non-park features are evident) and also from ecology. They lack ancient park indicators but may have indicators of medieval woodlands, hedgerows, and perhaps veteran pollard trees. This can give what I describe as 'acquired antiquity', the landscape having elements normally associated with a genuinely ancient feature or area, but which are incorporated into a later design, thus acquiring or 'borrowing' fragments from an earlier period. This is presumably what designers hoped to achieve, though perhaps not at the ecological level.

Wooded landscapes, forestry and gardening

As discussed above, the relationships between people and nature, and politics and fashion, were important in determining the lineage and evolution of park landscapes over time. Nature and landscape were becoming the concern of

FIGURE 30.
Veteran oak with
extensive dead and
decaying wood and rot
pocket with bird's nest.
IAN D. ROTHERHAM

the cultured British, whether they were philosophers, poets, writers or artists. The eighteenth century brought a revolution in parkland design with, at the highest social level, symmetry and orderliness displaced by informality and naturalness. This was the era of the great landscaped park, characterised by large areas of rolling grassland. Some parks were substantially recontoured, with naturally shaped woods, clumps of trees (and roundels), individual large trees, and expanses of water. Such natural-looking – but mostly artificially created – landscapes had necessary buildings, such as lodges and boat-houses, and features such as temples, obelisks, mausoleums. From the 1700s onwards new plants (species and varieties), particularly new tree species, were imported and used, beginning a distinctive phase of the ecology of these parks. Still with us today are the exotics and in some cases invasives *Rhododendron ponticum*, Giant Hogweed, Japanese Knotweed, and many others.

Lancelot 'Capability' Brown left a dramatic legacy of designed parkland landscapes, within which key features were the serpentine grouping or dotting of trees, irregularity, and gentle landscape undulations. Water was manipulated in the form of lakes, pools and canals or rivers, with partly wooded banks. Strategic clumps of trees and isolated specimen trees were placed to carry the eye and mind into the distance. Winding ribbons of trees around the periphery of the park implied continuity (and ownership beyond), cleverly blotting out undesirable views. Brown's landscapes are typically impressive vistas which were designed to be viewed, uninterrupted, from the main rooms of the great house. He generally used long-established and native trees, though for special effect also employed exotics. However, Brown and many of successors were great destroyers of what went before, with implications for the survival of early elements in parks subjected to his designs. We know that great avenues of lime and elm were destroyed, as were formal gardens, but little is written about the earlier landscape elements that were lost. Old trees and other features were sometimes saved, but much was removed, and not everyone appreciated Brown's work. Sir William Chambers, for example, described his landscapes as resembling:

> ... a large green field, scattered over with a few straggling trees ... (where) he finds a little serpentine path, twining in regular S's along which he meanders, roasted by the sun, so that he resolves to see no more, but vain resolution! There is but one path; he must either drag on to the end, or return back by the tedious way he came. (Chambers 1772, v–vi)

The Brown-style landscape may superficially have resembled an ancient deer park, but it was a synthetic landscape designed to please, with simplified ecology.

The Picturesque

Humphry Repton, one of Brown's successors, acquired Brown's reputation as 'an improver of landscapes'. He made less use of water than Brown, but his imaginative designs included cattle grazing under mature clumps of trees, dotted individual trees, and surrounding belts of woodland. Brown's landscapes were designed to be seen *from* the house, whereas Repton designed his as settings for the house, to be viewed by those passing by or approaching. In his *Theory and Practice of Landscape Gardening* (1816), Repton used 'before' and 'after' views of a recently improved estate, and argued against improvement merely for profit, suggesting that he had some sympathy for the past and its landscapes. Perhaps in his landscapes there was a chance for continuity and for survival:

> By cutting down the timber and getting an act to enclose the common, he had doubled all the rents. The old mossy and ivy-covered pale was replaced by a new and lofty close paling; not to confine the deer, but to exclude mankind, and to protect a miserable narrow belt of firs and Lombardy

poplars: the bench was gone, the ladder-stile was changed to a caution about man-traps and spring-guns, and a notice that the footpath was stopped by order of the commissioners. As I read the board, the old man said 'It is very true, and I am forced to walk a mile further round every night after a hard day's work'.

The Picturesque movement was important for the survival of elements of antiquity and ecological continuity from medieval parks; Sir Uvedale Price (1747–1829) wrote of landscapes in a way that reflected the past but looked to the future. Price promoted the retention of fine old trees, and the making of new plantations, to give an effect of natural vigour:

> ... the rugged old oak, or knotty wyche elm ... are picturesque; nor is it necessary that they be of great bulk; it is sufficient that they are rough, mossy, with a character of age, and with sudden variations in their forms. The limbs of huge trees, shattered by lightning or tempestuous winds, are in the highest degree picturesque; but whatever is caused by those dreaded powers or destruction, must always have a tincture of the sublime. (Hayman 2003)

He also suggested planting exotics in remote parts of landscaped grounds: 'There seems to be no reason against the familiarising our eyes to a mixture of the most beautiful exotics where the climate will suit them'. This advocacy of exotics was passed down to Victorian gardeners and now is a matter of concern for many conservationists.

The Victorian landscapers

By the time of Victorian gardeners and municipal parks many ancient parks were faded memories or fragments of ecology and landscape. Although some were swamped by urban sprawl or agricultural improvements, others survived in whole or in part, and were incorporated into the final great phase of parkland creation. Sir Joseph Paxton (1801–1865), generally considered the finest of the Victorian horticulturalists (he was famed for Chatsworth and, later, the Crystal Palace), had a beneficial and permanent influence on public parks and their planting, as the boundaries between parks and gardens blurred (Lasdun 1992). William Robinson (1838–1935), whose publications, such as *The Wild Garden* (1870) and numerous books advocating the Gardenesque style, were hugely influential, emphasised the strong use of 'wild', naturalised, exotic species. A pioneer of what are now local authority parks, he is generally held to have had a positive influence on landscape design. One of his main legacies to park ecology was his advocacy of naturalised exotic herbs, shrubs and trees alongside natives, in 'wild' landscapes. These are often amongst the most striking features of parklands today, imposed and imposing on earlier palimpsests.

Conclusions: decline, fall, and re-emergence in the twentieth century

By the late nineteenth and early twentieth centuries many houses, parks and gardens were subject to neglect or became financial liabilities. In the 1950s even famous and now highly valued locations, such as Chatsworth House in Derbyshire, were seriously considered for demolition. The losses and severance of the landscape lineage is beyond calculation. The destruction of Ongar Great Park, Essex, a pre-Conquest survival, was possibly 'the worst loss of a visible Anglo-Saxon antiquity' in the twentieth century (Rackham 1986). So what have we left? The nineteenth-century clergyman and diarist the Revd Francis Kilvert gives some idea, describing the ancient oaks of Moccas Park, Herefordshire:

> ... grey, gnarled, low-browed, knock-kneed, bowed, bent, huge, strange, long-armed, deformed, hunchbacked, misshapen, oakmen with both feet in the grave yet tiring down and seeing out generation after generation ... (Harding and Wall 2000, frontispiece)

Parks and great trees may 'survive' in new landscapes of housing or agriculture, but most are erased from land and memory. Even if the trees survive there is no means to replace them as time and nature run their course; so the remaining sites are conservation icons, often isolated in time and space. They possess a unique resource of ecology: lichens, bryophytes, insects, spiders and more, enmeshed with a cultural lineage from the great forests of north-western Europe (Figure 30).

Finding, preserving and conserving this heritage is a huge challenge. There is no single approach and correct answer, although involving local people and engaging with local communities must be key. It is now suggested and accepted, at least in part, that remnants of medieval parks are vestiges of landscapes that preceded human domination and agriculture (Vera 2000). Vera's vision of a forested savannah suggests links back to the great primeval origins of the European forest through the extant remnants of medieval pasture-woodland landscapes. Harking back evocatively to the past, this view also informs the future: the vision of landscapes is freed from anthropogenic constraints of medieval agricultural and pastoral scenes, setting new challenges for deeply embedded precepts of nature conservation. The best working examples are in the remains of once-numerous medieval parks. Individual case studies prove hugely rewarding and informative and the recent seminal volume on the Duffield Frith in Derbyshire (Wiltshire *et al.* 2005) is a wonderful example of what can be achieved.

Acknowledgements

The author is grateful to Melvyn Jones for access to his research notes on parks, and to Robert Liddiard for thoughtful comments.

PART TWO

Parks in the Landscape

CHAPTER SIX

The Medieval Parks of Yorkshire: Function, Contents and Chronology

Stephen Moorhouse

Much has been written about the medieval parks of Yorkshire. A pioneering study, typical of much of the early work on the medieval landscape, but still invaluable, was carried out by Maurice Beresford (1957, 187–236). Cantor produced a preliminary list of parks amongst his national survey (1983), which has been greatly extended by subsequent work on a wider range of documents. An important study of late-medieval and post-medieval parks in the historic East and West Ridings has appeared (Coates 1960; 1969). Excellent regional studies have taken place, covering the North York Moors (Rimington 1970–78) and East Yorkshire (Neave 1991). Two detailed studies of contrasting parks have been produced: that on the development of the parks at Tankersley and Wortley in South Yorkshire (Hey 1975) and that on Holden Park, one of five parks in the Honour of Skipton (Steel 1979, 1–4). A multi-disciplinary approach to Sheriff Hutton Park has also recently appeared (Dennison 2005).

This present study started life in the late 1970s as part of work on the medieval landscape of West Yorkshire (Moorhouse 1981). It was expanded subsequently to other parts of Yorkshire, primarily the Yorkshire Dales. From its inception this research considered parks as economic units with a number of internal functions that developed throughout the medieval period and into the post-medieval period. It is these varied and changing uses that have produced a series of different and unique landscapes within often changing park boundaries (Figure 31).

Sources

Alongside those documents that provide evidence for the existence of a park, there is a range of other source material, often overlooked in earlier lists, which reveals the working of parks. These sources mainly include those produced by the manor, particularly manorial account rolls and also the long runs of accounts from property held by the Crown. During the first half of the fourteenth century the park attains its own section in manorial accounts under the heading 'costs of the park'. All expenditure on the park is itemised, providing evidence for the growing importance and complexity of the park, and hence the development of the various landscape features in the park. All types of cartographic material are helpful, particularly estate maps and tithe award maps. A wide range of minor names often provide the only evidence for parkland features. The vast range and quality of Middle

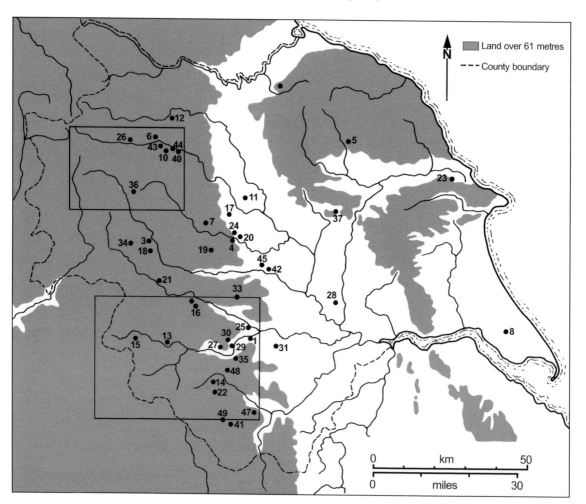

FIGURE 31.
Location of medieval parks mentioned in the text: 1. Altofts; 2. Addlethorpe; 3. Barden; 4. Bilton; 5. Blandsby; 6. Bolton; 7. Brimham; 8. Burstwick; 9. Calverley; 10. Capplebank; 11. Cranswick (or West Park, Snape); 12. Downholme; 13. Elland; 14. Emley; 15. Erringden; 16. Farnley; 17. Fountains; 18. Halton East; 19. Haverah; 20. Hayra; 21. Holden (Silsden); 22. Hoyland Swain; 23. Humanby; 24. Little Park (the home park next to Knaresborough Castle); 25. Methley; 26. Nappa; 27. New Park (Wakefield); 28. North Duffield; 29. Old Park (Wakefield); 30. Outwood (Wakefield); 31. Pontefract; 32. Rothwell Haigh; 33. Roundhay; 34. Rylstone; 35. Sandal; 36. Scale Park (Kettlewell); 37. Sheriff Hutton; 38. Sicklinghall; 39. Spofforth; 40. Sunskew (Middleham); 41. Tankersley; 42. Thorp Arch; 43. Wanlace (West Witton); 44. West Park (Middleham); 45. Wetherby; 46. Whorlton; 47. Woodhall (Wombwell); 48. Woolley; 49. Wortley. The inset boxes locate Figures 32 and 33 within Yorkshire.

English literature, both prose and poetry, has much to offer for its content in describing not only parks and gardens, but the reasons for their existence and particularly the symbolism embodied in especially late medieval designed landscapes. For example, a late fifteenth-century Wakefield pageant play, written in the hinterland of the town, refers to a trist, or hunting stand (England and Pollard 1897, 373, line 207). Such a structure must have been a common sight to Wakefield folk in either the New or Old Parks close to Wakefield (Figure 32).

While there are many terms that describe parks or features found within them, the most common, 'park' has to be used with caution. 'Park' comes from Old French and Middle English, meaning 'an enclosed tract of land for beasts of the chase'. The Old English term *pearroc* developed into park and

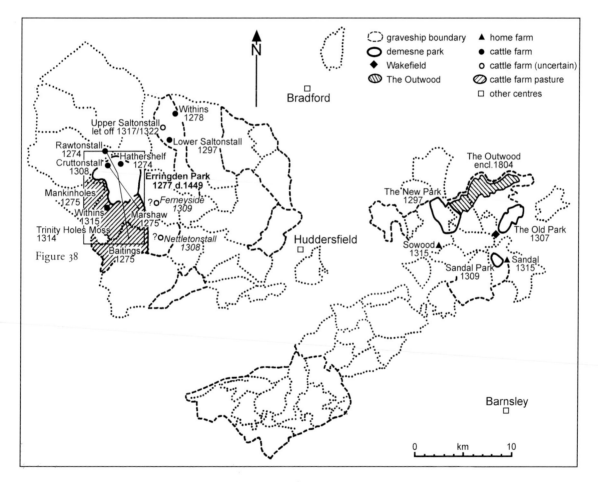

FIGURE 32.

Medieval demesne parks, farms and woodland of the manor of Wakefield. The parks had different functions and life spans: Erringden Park, used mainly for hunting, was officially dispaled in 1449 but was in decline by the early fifteenth century; Sandal Park was abandoned in the seventeenth century and the Old and New Parks survived into the eighteenth century, while the Outwood, although long-since felled of trees, was enclosed in 1804. The earliest recorded dates are shown, but it is likely that their creation pre-dates these. Adapted from Moorhouse 1979, figs 5 and 7.

means 'an enclosed plot of ground, a paddock, a field'. This sense is used frequently throughout Yorkshire from the twelfth century. It refers to many types of small enclosures, from assarts to pinfolds. A detailed late thirteenth-century description of part of Drax Priory's land on their granges of Faweather and Halton in Bingley township lists *Calvepark, Oxpark, Overpark* and *Cotepark*, describing cultivated assarts (Bod. Lib. Top. Yorks. C.72, f.47).

Names have, however, been a crucial source of information for identifying the presence of parkland features, and, by their survival, their location. Names are often interpreted from existing element meanings (e.g. Smith 1962, 150–270). This has acute dangers. Over many years George Redmonds has collected names, and, from their context in the document, defined their meaning. He has recently published a small part of this work, a glossary of terms dealing with spring wood, or nurseries (Redmonds 2004, 211–18). This was the approach followed for the West Yorkshire Survey (Moorhouse 1981), for the work in the Yorkshire Dales (Moorhouse 2003) and for the work outlined in this paper. Had the established meaning of terms been followed, it would have led to much misunderstanding.

The park as an integrated economic and social unit

The park formed an integral part of the lord's demesne. Parks were owned by the Crown and by lay, monastic and ecclesiastical lords alike. The size of the estate and the social position of the owner would determine whether there were a number of parks scattered across different types of terrain in order to suit a particular purpose or whether they were located conveniently for efficient integration into the management of the lord's property. The park of a minor lord, such as that at Thorp Arch, would contain most of the required features. Those on the extensive estates of tenants in chief would each concentrate on particular aspects of social and economic needs, and therefore their landscapes were potentially subtly different from one another. The distribution of parks on the great seigneurial estates is illustrated by those scattered across the manor of Wakefield (Figure 32) and those in the manor of Middleham (see Figures 33 and 34). Monastic and ecclesiastical parks had their own characteristics. The vast home park attached to the west and south of the precinct of Fountains Abbey (Beresford 1957, 196, fig. 18) was devoted mainly to timber production, with fishponds, a water supply, a horse stud and a rabbit warren. They also differ in that senior officers of monastic houses often retired to hospice accommodation in distant parks. Brimham Park was such a park on the vast estate of Fountains Abbey, and the small park at Halton East belonged to Bolton Priory. No two parks were the same. Who created them, what they were used for and why, and their geographical setting, would make each park and its development different. There are, however, a number of characteristics which are common to most parks.

FIGURE 33.
Parks of the Neville family in the manor of Middleham in the fifteenth century.

FIGURE 34.
Detail of the parks around Middleham (see Figure 33), showing their development (small letters). The site of the kennels and stables (now ploughed over with lynchets) in West Witton serving the parks of Wanlass and Capplebank are shown at (a), and the kennels in Middleham township serving the parks of West Park and Sunskew are shown at (b). Their details are to be discussed elsewhere when a multi-disciplinary study, particularly involving earthwork survey, has been completed.

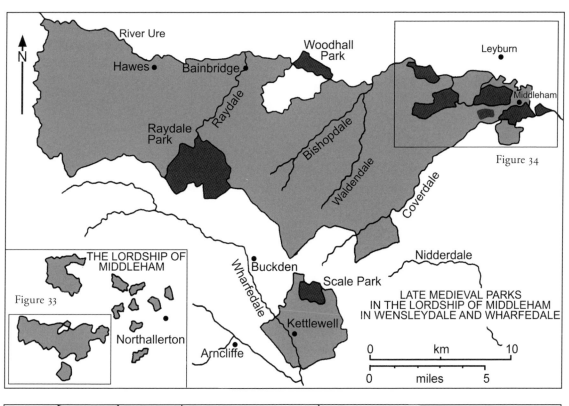

THE LORDSHIP OF MIDDLEHAM

Figure 33

Figure 34

LATE MEDIEVAL PARKS
IN THE LORDSHIP OF MIDDLEHAM
IN WENSLEYDALE AND WHARFEDALE

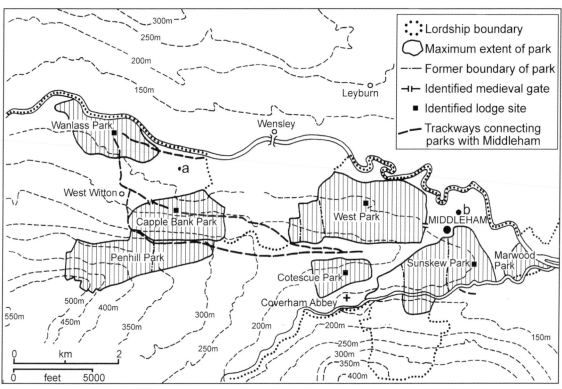

Lordship boundary
Maximum extent of park
Former boundary of park
Identified medieval gate
Identified lodge site
Trackways connecting parks with Middleham

The most obvious feature of the medieval park was that which defined its shape, the park pale. As surviving earthworks they normally appear as banks with a broad internal ditch. The documents demonstrate that, when in use, the banks would be surmounted by a quickset hedge, timber palisade or stone wall, or some combination of these, depending on geography.

The 'costs of the park' section of annual manorial accounts often record detailed repairs to the pale. Timber palisades appear to have been composed of a number of timber features, each having its own terminology. Parts of the pale could have a double boundary, while different forms of construction in timber, quickset and stone could occur around the same short stretch. The wide variation in construction and form are seen in the repair accounts for the Outwood, near Wakefield in 1391 (Taylor 1886, lxv), for Blandsby Park, the home park of Pickering Castle (Turton 1895; 1896; 1897, *passim*), and for the

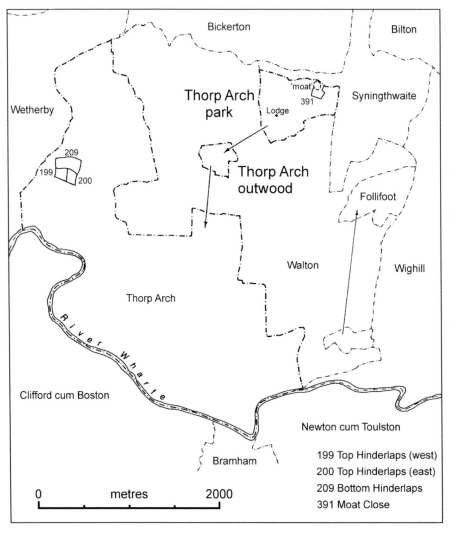

FIGURE 35.
The medieval park of Thorp Arch, lying in two detached parts of Walton township. The park and its outwood were in existence by the thirteenth century, and still lying in open country, with a substantial ditch round much of its boundary, but the outwood is wholly built over. The numbered fields are taken from the 1843 Thorp Arch tithe award, while the 'moat', possibly a stand site, is shown on the 1853 first edition 25-inch Ordnance Survey map, sheet 189. The 'hinderlaps' name is recorded from about 1230. It means the 'female deer leap', but refers to Wetherby Park in the adjacent township to the west, and not Thorp Arch Park.

FIGURE 36.
The wide sweep of
Emley Park boundary
around the top of the
curve of the Dearne
valley. The species-
rich hedge suggests
that this may be the
original line.

demesne parks throughout the Honour of Pontefract in 1420–1 (YAS MS580, ff.162–197r). It is likely that careful fieldwork and detailed field survey may identify the variations mentioned in the documents.

A number of features pierced the park boundary, providing different forms of access. The most common are gates, the numbers of which would vary. There would normally be one or more main gates but there could be a number of others providing access for the tenants of adjacent townships, where they had agistment rights. This was the case for Rothwell Haigh: the 1420–1 reeve's accounts for repairs to the park record the repair of two separate postern gates (*postern yate*) near Hunselt and Carlton (YAS MS 508, f.184). These and others are shown around the perimeter of the park on a map of 1531 (Hoyle 1991, 96–7; pl.1; TNA:PRO DL 31/248. MPC204).

Deer leaps were common on park boundaries, allowing deer to jump into the park or its woodland, but not out. Their creation was strictly controlled. Illegal leaps were created by lords who wished to encourage animals into their parks to increase herds (Cox 1905, 57–8). Expenditure on their construction, repair and demise provide details of their form, while minor place-names and field names help to locate them on the ground. A number of different forms are recorded. Repairs to a leap on the boundary of Wakefield Outwood in 1391 suggest two parallel barriers (Taylor 1886, lxv), while at Blandsby Park, Pickering, some 50 feet of hedging was used to stop up an old leap (Turton 1895, 21). While names can help locate deer leaps, they have to be used with caution. The name *Hynderlopehyll*, meaning 'female deer leap hill', occurs in Thorp Arch about 1230 (Purvis 1936, 74), where there is a well-documented park (Figure 35). The name 'Hinderlaps' occurs in the list of field names in Thorp Arch's tithe award (Smith 1961, 245), but examination of the Thorp Arch tithe award map shows that the name lies near the Wetherby township boundary, and does not relate to the Thorp Arch park, but to Wetherby Park, which lay adjacent to the Thorp Arch boundary in the area of the modern Wetherby Racecourse.

Park boundaries utilised natural features wherever possible. The northern boundary to one of the successive parks in Emley township lies cunningly on the lip of the northern edge of the curving Dearne valley (Figure 36), making it difficult for animals to run up the steep slope and jump out. A quickset hedge still defines the line, the number of species suggesting it may be part of the original boundary (Moorhouse 1978). The southern boundary of Capplebank Park, West Witton, lies on the edge of a very steep slope (Figure 37). The park wall has been built on the top of a rock-cut ledge, the ledge forming a quarry for the stone wall that sits on its edge. This form of boundary is common elsewhere, as on the southern side of Errington Park (Figures 38, 39 and 40). Wherever possible, boundaries incorporated streams just within the park pale. This had a dual function: it provided an important source of water for the animals but also acted as a further barrier, preventing animals getting close enough to the pale to jump over. The incorporation of watercourses and the use of natural features for boundary lines are two important factors in park location.

Changing shapes

Many parks changed their size and hence their shape through time. The various parks in Farnley township, which not only moved their site, but extended into the adjacent township of Bramley (Figure 41), provide an extreme example. Many other parks are less peripatetic, but could extend their boundaries more than once, as in Sunskew Park, east of Middleham, where four extensions have been identified. Some of these extensions were undertaken by agreement. In 1302 2½ acres in the arable field of Sicklinghall was granted to extend William Vavasour's park there (WYAS/L/1514/9). In other cases, and probably more often, it was done illegally. In 1331 it was found that the Earl Warenne had illegally enclosed 16½ acres and four bovates within the New Park (Walker 1945, 197). In this case, as in others, the land was returned, suggesting that some park boundaries could ebb and flow often through their life, either through legal means or otherwise.

Preserved landscapes

The creation or extension of parks could preserve landscapes brought within their boundaries. These landscapes might contain features from the prehistoric and Roman period, as has been shown in Sunskew Park, Middleham. When existing grazing landscapes were enclosed, sheephouses and their attached enclosed pastures formed important imparked features. The sheephouse complex at Cranswick near Bedale went out of use in the mid-fifteenth century, for in 1457–8 a lack of income is explained by the sheephouse 'now enclosed within the west park of Cranswick [Snape]' (Askwith and Harrison 1975,

54–5). Sunskew Park also provides a typical example: in 1474–5 the *Eastcote* sheephouse complex was enclosed within a third-phase extension, with some of the earthwork buildings lying under the wall and others outside to the north. Earthwork survey has shown that parts of the extensive medieval hospital (now represented only by earthworks) on the north-east was reduced in area and the abandoned part included within the original park (created in 1335), while, further south, clearly defined ridge and furrow is cut by the park wall of 1335. Parts of arable fields are commonly found elsewhere underlying dated park walls, providing potential and invaluable environmental evidence with a *terminus ante quam* date.

Riverside meadows

Sometimes a narrow strip of land was left between the park boundary and a river. The best-known example is perhaps Sowerby Ramble, dividing the northern side of Erringden Park from the river Calder. This varies in width from 2 to 440 yards, and is over 5 miles long (Newell 1915) (Figure 38). The Wakefield court rolls show that, by the mid-fourteenth century, the strip was gradually mostly enclosed, both legally and illegally, by tenants. A similar strip separates the northern boundary of Rothwell Haigh from the river Aire. The strip was in existence by the early twelfth century, when part of it was granted to Nostell Priory, while in 1425 a tenant was recorded as holding demesne land, meadow and pasture between the park boundary and the river Aire (Michelmore 1979, 6, fig. 4; 1981, 488–9). These strips appear to be more common, as illustrated by the example of Altofts Park (Appendix 1). These strips were left outside the park in order to provide waterside meadowland, which was highly prized for its rich grass crop (Moorhouse 1981, 696); slow-flowing streams were ideal for this purpose. The notion that these strips were generally used for hay crops is supported by Nostell's use of the strip at Rothwell Haigh for hay, and the name 'Ings' given to the strip at Altofts. Narrow park-side strips were not restricted to riversides, however: a narrow strip about 11 yards wide divided the northern side of The Outwood from the boundary of the manor of Wakefield (Figure 32).

The park lodge

The park lodge was both the administrative and economic centre of the park. The wide range of facilities offered by the park and the heavy responsibilities for management which these produced created not only the need for a centralised place where these could be co-ordinated, but also someone who could do this: the parker. The status of the landowner and the size and function of the park would determine the form of the lodge. The 'costs of the park' section of manorial accounts shows that the lodge complex would act like a small farm, with somewhere for the parker to live and agricultural buildings, particularly hay storage barns. Long runs of accounts can provide considerable detail about such complexes. The most common feature repaired is the lodge building itself. The complex in Roundhay Park near Leeds is typical;

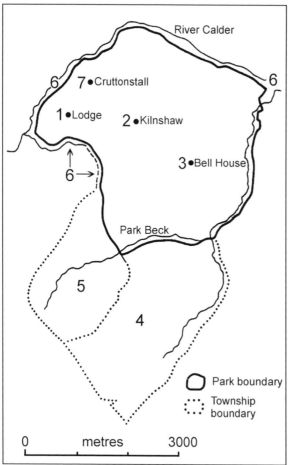

River Calder

6 7 •Cruttonstall   6

1 •Lodge   2 •Kilnshaw

3 •Bell House

6→

Park Beck

5

4

⬭ Park boundary
⋯⋯ Township boundary

0   metres   3000

FIGURE 37.
(*above*)

The southern boundary of Capplebank Park, West Witton (Figure 34). The wall stands on the top of the back of a ledge cut along the top of a steep slope, reducing the need for a high wall by making it easy for animals to get in, but impossible for them to jump out.

FIGURE 38.
(*left*)

Detail of Erringden Park, located in Figure 32, showing principal features with their modern names. 1. lodge site; 2. kennel site; 3. hunting stand site; 4. vaccary of Turley Holes; 5. vaccary of Withins; 6. Sowerby Ramble; 7. vaccary of Cruttonstall.

FIGURE 39.
(*opposite top*)

The southern boundary to Erringden Park (Figure 38), where the wall sits on the front of a rock-cut ledge slightly above the valley floor, above the Park Beck. The view is located on Figure 40.

FIGURE 40.
(*opposite*)

View of the southern boundary of Erringden Park from within the park looking south (Figure 38), showing a common feature: a park wall runs slightly above a stream, which runs within the park; animals could easily jump in but would find it difficult to jump out. Figure 39 lies halfway along the wall looking east.

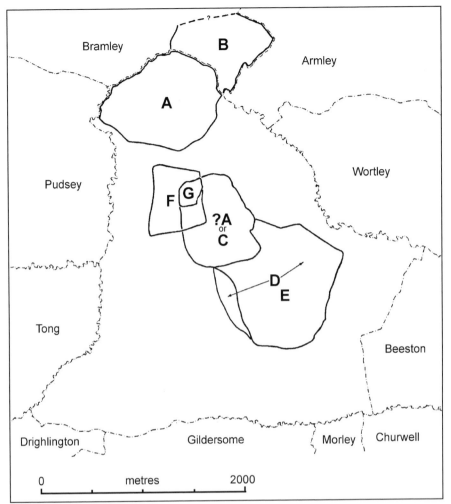

FIGURE 41.
Development of
medieval parks within
Farnley township from
the thirteenth to the
twentieth century:
A, by 1268; B, 1268;
C, possibly by 1268;
D, late medieval,
possibly 100 acres
illegally enclosed by
Christopher Danby
between 1488 and
1507 (Leadam 1893,
241); E, early post-
medieval; F, by 1805;
G, early twentieth-
century. Overlapping
boundaries (F
and A/C) suggest
discontinuity, while
the early park (A) was
extended northwards
in 1268 into Bramley
township (B), onto
land of the abbot
of Kirkstall. Based
on work by S. and
C. Moorhouse and
A. Rymer in the early
1980s.

among many annual repairs, the lodge roof was repaired in 1384–5 (Morkill 1891, 230), while a new three-bay lodge was erected in 1442–3 (TNA:PRO DL 29/510/8251). While the form of the lodge complex may vary, its siting was consistent. Wherever possible, lodges were placed at the highest point of the park, even on a slight rise in low-lying parks, as in Altofts (see Figure 46). Where the manor house lay on the edge or within the park there would be no need for a lodge, as at Sandal Park (Figure 32) and Elland Park (Evans and Lawrence 1979, 92, pl. 13).

Parks within the manor of Wakefield illustrate the variation between lodges (Figure 32). The principal residence lay at Sandal Castle within its own small park, which was administered from outside the eastern boundary of the park. The Old Park, to the east of Wakefield, contained two lodges, their sites surviving as Old Lodge and New Lodge on the first edition six-inch Ordnance Survey map. The New Park, to the west of Wakefield, had only one, the surviving Lodge Farm, perched, typically, on the highest point and dominating the park landscape. The lodge in the hunting reserve of Erringden Park was small and, less typically, the main lodge here lay outside the park; substantial parts of the medieval timber building can still be found within a house in the modern village of Sowerby, with earthworks of gardens surviving to the north. Early fourteenth-century account rolls and fines in the court rolls for the failure to carry out contracts show that the complex had a hall, chamber, kitchen, stables and barns. The lodges within the manor of Wakefield parks illustrate some typical features of those elsewhere, but they also show that there is no stereotypical lodge. While many lodges have disappeared, some have survived the parks of which they formed the administrative centre as working farms with 'Lodge' in their names. Elsewhere, they took on a life of their own: Sheffield Manor started life as a lodge in the park attached to Sheffield Castle, but was enlarged when Sheffield Castle declined.

Woodland

Many early parks were created by simply enclosing woodland for hunting, a process which continued well into the fourteenth century. The origin of the important complex of parks around Middleham (Figure 33) came in 1335, when Ralph Neville obtained licence to enclose his wood of Middleham (CPR 1334–8, 79), probably Sunskew Park. Names play an important part in locating park woodland. Following 'park' and 'lodge', the most distinctive name with which parks may be identified is OFr *launde*, 'a grassy enclosure within parks', which usually develops as laund, sometimes as lawn.

Park woodland, like that elsewhere on the estate, was managed to supply a range of timber and woodland facilities. Often this created a number of separate enclosures where trees of different species would occur. The park at Thorp Arch in 1301 contained 30 acres of alder and hazel (Brown 1902, 167), almost certainly within the park boundary, for there was a separate Outwood (Figure 35). The most-documented species grown either as woodland or hedging was holly, the upper branches of which were an important source of winter feed. The importance of holly has left its mark in many ways, but none more clearly than OE *holegn* in such names as Hollins (Moorhouse 1981, 595, 611, n.113–37; Radley 1961; Spray and Smith 1977). Typical is Hollins Close, shown within Downholme Park in Swaledale on a map of 1730 (Fleming 1998, 92, fig. 6.7).

The name 'Outwood' is often associated with medieval parks. It means precisely what it says: a piece of woodland outside the park boundary. Perhaps the best example is The Outwood of Wakefield, which linked the New Park and the Old Park and occupied an extensive arc of land around the northern part of Wakefield (Figure 32). Often outwoods are physically detached from the park. Some extreme examples are known, such as Thorp Arch Park and its outwood, which are both detached parts within the adjacent township of Walton (Figure 35).

Large carpentry workshops often existed in park or related woodland. The accounts for the manor of Middleham for 1465–6 records 23d for the carriage of a pair of trundle wheels for the water mill at Bainbridge from Middleham

(TNA:PRO SC6/1085/20, m.5d), over 10 miles westwards along Wensleydale. Other evidence suggests that the carpentry shop lay in Sunskew Park and the workman was a manorial carpenter. The Leeds graves accounts demonstrate the extensive use of timber from the manor's park woodland (Le Patourel 1957; Kirkby 1983). For example, in 1383–4 they record the wages of twenty-three carpenters who were felling timber in Rothwell Park and Seacroft Wood (Le Patourel 1957, 61, 115). Other timber in the same account came from a place called *Hope*, a now lost name which can be located on the 1531 Rothwell Haigh map (Hoyle 1991, 96–7, pl.1). The Spofforth accounts of 1441–3 record the making of ten posts for a house that were cut in Agglethorpe Park, worked, and then moved to Linton, 3 miles south-east, for erection (YAS MS880, accounts/19).

Barns and animal shelters
A wide range and large number of barns and shelters existed in medieval parks in the county. They are documented by references to their construction and repair in manorial accounts and through a variety of name elements. They are discussed elsewhere (Moorhouse 2007c; 2007d) and will be mentioned only briefly here. The most common of these constructions referred to are helms, open-sided shelters set within stone wall lines, which are found throughout the medieval farming landscape (Moorhouse 2007c; 2007d), particularly in parks – for example, those in Wanlace Park, West Witton (Figure 42) – and

stackgarths, freestanding stands for drying hay. Undefined structures were built for sheltering the deer. Surviving medieval hay-storage barns in parks show that their form and structures are different to those of barns found on farms.

The lord's private facilities

The special conditions within parks often provided the lord with a range of facilities, for which extra protection was offered by the park's not inconsiderable boundaries.

The home park

Home parks were attached to the main house. Their size would vary both through circumstance and through time. Their purpose was two-fold: most commonly, they provided grazing for the fluctuating but often large numbers of horses corralled; but they also afforded temporary grazing for animals on hoof brought with visiting households. An exceptional case, but one that illustrates the sudden increase in horse numbers as a result of the arrival of a household, occurred in 1318, when Thomas Earl of Lancaster used his castle at Pontefract as his base before going to the Parliament at York (WYAS/L/GC/DL2). The account roll suggests that there would normally be 160 horses at the castle for riding and as pack and draught animals. Between 20 and 24 October, immediately before the Parliament, the number of horses rose from 296 to 682. They clearly could not be accommodated within the outer castle walls, and the most likely place for grazing and perhaps stabling was in the adjacent Pontefract Park. The frequently large numbers of horses and cattle involved meant that they would need considerable management. The court rolls of the manor of Wakefield record that rights to drive the chase and looking after the animals in the Old and New Parks were commonly attached to particular copyhold tenements (e.g. Baildon 1906, 114, 117, 177, 222; Lister 1930, 159; Walker 1945, 114; YAS MS759add, 29). These were some of the many duties regulated by the community of the vill or *byer-law*.

Rabbit warrens

Rabbits were important for their meat and fur, particularly in the later Middle Ages. They were managed in warrens, or coneygarths. Apart from direct references, they are described by a number of distinct name elements and take on a variety of distinctive forms (Moorhouse 1981, 753–6). The range of warrens is illustrated by those within the designed complex of Henry Clifford, the 'Shepherd Lord', at Barden Tower from 1484 (Moorhouse 2003, 345–8) and those created by the Norton family at Rylstone, set within an extensive designed landscape within the park (Villy 1921). Other coneygarths form unusual features: a singular accentuated pillow mound with side quarry ditches is seen in profile from the viewing window at Middleham Castle and forms part of the extensive designed landscape there.

FIGURE 42.
Earthwork of a helm site in Wanlace Park, West Witton. The view looks along the helm, with the large tree on one gable, the other in the foreground. The back wall lies on the right at the bottom of the shallow slope, the other side is defined by arrows. Helms were open-sided shelters mainly for the storage of winter hay, but were also used for agricultural equipment. They are well documented by name evidence, and are common in the landscape. Although they cannot be seen from the air, they are particularly well evidenced by field survey.

Gardens are now seen as part of designed landscapes: principal building, garden and park, all designed as one and meant to be viewed from one or more elevated viewpoints. The ornamental gardens within parks often contain extensive waterworks. Those in the parks at Rylstone, and the West Park and Sunskew Park, either side of Middleham (Figure 34), are mentioned elsewhere (Moorhouse 2003, 329–32). West Park and Sunskew Park at Middleham are well documented; they preserve much of the elite landscape created by Richard III and are currently the subject of detailed field survey.

Animal husbandry

Sheep, cattle and horses were all reared in parks in varying proportions and at different times. Each would require distinct accommodation and grazing pastures; horses could not be grazed with cattle. The appearance of the buildings and pastures for each would be distinct. The physical form of medieval sheephouse complexes, incorporating their closes and grazing pastures, are now well known (Moorhouse 2003, 328–9), and it was the importance of their grazing pastures that attracted landlords to include them in parks. Cattle-rearing was expanded in the fifteenth century at the expense of sheep, and parks became grazing grounds for cattle (Pollard 1990, 202–6). Park grazing grounds could be linked with external vaccaries, as in the manor of Wakefield and the Neville parks around Middleham.

The least well-known but best-documented of these facilities are horse studs, with large quantities and a wide range of horses being reared (Ayton 1994; Davis 1989; Hewitt 1983; Hyland 1999; Langdon 1986). The remains of the range of horse studs and their grazing pastures are now being recognised from place-name study, fieldwork and field survey (Moorhouse 2003, 332–4; 2006a). Many were sited in parks for their ideal grazing pastures and the extra protection afforded by their boundaries. While large numbers are now recognised across the county, such as that at Agglethorpe, in the mouth of Coverdale (Figure 43), the best-documented are the royal studs. The most important royal studs north of the Trent lay in Haverah Park, Little Park (the home park next to Knaresborough Castle) and Bilton Park, all in the Forest of Knaresborough, and Burstwick Park near Hedon in the East Riding (Davis 1989, 41, 91). The extensive documentation for the royal studs (mainly the as-yet largely unstudied *equitata* (horse-business) accounts from 1282 onwards (TNA:PRO E/101)), is now being matched by the recognition of earthwork stud complexes for mares, foals and stallions (Moorhouse 2007a). Some are recognised from a wide range of park names, such as Capplebank Park in West Witton. The name means 'nag, or riding horse bank', which probably explains the extensive earthwork landscape of enclosures and buildings across the southern side of the park. The documentation demonstrates that there are many more stud types that await discovery, potentially made possible by the distinctive plans that could survive in the pasture conditions still prevailing in upland parks.

FIGURE 43.
Earthworks of a medieval horse stud at Agglethorpe, Coverdale. This horse stud, next to the extensive earthworks of the medieval manor and farm complex, lies within the medieval park, whose boundaries are as yet uncertain. The classic courtyard arrangement, with attached closes of different functions, represents one of many different plans now being recognised. Horse studs were very common, are extremely well documented, are often found within parks, and their presence is now being recognised on the ground.

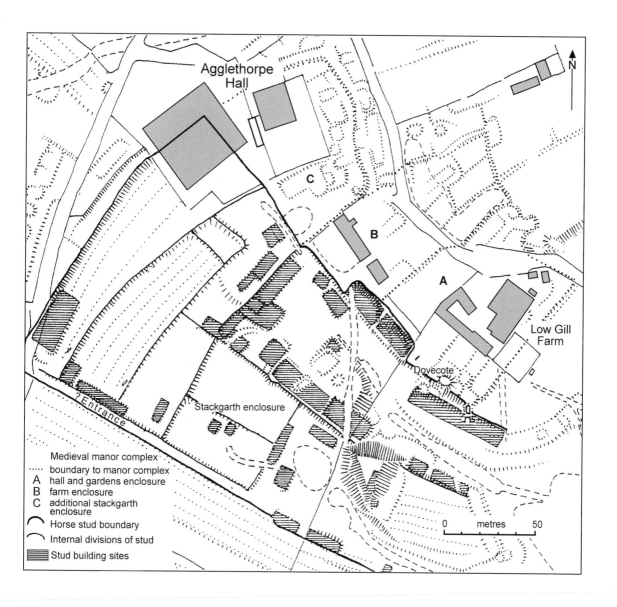

Agglethorpe
Hall

C

B

A

Low Gill
Farm

Dovecote

? Entrance

Stackgarth enclosure

Medieval manor complex
boundary to manor complex
A hall and gardens enclosure
B farm enclosure
C additional stackgarth
enclosure
Horse stud boundary
Internal divisions of stud
Stud building sites

0   metres   50

The hunting reserve

One of the main functions of parks, but by no means the only one, was as a reserve in which a variety of game could be bred and hunted for sport – a private reserve, as opposed to the warren or chase (Cantor 1982). Within the park landscape and adjacent to it, a number of features existed to allow these various activities to take place (Almond 2003; Cummins 1988; McLean 1983, 36–57).

Kennels

The most popular form of hunting was with dogs (Cummins 1988, 21–31, 212–13). Medieval hunting treatises show that different types of dogs were used at different stages of the hunt, often in large numbers. Not only was the knowledge of breeding and the care of dogs highly developed, but sophisticated kennelling arrangements were in use (Cummins 1988, 175). The most typical appears to be a timber structure raised on stilts and surrounded by a stout fence, as illustrated in Gaston Phoebus's *La Livra de la Chasse*, completed in 1387 (Figure 44). Other less sophisticated structures were also built, as seen in a late medieval treatise (Bod. Lib. Doe MS 335, F. 46r).

Some kennels were sited within large parks. Those at Erringden Park (West Yorkshire) probably lay close to the farm now known as Kilnshaw Farm (Figure 38), a name which developed from *Kenalshawe*, 'the wood near the kennel', from 1621 (Kendall 1918, 27–8). Neither the wood nor kennel site has been located in this remote park, which was dispaled in 1449, and had been on the decline since the beginning of the fifteenth century.

Surprisingly, more evidence exists for kennel sites associated with parks

of lower seigneurial classes. A number of parks, for example, have associated names with dog-related elements. The most common is OE *hund*, ON *hundr*, 'hound'. The now obsolete *Hundell*, 'hound hill', referred in 1420–1 to a place near Pontefract Park (YAS MS508, f.164). Hundhill is the name of the hall surviving from within the medieval park of Ackworth, recorded from 1200. A lane leading into Ackworth Park from the adjoining township of Purston Jaglin is called Hound Hill Lane. The most common dog-related name is Hundgate, meaning 'the way used by the hounds', almost certainly referring to the way along which the hounds were taken from the kennel to the park. Hundgate is the name of a settlement in Methley, recorded from 1365 (Darbyshire and Lumb 1934, 142, *passim*) along a medieval road to the east of the medieval park. It is also the name of a street in Hunmandy village (East Riding), adjacent to the medieval manor and park. The place where the Earls Warenne kept their hounds in Wakefield is still called Bitch Hill. The hereditary family who looked after them from the thirteenth century were known as Withehounds – 'with the hounds'. The kennels were sited midway between the two parks of New Park and Old Park.

Map sources, and particularly tithe award maps, are helpful for locating kennels and related sites. The West Witton enclosure map for 1780 gives the names Hound Hill and Stable Close (NYCRO ZKW 2, nos 87, 82) to fields midway between the parks of Wanlace and Cappelbank in the township; surviving lynchets show that their sites have been destroyed by agriculture (Figure 34). A series of dispersed fields called Dog Hill and Whennel, to the north of Middleham in Wensleydale on the 1839 tithe award map (NYCRO MIC1797, nos 69, 469–79), locate the area of these kennels midway between the important home parks of West Park and Sunskew Park, either side of Middleham. The positioning of kennels between major parks is not uncommon. They are usually on major estates and positioned to make it easier to get the dogs to the various places in which they worked. Beech Hill, from Bitch Hill, lies between two important parks, Bilton Park and Haya Park in the Honour of Knaresborough. It is likely that names with OE *bicce*, 'bitch', as opposed to *hund/hundr*, 'hound', refer to places where the various types of hunting dogs were bred, and therefore the physical remains of these kennels may take on different plan forms from those of kennels which housed hunting dogs.

Towers

Towers are often found in parks, but they cover a variety of functions which are often difficult to distinguish by their remains on the ground. The most obvious and best-documented are associated with hunting: the hunting stand. Tower-like structures forming parts of ornamental gardens, often overlooking parks, are better documented in the south of England, such as those constructed at The Pleasance at Kenilworth Castle (Warks.) in 1414–17 and at Broughton Castle in Oxfordshire in *c.*1380 (Harvey 1981, 98, 106–7). One of the most detailed descriptions of a permanent hunting stand in a park

FIGURE 44.
Large square raised kennel within a palisaded enclosure. From a mid-fifteenth-century version of Gaston Phoebus's *La Livra de la Chasse*, illustrated in Bice 1978, 42. Kennels are rarely mentioned in manorial accounts, yet field names suggest that they were common, emphasising the importance of a multi-disciplinary approach to studying parks and their associated features.
BIBLIOTHÈQUE NATIONALE DE FRANCE MS FR.616

is given by Edward, Duke of York, in his early fifteenth-century treatise (Baillie-Grohman 1904, 107). Permanent raised stands developed from ground stations known, significantly, as stable-stands (see below), of the type recorded in the 1327 treatise by William Twiti (Danielsson 1977, 48–9, 110).

Some survive as part of the park lodge complex, which is normally sited on the highest point in the park (see above). Typical is that at Cappelbank, in West Witton. Although only the foundations of the tower survive now, the lodge complex is shown on the West Witton enclosure map of 1780 (NYCRO ZKW 2). A number of typical stand complexes are known, similar to the classic one at King's Standing in Ashdown Forest (Tebbutt 1974). Perhaps the best-preserved example known to date is to be seen in the park attached to Bolton Castle. The foundations of a square stone tower are surrounded with a ditch and berm set on the edge of, and high above, a series of enclosures to the west of the earthworks of the lodge. A similar arrangement is found in Scale Park in Wharfedale. Here a square earthwork lies above the lodge site, now East Scale Lodge Farm, in a park created in 1410, the boundaries of which are, unusually, shown on the first edition six-inch Ordnance Survey map.

Hunting stands can be identified through a series of name elements. Typical are OFr *tristre*, and ME *trystor*, *stable* and *stand*, all meaning 'a hunting stand or position'. The now lost name *Trysterlandes* is found in a Hoyland Swaine (South Yorkshire) charter of 1362 (Hebditch 1948, 104, no. 262). The name Tristor Hill in adjacent Denby township is almost certainly the same place, the change in township created by boundary movement. The name refers to a prominent hill with two platforms, which are surrounded on the northern hill slope by a series of banked earthwork enclosures. In keeping with many other names, this is the only documented evidence known for the park here. The present farm name Bell House, in Erringden Park (Figure 38), can be taken back to 1307, and almost certainly refers to a hunting stand, for there are a series of earthwork enclosures around the farm. 'Stable' and 'Stand' can have dual meanings, but their association with early hunting is documented in the works of William Twiti and others (see above). However, their presence within medieval park boundaries cannot be taken as evidence for hunting stands on their own, and need further confirmation via fieldwork. Many have been identified from tithe awards; typical are Stand Close within Rothwell Haigh in Rothwell township, and Stand Flatts within Sandal Park. Clearly their position is important and in both cases their elevated position helps support the interpretation of the name.

Towers associated with the protection of medieval rabbit warrens are better known in East Anglia (Bailey 1989, 254–5), but they do occur in Yorkshire. Typical is Norton Tower in Rylstone Park (Villy 1921). The lower part of the stone tower (with fireplace) lies at the head of a rabbit warren enclosed with a stone wall. The whole is in a lofty position overlooking the extensive park of the Norton family, with drained ponds around the now-demolished manor house and drained lakes in the undulating former parkland. In keeping with many park towers, it has multiple purposes: protecting the isolated warren from poachers, and acting as a banqueting tower and as an observation tower.

Towers were also built in medieval parks for other purposes. Banqueting towers are known in the late medieval period. The stone foundations of a tower and attached building, with terraced gardens at its front, have been located in the park at Bolton Castle. Its function as a banqueting tower is suggested by its elevated position and by the large quantity and wide variety of high-class English and northern European ceramic tablewares found across the gardens. A complete example exists at Barden Tower in Wensleydale, attached to the chapel. Traditionally thought to be the porch to the chapel, its position within the building complex, the existence of a blocked-in door giving access from the top storey to the roof of the attached chapel, the location of large windows in the top storey only, a kitchen on the first floor and the magnificent all-round views up and down the valley, across the gardens and across the park from the top floor all suggest that this is a purpose-built banqueting tower created by Henry, Lord Clifford. The building accounts for the chapel (1515–17) show that this is one of the earliest surviving purpose-built banqueting towers in the historic county (Moorhouse 2003, 347–8). This tower demonstrates that features associated with parks may not be found *within* the park landscape. A number of towers are found either within or attached to the house complex as places for observing gardens and parks. Typical is the raised west tower of Nappa Hall in Wensleydale, with its elevated corner turret, from which the extensive water-based ornamental garden and park landscape can be viewed.

Traps and snares
A wide variety of traps and snares were used to entrap many types of animals of all sizes, from the rabbit to the deer (Sayce 1946), generally being placed across natural animal runs. Many of these traps were made from rope, and were designed so that they collapsed around the animal when it ran into the mesh. They had many advantages: they preserved the edible meat, which might otherwise be damaged if the animal – particularly smaller species – were shot; they prevented the animal from running away, and allowed the all-important climax of the hunt, the kill, to be carried out in a less hurried fashion; their construction allowed ease of relocation from place to place; and they were easily constructed and re-erected after a capture. A wide range of collapsible rope nets are seen in manuscript illustrations, particularly those accompanying late medieval hunting treatises (Lacroix 1874, 178–216; Sayce 1946). They are best known from the illustrations in Gaston Phoebus's *La Livra de la Chasse*, completed in 1387 but surviving in a number of fifteenth-century copies (Bice 1978, 43, 72–3, 81, 84, 99–101, 104) (Figure 45). The quantity of rope used for nets can be illustrated from the costs of rope sent from Scarborough to Pickering in September 1323. A total of £5 0s 9d was spent on twenty-six stone of small cord and sixty-nine stone of thick cord for the king to trap deer on his journey. A few days earlier 2s was paid to

two people for setting nets for the king to catch roe deer in Whorlton Park, on the western edge of the North York Moors (Turton 1896, 225–6). Illustrations and documents show that rope nets were common, but they leave no physical trace.

A variety of names were given to the different types of trap. Those most commonly referred to are 'deer hays' or 'buckstalls', used for catching deer (Cox 1905, 56–60). They are the traps about which most is known because they are often referred to in accounts of royal or lordly expenditure and, more particularly, in forest court cases brought against minor tenants for the illegal use. In 1488 a number of individuals illegally entered Brandsby Park, near Pickering, at midnight with a horse laden with 'nets called *buckstalles* and ropes', and killed twenty does (Cox 1905, 57). In the Forest of Pickering, during the mid-fourteenth century, tenants were obliged to drive deer to a buckstall as a customary service, from which the Gilbertine canons of Malton and Ellerton, who held land in the Forest, were exempt (Cox 1905, 104–5, 109). It is clear that, while many buckstalls were made from hurdling and rope, some were of earthern banks and were therefore more durable and permanent, as recently shown elsewhere (Taylor 2004).

Other terms were used for traps. For example, a fifteenth-century description of Healaugh Priory's property in Wombwell (South Yorkshire) describes land as lying in *le Gyldersteds* (Purvis 1936, 207); the park implied in the document is Woodhall Park, and not, in fact, Wombwell (Hey and Rodwell 2006). The name comes from ON *gildri*, 'snare', and OE *stede*, 'site of', meaning the site of a snare. Some terms include the name of the animal to be trapped: the name 'wolfpit' is frequently found in medieval minor names in West Yorkshire (Moorhouse 1981, 836–7). Medieval manuscripts show that wolf and boar pits were more sophisticated than simple holes in the ground (Bice 1978, 85–87, 93).

More common and widespread were the various types of bird trap or snare. Medieval manuscript illustrations, many accompanying hunting treatises, show that a variety were in use, from hand-held nets to those fixed in the ground (Lacroix 1874, 178–216). Many of the trapping and snaring sites have gone unrecorded, but some are preserved in minor place- and field names. Early modern English *springle*, 'a snare for birds', may be the root of some of the modern names such as 'Spring Hill', where no medieval ancestry is known, for Spring Hill in Erringden Park has developed from *le Springle Cliff*, recorded in 1462–3 (TNA:PRO DL 29/560/8900, m.3).

The most popular of the minor birds hunted, or at least the best-documented, is the woodcock. Its capture is described in medieval hunting manuals, which describe a netting technique that was in use in some regions until recently (Cummins 1988, 244–6; Almond 2003, 103–5). The most common method was the creation of a passageway through woodland, in which a net was suspended between the trees. This technique gave rise to the common term of 'cockroad' for the netting sites (e.g. Smirke 1848, 118–21), which are generally referred to in the plural, implying that it was customary to create more than one in any given location. The sizes of nets are uncertain. Medieval manuscript illustrations suggest different shapes, but their lack of proportion and perspective do not allow suggestions of their size. In 1617 2s 4d was spent on three pounds of 'merchant thread' to knit a woodcock net 19 yards 'masted' and 11¼ yards deep, clearly a very large net (Ashcroft 1988, 149). The term most commonly found in the county is OE *cocc-(ge)sciete*, 'cock-shoot, place where woodcock were netted'. This frequently occurs as 'cockshot', and it is often found within medieval parks, or the woodland attached to them; for example, two fields called 'Cockshott' occur on the Woolley tithe award map within the area of the medieval park. The netting sites were of sufficient importance to form the subject of property transactions. In 1462–3 12d was recorded for the lease of two *cokeschotes* in the Outwood (TNA:PRO DL 29/560/8900, m.4) north of Wakefield, while an indenture of 1474 grants rights in the park of North Duffield (East Riding), including 'a *cokshote* in the said park' (Clay 1926, 35, no. 67). The small clearing often attracted the term 'glade', hence 'the cock glade' shown on the 1597 map of Elland Park (Evans and Lawrence 1979, 92, pl. 13). The presence of cockshots is also implied: the 1416–17 household accounts of Robert Waterton, lord of Methley, distinguish between the woodcock received by gift and those from the lord's *cokshotys* (Woolgar 1993, 517). They were a source of manorial income. Nothing was recorded from the rent of *lez Cokeshotes* in the park of Spofforth in 1442 (Fisher 1954, I, 166). Woodcock were not only highly prized, but were also easy to catch, and tenants were occasionally fined in manor courts for taking them; at a Wakefield court in 1285, for example, four Ossett tenants were fined the large sum of 12d each for killing *wytecokes* in the Outwood (Baildon 1901, 197).

Enclosure

Rackham has drawn a distinction between uncompartmented parks, uninterrupted by internal divisions, which were used for woodland, and compartmented parks, used for grazing (Rackham 1976, 142–51; 1986, 122–9). The two are not mutually exclusive and any distinction has more to do with chronology, the open parks generally belonging to an earlier period in which woodland was enclosed for hunting. Certainly, by the thirteenth century woodland was being cleared and enclosures created for a variety of uses.

An increasing variety and number of animals were kept in some parks. This often meant that large areas of hay meadow were set aside either within, adjacent to or near to the park, for a good supply of winter feed. At Blandsby Park in 1326–7 enclosure boundaries were repaired to keep the deer out before the meadow was sown (Turton 1897, 251). Sometimes the internally grown hay was insufficient; at Blandsby a year earlier three different sources of hay, including six cartloads from 9 miles away, were needed to feed 50 horses on the stud there, and 1,300 deer (Turton 1897, 227).

The extensive Wakefield court rolls show that tenants played an important role in enclosing within parks. In 1308 4 acres of new land were enclosed 'from the waste land within the New Park', and in 1331 a number of enclosures were created in the same park, one being of 15 acres (Baildon 1906, 175; Walker 1945, 197). The impression gained is that the interiors of parks changed with time. The map of Altofts Park of 1602 shows the interior undivided and without any features, except the lodge, yet a series of medieval reference show that it was enclosed with a number of structures (Appendix 1).

A number of parks include a distinctive feature, the 'inner' or 'little park'. These are usually found in the centre of the park and are completely enclosed. They are sometimes shown on post-medieval maps, such as the 1531 map of Rothwell Haigh (Hoyle 1991, 96–7, pl. 1). In 1297 a number of tenants were fined for trespass within the Old Park of Wakefield, including incursions 'within the middle park' (Baildon 1901, 93). An estate map of Barden township, dated 1731, shows the landscape created by Henry Clifford, the 'Shepard

Lord' from 1484 (Bolton Abbey Estate Office), comprising park, rabbit warren and the 'little park' encircling Barden Tower; a designed landscape which survives intact within the present-day countryside. At Barden it is clear that the little park formed the private reserve of Henry Clifford, and at Rothwell Haigh the little park surrounded the substantial lodge, which no longer survives and whose site is unclear.

Mineral working

Many parks over the Coal Measures and in the uplands were sited over natural mineral resources that were a profitable source of income to the landlord. Even park landscapes were not spared in such situations. In 1322 the grave of Rothwell reported that the ironworkers in the park there were the cause of the drastically reduced incomes from nesting herons, sparrow hawks and honey (Vellacott 1912, 349). The park boundary did not exclude often extensive working.

Iron working

Medieval iron production in Yorkshire was widespread, in some cases long-term, and was run on an industrial scale (Moorhouse 1981, 774–89; 1985; Vellacott 1912; Waites 1964). Parks and associated woodland over the Coal Measures had extensive iron mining and smelting: Rothwell Park, Erringden Park, the Old and New Parks at Wakefield and Roundhay Park are some of the well-documented examples (Moorhouse 1981, 774–89; Vellacott 1912, 349–50). Some works were water-powered, emphasising their permanency, and could be very sophisticated, as illustrated by two examples: the water-powered complex in the small park at Creskeld in 1352, and the late fourteenth-century complex in Calverley Park (Moorhouse 1981, 774–86). The scattered documentation for the latter shows a small self-contained community, with bakers and brewers, lasting for at least forty years. The well-documented smelting complex of the Short family in the Outwood near Wakefield lasted over 150 years from the late fourteenth century. Extensive iron-ore mining could take place, making it important that shafts were backfilled; in the New Park, Wakefield, in 1331, four tenants were fined because they left nineteen of their shafts open (YAS MD 225/1331, m.3). While some landlords exploited their iron resources, others took steps to prevent such work. Separate grants of land in Emley from the Fitz William family to Byland Abbey excluded any iron working within their park there (Loyd and Stenton 1950, 322–3, no.464; WBA DDSR/1).

Stone quarrying

Medieval stone quarrying complexes were much more than just the quarry. They were well-organised enclosures, usually on the edge of or within the park boundary, with places to work the stone and store the three levels of waste created during the successive stages of the working (Moorhouse 1990;

2007d). Quarrying was normally for home consumption rather than for commercial gain, the stone being used for the building of manorial structures, particularly associated with the principal residence. Quarries are known in parks at Methley, Middleham, Barden, Fountains Park and Nappa, but by far the best-preserved complex is that associated with the building of Bolton Castle between 1378 and about 1396. They are partly covered by the extensive ornamental gardens, which in turn are surrounded by the contemporary park (Moorhouse 2007d).

Communications

As parks were essentially private reserves and contained a wide range of facilities and activities enjoyed by landlord and tenant alike, movement within them was strictly controlled. Principal access was limited, although there could be a number of minor access points through the pale for specific use, such as access for agistment from surrounding townships, as seen on the 1531 map of Rothwell Haigh (Hoyle 1991, 96–7, pl. 1). The 1420–1 graves accounts for the Honour of Pontefract provide vivid details of the repair and maintenance of the numerous types of gates in the parks across the extensive honour (Moorhouse 1981, 646). The Wakefield court rolls suggest one of the possible main reasons for their repair – accidental or deliberate damage by the tenants.

Existing routeways could be moved during the creation or extension of parks. In 1314 license was granted to move a way in Little Bolton (Wensleydale) in order to allow Henry le Scrope to create the first of a succession of parks on carefully chosen sites throughout the medieval period, which ultimately ended up around Bolton Castle (NYCRO ZBO/MC/27); both old and new routes can be defined.

The importance of specialised areas such as rabbit warrens, fishponds, meadows and woodland would have necessitated specific routes within the park, and hence gates. At Blandsby Park in 1326–7 an internal gate 18 feet wide was repaired (Turton 1897, 252), while tenants were fined in the manor of Wakefield in 1316 for failing to repair gates in their 'tenements' in the [Old] Park (Walker 1945, 105). Fines throughout the Wakefield rolls for a variety of offences show abuse of gates and routes in the New Park, Old Park and Outwood.

Epilogue

This chapter has covered a wide range of parkland uses. It has been approached through the eyes of a landscape historian, where evidence is amassed, assessed and then interpreted. The methodology is taken from a wide range of disciplines, but includes primary documentary work, place-name study, fieldwork and particularly field survey. Yorkshire is a county of geological contrasts, each region creating its own man-made landscape. The function of parks, their plans, internal details and the material from which they were made all vary, both in time and space. During the above exploration of the main themes, groups of parks in two geographical areas have been examined: the parks on the manor of Wakefield in West Yorkshire, and those in the manor of Middleham, mainly in Wensleydale. While general trends can be identified across the groups, each park was governed by its own unique set of influences. The parks of the sub-infeudated tenants varied from those of their overlords, in as much as the undertenant may have had only one, with a concentration of resources, while the tenants in chief were able to spread their resources amongst a number of parks spread throughout their estate. Parks have to be understood against the background of their creators and their uses, and seen against the society in which they were created. Their layout, content and development can be understood through the important 'costs of the park' section of manorial accounts, which records all expenditure on the park in that year. The various uses enjoyed by tenants often led to abuse, which were punished by the manorial court, providing another important source of information, and showing, for example, the important part played by ordinary tenants in enclosing park landscapes.

Parks were rarely simply deer parks, nor used solely for hunting. Using terms such as 'deer park' or 'hunting park' risks limiting their understanding by focusing on one aspect of use. A much more appropriate term would be, simply, 'park'. Moreover, parks cannot be understood in isolation. They frequently formed parts of designed landscapes which incorporated the principal residence, gardens and park, and which were often created as one unit. Equally, they are often associated with landscapes outside the park, such as grazing pastures and their impact on associated routeways. A number of topics discussed here are to be developed elsewhere, hence their brief treatment here. Many well-documented parks have no surviving evidence on modern maps through either field boundaries or names, an example being Altofts Park (Appendix 1). Often the only documentary indication is a name appearing in medieval documents, be that a field name or the name of one of the many internal features, which has then led to the feature's identification in the field as earthworks, and hence to the presence of the park.

This work is being developed through the execution of detailed surveys of particular parks. These include the parks of the Neville family, around Middleham. Field survey at a scale of 1:1000 is an important tool and has revealed some remarkable results so far, demonstrating that good documentation for parks like those around Middleham can only reveal part and in some cases a small fraction of the story. In effect, therefore, this chapter is an interim report, representing thoughts in progress.

Appendix 1

Altofts Park: a case study, by R. E. Yarwood and Stephen Moorhouse
Altofts Park is an example of a park documented in scattered sources, but for which no evidence exists on first edition Ordnance Survey maps or in local

memory. Its fate is typical of many medieval parks in Yorkshire. The park was in existence in 1602 when Christopher Saxton made a plan of it (WYAS/L/DB 216/23), but the only internal feature shown is the park lodge, whose demolished site is marked today by a clump of trees on a slightly raised area at SE37452424. The park is mentioned in the national survey of royal forests, parks and chases made in 1608 (*House of Commons Journal* 47 (1792), 286), but it is not shown on Speed's map of Yorkshire of 1610, usually a good guide for existing parks, suggesting that the park may have gone out of use between 1608 and 1610. The manor was in decline some years earlier, for a report on the manor house of Altofts in 1594 states that it had been 'decaid of Ancient tyme' and that its ruined walls were not fit to repair for habitation (TNA: PRO DL 44/512). The boundary of the plan produced by Christopher Saxton can be traced in the surviving field system of Altofts (Figure 46), with the exception of the northern line. This has been destroyed by the Aire and Calder Navigation, which received royal assent in 1699.

The 1602 map shows that the interior of the park was open and by then devoid of any features, except the park lodge, but during the Middle Ages it was a hive of activity. The 1304–5 steward's and sergeant's accounts record the large sum of 27s 6d for the construction of a new bercary, or sheephouse complex, at *Fernley* (TNA:PRO DL 29/1/2), and this possibly marks the foundation date for the farm at Fernley Hill, adjoining the eastern boundary of Saxton's park at Foxholes Lane. In 1356–7 18d was spent on digging ditches around land within the park (TNA:PRO DL 507/8226), boundaries which had disappeared by 1602. The graves account for 1420–1 records 4s 9d spent on nine wagon-loads of hay from the meadow of Altofts, and their transport 'as far as *les Helms* within the park there' (YAS MS508, f.168). The plural implies that more than one helm was involved.

The northern boundary, now destroyed, may have been moved southwards, for a commission report in 1587 recommends that the pail 'towards the *Inges*' be moved to dry land within the park (TNA:PRO DL 44/403). The name Altoft Ings still survives, now appended to a strip of meadow along the southern bank of the river Calder. It is probable that here we have another example of a narrow meadow strip between park pales and rivers which produced a highly prized hay crop of the type discussed above.

This outline history was arrived at not through detailed systematic work carried out on the history of the park, but through documentary work and fieldwork evidence carried out for other purposes. It illustrates the wealth of evidence which is available for the history and landscapes of small medieval parks, the evidence for and memory of which was lost generations ago.

Acknowledgements

I am grateful to many people and organisations who have helped in various ways during the preparation of this paper over the past three decades. Professor David Hey drew my attention to his work on Wombwell and saved me from

FIGURE 46. Altofts Park, recorded by Christopher Saxton in 1602 and superimposed on the first edition 25-inch Ordnance Survey map of 1911. The park is typical of many: its presence is not found on the first edition Ordnance Survey map, it cannot be identified from surviving names, and there is no local memory of a park, which often survives in oral tradition. Medieval documentation shows it to be a typical park whose interior plan had disappeared by 1602.

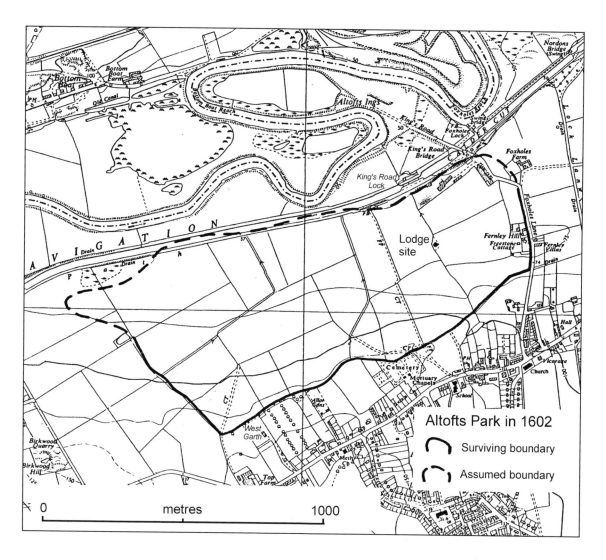

Altofts Park in 1602

⌒ Surviving boundary

⌒ Assumed boundary

misidentifying the park there. Bill Conner (former Principal Archivist) and his staff at the Leeds District Archives: West Yorkshire Archives Service, were, as always, most helpful on numerous occasions, as were the staff of numerous other record offices who held material. Bob Yarwood has helped in numerous ways in the initial work on the paper in the 1980s, not least in allowing his work on Altofts Park to be put together as Appendix 1. Finally, I would like to thank my wife who, as ever, has helped in many ways, particularly in reducing a much larger article to its present length.

CHAPTER SEVEN

The Distribution of Parks in Hertfordshire: Landscape, Lordship and Woodland

....

Anne Rowe

At the end of the sixteenth century John Norden wrote of Hertfordshire, 'This Shire at this day is, and more hath beene heretofore, much repleat with parkes, woodes, and rivers' (Norden 1598, 2) and, from the medieval period onwards, parks have formed an important element in the character of the county's landscape. Lionel Munby described Hertfordshire as 'a county of parks' and found evidence for about forty medieval 'hunting parks or game preserves'; Leonard Cantor listed forty-four parks in 1983 and Oliver Rackham considered it 'the most parky county of all ... with ninety known parks', but the evidence for the latter figure is not stated (Munby 1977, 131; Cantor 1983, 38–9; Rackham 1980, 191). Current research puts the total number of medieval parks in the county at about sixty-six, but there may well be more awaiting discovery (Rowe forthcoming; Figure 47). Surprisingly perhaps, considering the extensive royal forest in neighbouring Essex, no part of Hertfordshire was ever subject to forest law.

The chronological development of parks in medieval Hertfordshire

The earliest parks recorded in Hertfordshire appear in the Domesday returns of 1086 at St Albans, Benington and Ware, each of which was described as 'a park for woodland beasts' (Morris 1976, 135 c, d; 138 c, d; 141 a). Parks have long been considered a Norman introduction but recent work has suggested that several were already in existence in England in the decades before 1066 (Liddiard 2003). Although clear evidence on this point is lacking in Hertford-shire, the possibility that all three Domesday parks had pre-Conquest origins needs to be examined.

There are perhaps three abbots of St Albans who could have established a park. Abbots Leofstan (*c.*1048–1066) and Frederic (1066–1077) both had close connections with the Crown and could have enclosed a park as part of their improvements to the abbey's estates. However, Abbot Frederic and many of the aristocratic English inmates of his wealthy abbey were seen as

FIGURE 47.
Distribution of medieval parks in Hertfordshire. Named parks are mentioned in the text.

a threat by William I, who sought to lessen the abbey's power and influence by confiscating some of its lands. The first Norman abbot, Paul de Caen (1077–1093), recovered some of these lands, including a wood called *Eiwoda* (Riley 1867, 53). Eywood, an extensive area of woodland which lay in a bend of the river Ver south of the town, has been identified as the most likely location for the Domesday park (Hunn 1994, 176–8). The fact that Eywood was not described as a park when recovered by Paul perhaps suggests that, of the three abbots, he is the most likely to have created the park recorded at the time of Domesday.

The two remaining Domesday parks were held by powerful Norman lords with close connections to William the Conqueror, both of whom acquired the lands of an important member of Hertfordshire's pre-Conquest aristocracy. The park at Benington was held in 1086 by Peter de Valognes, nephew of William I and Sheriff of Essex and Hertfordshire. He held land in six counties in the east of England but he made Benington the *caput* of his barony. Before the Conquest, the majority of his lands in Hertfordshire had belonged to a thegn called Aelmer of Benington, one of the chief English landowners

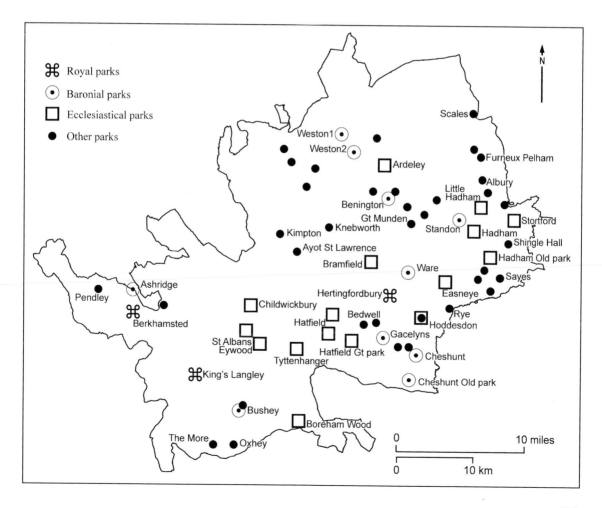

in the shire, who held not only Benington but also five other estates in the county. His main residence (as his name suggests) was probably at Benington and the possibility that he possessed a park might explain why de Valognes chose to locate his *caput* here.

The park at Ware was held in 1086 – although he was not the first Norman to be granted the wealthy manor of Ware – by Hugh de Grandmesnil, a man who had fought alongside William at Hastings and was one of his most trusted followers (Keats-Rohan 1999, 262–3). Grandmesnil acquired the manor in exchange for other lands and the vineyard recorded in Domesday Book suggests that he had a residence there, although most of his interests and extensive estates were in Leicestershire. It is possible that a pre-existing park, created perhaps by the English thegn 'Askell of Ware', was one of the attractions of Ware for Grandmesnil. Askell held extensive lands in Bedfordshire but Ware was by far his most valuable manor and a man of his rank may well have aspired to a park. In any event, the topography of the park at Ware, a spur of high ground between two rivers, would have made a natural hunting ground, with or without deliberate imparkment.

Whether these three parks originated before or after the Norman Conquest will probably never be known for certain and a lack of evidence makes it impossible to ascertain how many parks were created in the county during the late eleventh and twelfth centuries. The first record of a park after Domesday dates from 1199, when the bishop of London granted a portion of land from his 'Old Park' in Much Hadham. The implication is that the park had been in existence for some time and had, perhaps, already been replaced. Another park likely to date from the twelfth century was at Cheshunt. The earliest reference to this park dates from 1226, when Alan de Bassingbourn held it by serjeanty, a position he had inherited from his father and his 'antecedants' before him. This suggests that, by 1226, at least three generations of men had held the park as part of their tenure (CRR 1225–26, 486).

In the eighty years from 1220 to the end of the thirteenth century thirty-two parks appear in the documentary record for the first (and, in some cases, only) time (Figure 48). For none of these parks is the date of their creation recorded; we can only deduce that they were created before the date of their appearance in the historical record. In the first half of the fourteenth century another thirteen parks were recorded for the first time but, with one exception, these could well have been established during the previous century. The exception was Easneye Park in Stanstead Abbotts; the abbot of Waltham Holy Cross obtained a licence 'to impark his wood of Isneye' in 1332 (CPR 1330–34, 259). In the decades immediately after the Black Death three manorial lords obtained licences to enclose parks: Roger de Louthe was granted permission to 'impark his woods of Gippes and Edeswyk' at Oxhey, Watford, in 1360 (CChR 1341–1417, 167); John de la Lee was permitted to enclose '300 acres of pasture and wood in his demesne lands, pastures and woods in the towns of Braughing and Albury' in 1366 (CChR 1341–1417, 192); and, in the same year, Sir Nigel Loryng, chamberlain to the Black Prince, was licensed to enclose

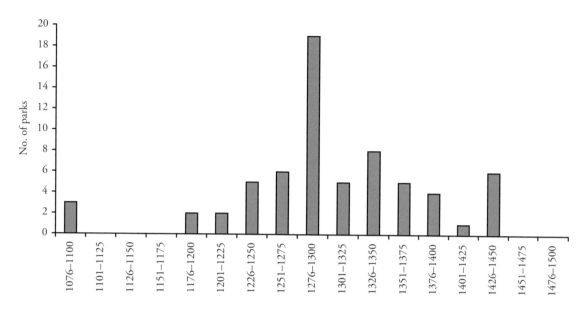

FIGURE 48.
First documentary
reference to parks in
Hertfordshire.

woods at Kimpton (CChR 1341–1417, 193–4). In each case the land being imparked was apparently not abandoned arable land but manorial 'waste'.

In addition to the creation of three new parks, at least two parks were enlarged following the Black Death. These were royal parks in the west of Hertfordshire, both of which were enlarged by enclosing land which had previously been cultivated: 54 acres of land and 10 acres of wood were added to Berkhamsted Park by Edward, the Black Prince, in 1354 (CPR 1354–58, 137) and at King's Langley Edward III added more lands to the park in the 1360s, including 160 acres of former arable land (CPR 1361–64, 93; CCR 1396–99, 107).

The early fifteenth century saw another flurry of imparkment, beginning with a licence granted to John Norbury to enclose 800 acres of his land at Bedwell in 1406 (CChR 1341–1417, 430). The second quarter of the century saw the granting of a further four licences: for the enclosure of '600 acres of land in wood' in Rickmansworth and Watford to make a park at The More in 1426 (CPR 1422–29, 351); for the enclosure of 200 acres of land at Pendley in Tring and Aldbury in 1440 (CChR 1427–1516, 8); for the enclosure of a 157-acre park comprising land, meadow, pasture and wood on the Island of Rye beside the river Lea in Stanstead Abbotts in 1443 (CChR 1427–1516, 38); and for the enclosure of a 520-acre park comprising land, meadow and wood in Sawbridgeworth and Thorley at Shingle Hall in 1447 (CChR 1427–1516, 98). The parks at Bedwell, The More and Shingle Hall were amongst the eight largest medieval parks in the county and all five parks for which licences were granted in the fifteenth century were created in association with a substantial house. A further two parks were established in the fifteenth century, also in association with major houses, at Tyttenhanger (abbot of St Albans) and at Bushey (Earl of Salisbury) (Riley 1870, 261).

Figure 48 shows a notable peak in the last quarter of the thirteenth century, when the number of parks appearing in the records for the first time rose dramatically. Similar peaks have been observed in counties as diverse as Cambridgeshire, Hampshire and East Yorkshire (Way 1997, 21, quoting Bilikowski 1983 and Neave 1991) and probably had as much to do with changing patterns of record-keeping as with an actual increase in park creation. Therefore, many of the parks making their first appearance in the documentary record from 1275 onwards were created earlier in the century, or perhaps earlier still.

Lordship

According to Cantor, 'The Crown and the great magnates, lay and ecclesiastical, continued to be the owners of the largest numbers of parks throughout the middle ages' (Cantor 1982, 76). In counties like Leicestershire and Buckinghamshire, however, he notes that 'long established knightly families' were the predominant class of park-maker and this also seems to have been the case in Hertfordshire (Cantor and Hatherly 1979, 78).

Of the county's sixty-six known medieval parks, only three were held by the Crown (Berkhamsted, Hertingfordbury and King's Langley), while ten were held by members of the baronage and sixteen by ecclesiastical institutions. The remaining thirty-seven parks (56 per cent) were held by lesser lay lords. These were lords of manors who had either inherited, or created, a modest park on their land: men like William de Say of Sawbridgeworth (whose park was first recorded in 1237), William de Ayot of Ayot St Lawrence (1268), Simon de Furneus of Furneux Pelham (1274), or Gerard de Furnival of Great Munden (1283).

Together with the Domesday parks at Benington and Ware, several other early parks occur on manors that were granted to high-ranking members of the Norman aristocracy after the Conquest. The manor of Cheshunt, where a park was first recorded in 1226, was held in 1086 by Count Alan, the son of the Duke of Brittany and son-in-law of William the Conqueror. The manor of Standon was held in 1086 by Rothais, the wife of Richard de Tonbridge, the head of a barony based at Clare in Suffolk. Gilbert de Clare became Earl of Gloucester *c*.1218 and it was probably his son, Earl Richard, who created the park at Standon, which was first recorded on his death in 1262. Another branch of the de Clare family held Weston, whose illustrious twelfth-century lords included Gilbert, Earl of Clare and Pembroke, and William Marshal, Earl of Pembroke from 1199 and Regent from 1216 until his death in 1219 (Gardiner 2000, 550). A park was first recorded at Weston in 1231 (CCR 1227–31, 489).

The manors on which these Norman aristocrats made their parks shared several important characteristics. Benington, Ware, Cheshunt, Standon and Weston were held before the Conquest by high-ranking members of the English elite: Aelmer of Benington (Benington), Askell of Ware (Ware), Edeva the Fair (Cheshunt), Archbishop Stigand (Standon), and Alstan, a thegn of King Edward (Weston). Benington, Ware, Cheshunt and Standon were all classified by Williamson as 'Category 1' vills based on their Domesday entries; that is, they were all 'very large vills, assessed for taxation at more than ten hides, with simple tenurial structures' and 'contained only one manor or estate' (Williamson 2000, 157). Weston, the fifth manor in this group, was assessed at ten hides and also contained only one manor, but had lost several pieces of land to neighbouring vills by 1086. With the exception of Ashridge (created *c.*1270 by the Earl of Cornwall), all of the parks held by members of the Norman elite were located in the eastern two-thirds of the county, and most were relatively large. Those at Ashridge, Benington, Ware, Standon and Weston, for which the acreages can be calculated reasonably reliably, contained an average of 340 acres each. Only Gacelyns (a late thirteenth-century park created by the Earl of Pembroke) was small, covering just 60 acres (CIM 6, 317).

Of the religious houses, the abbots of Ely held the largest area of parkland in the county, probably totalling over 1,650 acres. The areas of two of the three parks on their manor of Hatfield were recorded in 1251: the great park of 1,000 acres (but possibly up to 1,860 acres) and a small park (Middle or Millwards park) of 350 acres (BL Cotton Claudius C.xi, f.155). Innyngs park, covering 100 acres, was established next to their Hatfield residence probably in the late fifteenth century. In addition, Ely had a fourth park on their manor at Little Hadham by 1300 (Newcourt 1708, 829), which covered nearly 200 acres. The abbots of St Albans were also keen park-makers, establishing two parks less than half a mile from the abbey at Eywood and Derefold by the late eleventh and thirteenth centuries and, in the fifteenth century, a third 3 miles away at Tyttenhanger. They also created two parks on their more distant manors of Boreham Wood and Bramfield, both probably in the thirteenth century, and possibly another at Childwickbury in St Michael's parish (Hunn 1994, 178). The parks ranged in size from about 80 acres at Bramfield to perhaps over 400 acres at Eywood, and possibly also at Boreham Wood: probably well over 1,000 acres in total. The bishops of London held Stortford, where they had a 295-acre park, and also Much Hadham, where they had an old park of 190 acres and a newer park of perhaps 85 acres (CPR 1281–92, 45; Page 1914, 60). The canons of St Paul's, London, held the manor of Ardeley, where they had a park of 60 acres (Hale 1858, 21). The abbots of Waltham created a park of about 133 acres at Easneye in Stanstead Abbotts and the dean of St Martin-le-Grand, London, had a park in Hoddesdon (CCR 1288–96, 64). An average acreage for the ecclesiastical parks – where their sizes were documented, or can be estimated – was, therefore, about 250–70 acres.

The earliest parks were created by leading barons and ecclesiastical figures but, during the thirteenth and fourteenth centuries, a growing proportion of parks were established by men of a lower social rank. Most parks in the county, as already stated, were created by ordinary lords of the manor, Cantor's 'long established knightly families'. Although the medieval acreage of many of these parks is not recorded, a calculated guess, based on a combination of map and landscape evidence, would suggest an average size of 70 acres for eight of these early parks, although some, such as Knebworth or Scales, were substantially larger.

The geographical distribution of parks in Hertfordshire

Hertfordshire's parks fall into two distinct zones: those in the south-western part of the county and those in the eastern and northern part of the county (Figure 49). Forty-eight of the county's sixty-six known medieval parks lay in the eastern zone; eighteen parks lay in the west. There were ten parks created after the Black Death, five of which lay in each zone. If these late medieval parks are removed from the picture, it leaves forty-three parks in the eastern zone and just thirteen in the west.

Unfortunately there is no recorded acreage for eight of the thirteen parks in the western zone in the medieval period. Field and map evidence suggests that the parks at Great Gaddesden, Flamstead and Derefold were relatively small (no more than 120 acres), and that the early park at Bushey covered only 10 acres (Hall 1938, 19). Ashridge Park was probably about 200 acres and the parks of Eywood and Boreham Wood *could* have been substantial (Hunn (1994) estimates 418 acres for Eywood). The royal parks at King's Langley and Berkhamsted grew to be very large (approaching 1,000 acres) after the Black Death, but their size prior to 1348 is not known. Queen Eleanor's park at King's Langley covered at least 188 acres in 1276, but could well have been substantially larger, and it was expanded by Edward III in the 1360s (Munby 1963, 16). At Berkhamsted the 'boundary of the old park' shown on the tithe award map (HALS DSA4/19/2, 1839) enclosed an area of 991 acres, but whether the park reached this size as a result of the enlargements made by the Black Prince in the 1350s, or at some time later in the fourteenth or fifteenth centuries, is not clear. The two Hatfield parks for which the medieval acreages *were* recorded – Great Park, at 1,000 acres, and Middle Park, at 350 acres – are also not straightforward. The remarkably tidy 1,000 acres for the Great Park suggests a figurative total intended to convey the idea of a very large area, rather than a calculated measurement, and it may actually have been closer to 1,800 acres. As it is now probably impossible to know the extent of the early medieval park and because its great size would distort any calculation of averages, it has been ignored, as has the tiny 10-acre park at Bushey. A tentative estimate of the average size of an early medieval park in this western zone is therefore approximately 200 acres.

The forty-three pre-1349 parks that lay in the eastern zone ranged in size from just 20 acres at Little Munden to about 400 acres at Benington and Walkern and 560 acres at Standon. Based on the acreages of fifteen parks, for which we can be reasonably confident of the boundaries, the average size of the parks in the eastern zone of the county was approximately 220 acres. So, as far as we can tell from the patchy evidence, there was no significant difference in size between the parks in the western and eastern zones of the county in the early medieval period. What *is* significant, however, is the difference in the densities of distribution: in the eastern zone there were 4.5 parks per 10 km square (25,000 acres), but in the western zone there were 1.9 parks per 10 km square (25,000 acres). That is, the density of pre-1349

FIGURE 49.
Hertfordshire's medieval parks and parish boundaries. The park boundaries have been determined with varying degrees of confidence using a combination of documentary, cartographic and field evidence. 'X' denotes the *approximate* locations of parks for which either the site or the boundaries have not been determined. The dark line marks the hypothetical division between the western and eastern zones of the county. Berkhamsted and King's Langley parks are shown at their late medieval extents.

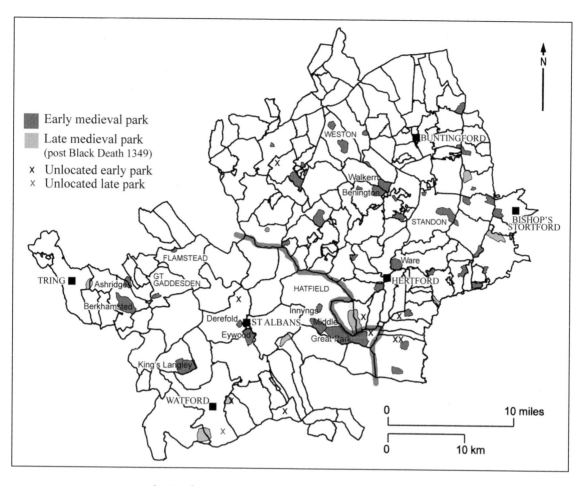

Early medieval park

Late medieval park
(post Black Death 1349)

x Unlocated early park
x Unlocated late park

parks in the eastern zone was nearly 2.5 times that in the western zone. After the Black Death the balance between the two zones evened out slightly but, taking all the county's medieval parks into account, the density of parks in the east remains double that in the west. The factors underlying this pattern of park distribution in the county will now be examined.

Parks and woodland

Previous commentators have consistently remarked upon a close correlation between the distribution of medieval parks and areas of abundant woodland, the latter largely deduced from information recorded in Domesday Book (Cantor and Hatherly 1979, 74–5; Cantor 1982, 77; Rackham 1980, 191). Cantor and Hatherly noted that 'a high woodland cover in the Domesday Book of 1086 was almost always the scene of much subsequent imparkment' (Cantor and Hatherly 1979, 75) and Liddiard states that 'large amounts of woodland invariably appear in conjunction with parks' (Liddiard 2003, 9). Examples quoted include Warwickshire, where the well-wooded area north of the Avon sustained forty-nine parks, in contrast to the well-cultivated and thinly wooded

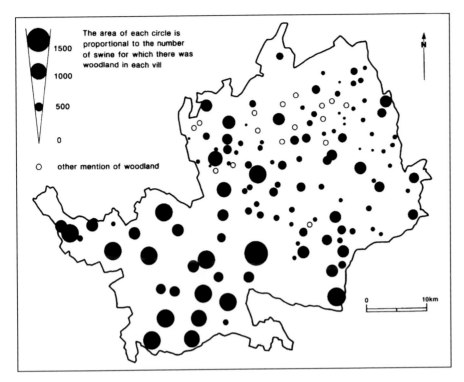

The area of each circle is proportional to the number of swine for which there was woodland in each vill

1500

1000

500

0

O   other mention of woodland

0   10km

area south of the river, which held just three parks (Cantor 1982, 80). Fertile agricultural land, such as the Vale of Aylesbury in Buckinghamshire, or the Vale of Belvoir in Leicestershire, were said to have been cleared of woodland by the eleventh century and were, in consequence, virtually devoid of parks (Cantor 1982, 81). Rackham, however, does note some exceptions to this general rule, including, for example, the densely wooded Sussex Weald, which 'had little above the average density of parks', and also poorly wooded areas, such as other parts of Sussex and also parts of Leicestershire, which had many parks (Rackham 1999a, 123).

Hertfordshire can also lay claim to being a significant anomaly in this relationship between Domesday woodland and medieval parks. Figure 50 reveals a marked concentration of Domesday woodland in the south and west of the county. In contrast, as we have seen, most of the medieval parks were located in the north and east (Figures 47 and 49). An explanation for this clear departure from the accepted 'norm' requires a detailed analysis of both the distribution and nature of the woodland in the county in the eleventh century and the reasons behind the variations in the intensity of park creation in the succeeding two centuries.

Woodland in Hertfordshire

There is abundant evidence to suggest that much of south-western Hertfordshire was still thickly wooded in the eleventh century. This area forms part of the Chiltern region and lay within what Rackham described as 'one of the largest wooded areas in England [which] extended from the Chiltern escarpment down the dipslope almost to the gates of London' (Rackham 1980, 123). A medieval monk at the abbey of St Albans claimed that 'the whole of the Chilterns was a dense and impenetrable forest, full of wild and fierce beasts' until the eleventh century and Abbot Leofstan (*c.*1048–1066) is said to have 'cleared the thick woods south of Watling Street from the Chilterns to London' in order to make the roads safer for travellers (Levett 1938, 180 quoting *Gesta Abbatum*, I, 39–40). Further south, a charter of King Offa (dated AD 785), granting land in Aldenham to Westminster Abbey, specifically mentioned the density of the woods (Birch 1885, 339), although several landscape features recorded in the boundary clause of this charter suggest a managed landscape of woods and clearings rather than an untamed wilderness. A similar woody landscape is suggested for the large estate further north at Wheathampstead in a charter confirming its ownership by Westminster Abbey in 1060 (Williamson 2000, 136–8).

Anglo-Saxon place-names indicating woodland and its clearance are curiously sparse in south-west Hertfordshire; indeed, they are completely absent from much of the area. There is a thin scattering of names in the south of the region, for example in the parishes of Ridge and Rickmansworth, and in the far west around Tring and Northchurch, but there are fewer than in some parts of central and eastern Hertfordshire, such as around Welwyn or Standon. The lack of woodland names is further evidence that the south-west of the county had not been extensively cleared and settled before the Norman Conquest – in contrast to the centre and east of the county, where woodland place-names are more abundant (Bigmore forthcoming; Brooker n.d.).

The Domesday survey of 1086 provides our first clear indication of abundant woodland in south-west Hertfordshire, which also extended into north Middlesex, south Buckinghamshire and the southern tip of Bedfordshire. Within this area, measuring approximately 40 by 25 miles and centred on the Chilterns, Rackham has noted that settlements were relatively sparse but that 'nearly every one had wood, usually for at least 500 swine' (Rackham 1980, 123). He estimates that 50 per cent of the land was wooded, but the high swine numbers, and an absence of entries describing 'wood for fences', suggests that these woodlands were not intensively managed. The soils over much of this area are of poor quality for agriculture: those on the Chiltern dipslope are derived from clay-with-flints and those on the 'Southern Uplands' (Figure 51) from London Clay.

Figure 50 suggests that the vills with the highest woodland totals in the western zone of the county in 1086 were concentrated on the higher (northern) parts of the Chiltern dipslope and also on the hills of the Southern Uplands to the south. However, the map needs to be interpreted with caution: each symbol indicates the location of a Domesday vill, rather than the woodland held by that vill and, in some cases, at least some of the woodland was probably located some distance from the parent vill. For example, the Abbey of

Ely had the highest swine total in the county, with 2,000 pigs on its manor of Hatfield. Hatfield Great Wood extended for many miles to the east of Hatfield but the Abbey's swine count probably also included those on its detached manor of Totteridge, 9 miles to the south. Similarly, the 1,000 pigs recorded at St Albans must include the Abbey's lands at Boreham Wood, Barnet and Northaw. These detached monastic holdings were all located on the densely wooded high ground bordering Middlesex and were not separately recorded in Domesday Book.

However, despite the concentration of woodland in south-west Hertfordshire, much of the remainder of the county was also relatively well-wooded in the late eleventh century. Over three-quarters of the Hertfordshire manors recorded in Domesday Book had woodland, more than in any other county (Rackham 1980, 123). The north-eastern two-thirds of the county was characterised by numerous small swine entries, plus a few large ones, and also a number of places with only 'wood for fences'. Rackham estimates that c.15 per cent of the north-eastern half of the county was wooded but, unlike the woods in the south-west, much of this was intensively managed, coppiced woodland.

The only part of the county that seems to have been virtually devoid of woodland, probably since prehistory, was a strip along its northern edge in the parishes bordering east Bedfordshire and south Cambridgeshire. Within this area Domesday recorded no swine counts for the manors in twelve vills, and another nine vills with sixty or fewer swine. Only Pirton in the west (500 pigs) and Ashwell in the north (100 pigs) had significant woodland. Place-names indicating woodland are very rare in this area and later documentary references to woods are largely confined to the high ground on the southern edge of this strip.

This high ground to the south of the 'wood-free' zone comprises the chalk ridge of the East Anglian Heights, which extends as a boulder-clay-covered plateau dipping gently southwards beneath north-east Hertfordshire. It appears to have been well-wooded in the pre-Conquest period, but the relatively fertile soils attracted settlement and by 1086 the ridge and the interfluves lying west and east of the upper Rib and Quin valleys were dotted with manors which had very little or no woodland, and thirteen holdings had only 'wood for fences'. Most of the woodland in this area, centred on the medieval market town of Buntingford, seems to have been cleared before the Conquest and those small woods that survived were probably intensively managed by coppicing. No medieval parks were established in this part of the county.

In the far east of the county several manors recorded reasonable swine counts, particularly in the upper reaches of the Ash valley and on its interfluves to the south. Further west, on the broad plateau between the Beane and Rib valleys, several manors also had Domesday swine counts in the hundreds, indicating much more abundant woodland; in several cases these were comparable with the swine densities in the west of the county. Numerous parks

FIGURE 51.
Relief map of Hertfordshire, showing locations of medieval parks (relief after Williamson 2000, 9).

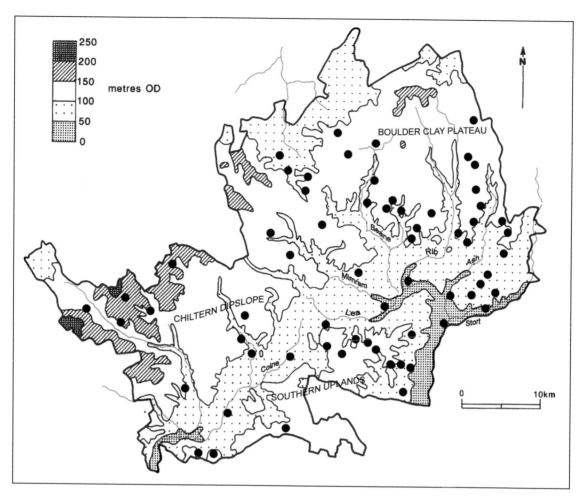

were created in this area, as well as in the far east of the county. Moving south-westwards, the watersheds between the Beane and the Mimram and between the Mimram and the Lea were also moderately well wooded and the particularly high number of 1,000 pigs was recorded at Knebworth. This central and western part of the 'eastern zone' of the county also had a scatter of medieval parks but, in the far north-west, where there were also several well-wooded manors, parks were largely absent. Some of the most abundant woodland in the eastern zone was in the far south on the high ground covered with poorly draining and infertile soils derived from London Clay. There were several parks in this area, some of them particularly extensive.

Clearly there was a relationship between parks and woodland at a local level because, within the less well-wooded eastern zone of the county, parks were generally only established on those manors which had significant Domesday swine counts. Where there was no woodland, as in the most northerly parts of the county, there were no parks. Similarly, where there was very little, and intensively managed, woodland, as in the area around Buntingford, there were no parks. However, the opposite did not necessarily hold true. There were many manors which did have abundant woodland in 1086, such as King's Walden in the north-west (800 pigs) and Wormley in the south-east (600 pigs), as well as most of the manors in the western zone of the county, but which did not, as far as we know, have medieval parks. So the abundance of woodland, although a desirable prerequisite, was not the primary factor influencing park creation in Hertfordshire, or there would have been far more parks in the west of the county, where the woodland cover was densest. Clearly there were other, more important, factors that influenced the distribution of the county's medieval parks.

Settlement pattern and territorial organisation

An examination of the distribution of medieval parks and parish boundaries (Figure 49) shows a positive correlation between the numbers of parks and the density of the parishes: that is, where the parishes are small and densely packed in the centre and east of the county, there were more parks. In contrast, parishes in the west are generally larger and there were correspondingly fewer parks. Perhaps in order to understand the distribution of parks in Hertfordshire we first have to understand the reasons behind the variation in parish densities and the underlying pattern of settlement.

By the late pre-Conquest period the east and north of the county was already densely settled. Rising population levels had resulted in the gradual clearance of woodland cover, resulting in the scatter of relatively small woods

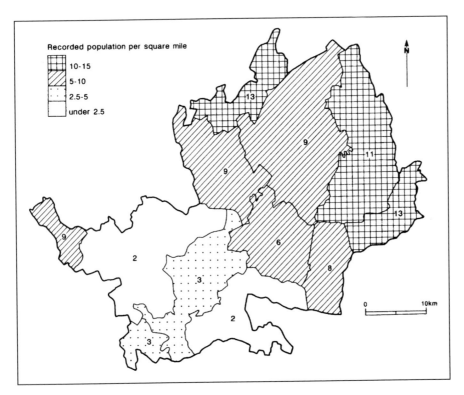

FIGURE 52.
Population density at Domesday, after Williamson 2000, 132; after Campbell 1962, 68.

indicated in Domesday Book. The density of the population in this part of the county in 1086 (9–13 recorded people per square mile) was comparable with much of East Anglia and is reflected in the multitude of small parishes and the numerous manors in Domesday Book. In the south-west of the county population density decreased sharply (2–3 recorded people per square mile). In the far west, where the county extends over the chalk escarpment near Tring and into the clay vale of Aylesbury beyond, the recorded population rose again to 9 people per square mile (Figure 52).

In the far north of the county, where the land falls from the escarpment of the Chiltern Hills down onto the Bedfordshire lowlands, a classic 'Midland' pattern of settlement was established, with nucleated villages and 'regular' open-field systems, and here population levels were particularly high in 1086. In the far east of the county was another area with equally high population levels. Here, in the parishes forming the west flank of the Stort valley, recorded population rose again to 13 people per square mile and yet, in marked contrast to the northern area, where there were no medieval parks, here nearly every parish contained a park by the end of the fifteenth century. The survival of significant woodland resources on the higher ground in these parishes, despite the high population levels, was no doubt a significant factor and the number of parks reflects the number of manors and lords wanting to enclose some of that woodland for themselves.

Between these two areas of maximum population density lies the bulk of northern and eastern Hertfordshire, where the majority of the county's medieval parks were established. Here there was an ancient, dispersed settlement pattern (with irregular field systems) which formed part of a much wider zone of 'ancient countryside' covering most of south-east England and southern parts of East Anglia (Rackham 1999a, 3). The recorded population in 1086 was generally 9 people per square mile, rising to 11 per square mile east of the river Rib. The rapid growth in population, which probably more than doubled between 1086 and 1307 (Bailey *et al.* 1998, xxii), led to a steady expansion of settlement and cultivation from the primary foci in the valleys up onto the clay-covered interfluves. Arable and pasture expanded at the expense of woods and wood pasture, which survived longest on the higher ground furthest from the settlements, often because there they had been preserved as enclosed woodland or as private parks.

By contrast, in the south-west of the county, as we have seen, there was abundant woodland and relatively sparse settlement at the end of the Saxon period. Precisely because this area was relatively 'undeveloped', large tracts of it were donated to religious houses in the middle and late Saxon period (Figure 53). As we have seen above, in AD 785 King Offa of Mercia granted land in Aldenham to Westminster Abbey and in AD 793 he founded the abbey at St Albans and provided it with a substantial endowment. The extensive Wheathampstead estate (including most of what later became the parish of Harpenden) was granted to Westminster Abbey *c.* AD 960 (Williamson 2000, 124), and Hatfield was given to King Edgar *c.* AD 970 and then granted to

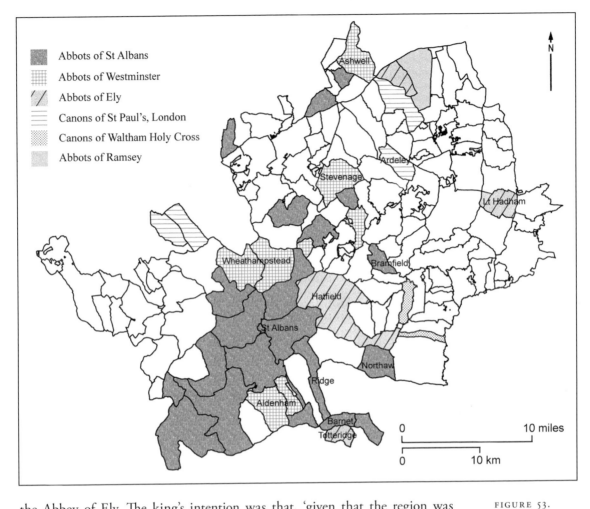

FIGURE 53.
Landed holdings of
major religious houses
in Hertfordshire.

the Abbey of Ely. The king's intention was that, 'given that the region was wooded in that place [Hatfield], the brothers would be able to have timber from it for the building of the church and enough firewood to satisfy their needs' (Fairweather 2005, 103). Ely also acquired Totteridge in the Saxon period (Williamson 2000, 129).

Under the control of large monastic houses, primarily St Albans but also Westminster and Ely, these mid-Saxon landholdings remained large and evolved into the extensive parishes that exist today. The main settlements on the Chiltern dipslope in the south-west were all located in the river valleys, leaving large areas of higher ground sparsely populated and covered in woods and pasture until after Domesday. As the population levels rose during the early Middle Ages settlement began to spread over the higher ground and the woodland was gradually cleared, initially providing fuel and then food for the London market. Only on the higher ground to the north did wood pasture survive well into the Middle Ages and much of that became incorporated into the medieval parks at Ashridge and Berkhamsted.

In summary, then, the area of the county with the most abundant woodland at Domesday did not become the area where most medieval parks were located. Rather, the distribution of Hertfordshire's parks had more to do with territorial organisation and lordship than with woodland *per se*. Large areas of south and west Hertfordshire were held by the abbeys of St Albans, Westminster and Ely, and their holdings remained substantially intact after 1066, allowing them to dominate this part of the county. In contrast, the north and the east was characterised by smaller properties in the hands of lay owners (Williamson 2000, 181). Various abbots of St Albans and of Ely were keen park-enclosers but, over most of their estates, monastic owners had an inhibiting effect on park creation and where those estates were particularly extensive there were relatively few parks during the medieval period.

A scarcity of woodland also inhibited park creation. The densely populated northernmost parishes lying on the well-drained soils of the chalk escarpment and also on the plains beyond can be compared with the aforementioned Vales of Aylesbury and Belvoir, where fertile land was cleared of woodland by the late Saxon period and where little or no habitat suitable for park-making remained in the Middle Ages. Where, however, some woodland *did* survive, even in the equally densely populated Stort valley, parks were numerous. In the populous east and centre of the county most parishes contained woodland in varying quantities in 1086 and the 'knightly families' in possession of the numerous manors were keen to enclose some of this rapidly dwindling resource for themselves, often by creating a park. Most parks seem to have been established in the thirteenth century or earlier, perhaps as a direct response to increasing pressure on woodland resources. In the Stort valley four parks were first recorded in the thirteenth century: Stortford (1282), Sayes (1237), Pisho (1294) and Hunsdon (1296).

It is interesting to note that those manors in the eastern zone of the county with the most abundant woodland in 1086 went on to become the sites of the largest medieval parks, such as Knebworth or Standon. In the western zone, the two largest parks were created by members of the royal family at Berkhamsted and King's Langley, but here surviving woodland was not a factor; both parks only reached their maximum extent as a result of expansion onto former farmland after the Black Death.

Parks in the landscape

An examination of the relationship between parks and topography is also necessary and enables us to address the question of whether there was a 'typical' landscape setting for a medieval park. A significant feature of approximately 70 per cent of Hertfordshire's medieval parks was their location on high plateaux and watersheds; a further 22 per cent lay on the sides of valleys. At a local scale, 36 per cent of parks were located on land which was either the highest, or amongst the highest, in their parish. The relationship between parks and topography is most clearly demonstrated in the far east of the county, where nine parks formed a line along the watershed between the river Rib (and its tributary the Quin) and the Ash, and another, parallel, line of parks lay on the watershed between the rivers Ash and Stort. Further west, nine parks lay on the broad interfluve between the Rib and the Beane, but here a preference for locations close to the margin of the plateau is apparent. A similar distribution can be seen around the margins of high ground in the south-east of the county. The highest parks (over 490 feet) lay on the chalk ridge of the Chilterns at Ashridge, Berkhamsted and Flamstead.

Not surprisingly, the views from many of these parks were extensive and, in some cases, very attractive. The most impressive of the early parks in terms of landscape quality were Berkhamsted, Standon, Walkern, Ware and Weston, but some of the fifteenth-century parks were equally striking, the best being Bedwell (Essendon). Rye Park was the only one established on entirely low-lying ground; several others, such as Ware and Hertingfordbury, lay beside rivers but also incorporated land which rose quite steeply above the floodplain.

About one-third of Hertfordshire's parishes had a medieval park and several had more than one: six had two parks, probably simultaneously; Sawbridgeworth and Hatfield, both large parishes, had at least three medieval parks each; and Cheshunt had four. About one-third of the parks had boundaries which coincided in part with a parish boundary and a further third (whose boundaries are less certain) are likely to have lain either at or very close to the parish boundary. As noted in other counties, medieval parks tended to be located on the peripheries of parishes for a complex combination of reasons: primary settlements often became established in river valleys close to the most fertile and easily worked land; the land further away, often on higher ground, became the manorial 'waste' – land not used for agriculture but nevertheless of value as common land for collecting firewood and grazing animals. Being relatively high and exposed, and usually with poorer soils, these sites were more likely to retain a covering of wood or heath than the rest of the parish. This largely unregulated land was particularly susceptible to enclosure, or 'privatisation', by a manorial lord seeking to ensure his supply of timber and wood, or to establish a 'venison farm' or hunting reserve.

The boundaries between Saxon estates and, later, parishes often tended to be on the higher ground of the interfluves, which was usually the furthest point between neighbouring valley settlements, hence the strong coincidence between park and parish boundaries. No doubt the large earth banks created to mark some parish boundaries were easily adapted to make an effective barrier for enclosing deer, thus allowing savings in labour for park owners. This may be one reason why high, remote corners of parishes seem to have been particularly susceptible to imparkment, as, for example, at Stortford, Scales, Hormead and Walkern. In some cases, however, the evidence points towards the parish boundary having being laid out around a pre-existing park or area of woodland, as, for example, at Wymondley.

In a few parishes the boundary takes a tortuous detour, presumably to include a resource that was important to the manorial lord at the time the boundary was established. For example, in the parishes of Great Munden and St Ippolytts there are marked extensions to the south and in both cases it is tempting to conclude that the important resource was an early park, or at least woodland which later became imparked. Similarly, the park of Pisho was located in a detached part of the parish of Sawbridgeworth, probably also an important area of woodland which was then enclosed to make a park.

Despite the 'rational' topographic and socio-agricultural reasons explaining the preponderance of parks on higher ground, it is difficult to avoid the notion when visiting the sites of former parks that their medieval creators were just as acutely aware of the pleasures of a beautiful vista as we are today. Given the recent conclusions of some landscape historians on the aesthetic aspects of parks in the Middle Ages, it is perhaps reasonable to at least question whether their location was predetermined solely and prosaically by the availability of suitable land and habitat. Perhaps some medieval lords exercised an element of choice in locating their parks in some of the most attractive parts of their local landscape.

CHAPTER EIGHT

Hunting Suffolk's Parks: Towards a Reliable Chronology of Imparkment

Rosemary Hoppitt

Within the period 1086–1602 documentary references confirm the existence of at least 130 parks in Suffolk (Hoppitt 1992, vol. II, 70–5).[1] Some of these parks remained in use for a considerable period; for example, parks at Eye and Hundon were extant for at least 500 years from the late eleventh to the early seventeenth century, and about another dozen parks remained intact for around 300 years (Hoppitt 1992, vol. I, 69–71). Other parks are more ephemeral in the record, and even more so in the landscape; for example, two early parks at Semer and Chelsworth are only mentioned once in documentary sources, with no evidence on the ground to suggest their location (Douglas 1932, 112–13). Between these extremes are a range of parks from those with good documentary records and clear landscape evidence – usually the property of substantial lords – to those more modest in terms of their record and ownership.

There are two clearly identifiable periods when parks initially make their appearance in the documentary record (Hoppitt 1992, vol. I, 76). The first extends from 1086 to the end of the fourteenth century; there is then a break of about 100 years in which very few new parks are recorded and many disappear from the record. The second period is the sixteenth century, when the numbers increase again, with over thirty parks being recorded for the first time in the period 1500–1602. These two periods display different characteristics in terms of the distribution, location and ownership of the parks first recorded in them, highlighting the changing socio-economic background against which imparking occurred (Figure 54). Within the context of Suffolk this chapter will examine two interrelated themes: the chronology of imparking, with particular reference to the reliability of the documentary record; and the location of parks, within which theme particular attention will be paid to the places where parks were established, and the possibility of establishing a predictive locational model.

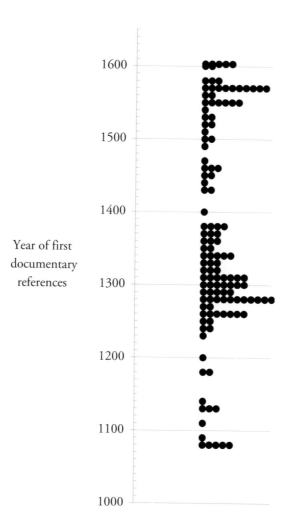

Year of first documentary references

FIGURE 54.
Chronology of the first documentary references for Suffolk parks.

The backdrop: the physical background and cultural landscape of Suffolk

Suffolk lies in southern East Anglia, bounded on the north by the Waveney and Ouse valleys, on the south and east by the river Stour and the North Sea, and on the north-west by fenland. The county's cultural landscape owes much to its physical background (Figure 55) and is generally divided into three or four distinctive zones, of which the dominant is the till-covered chalk escarpment ('High Suffolk') running from west to north-east, with the dipslope extending down towards the coast. Soils in this area (mainly clay-with-flints) are very varied, but characteristically heavy. The Gipping valley bisects the escarpment; the north-east side is between 130 and 195 feet above sea level, with broad level interfluves drained by mainly south-east-flowing rivers. To the south and west the land is higher, reaching over 330 feet, with drainage southwards into the Stour, while northwards the larger catchments of the rivers Lark and Blackbourn feed into the Ouse rivers. The whole area

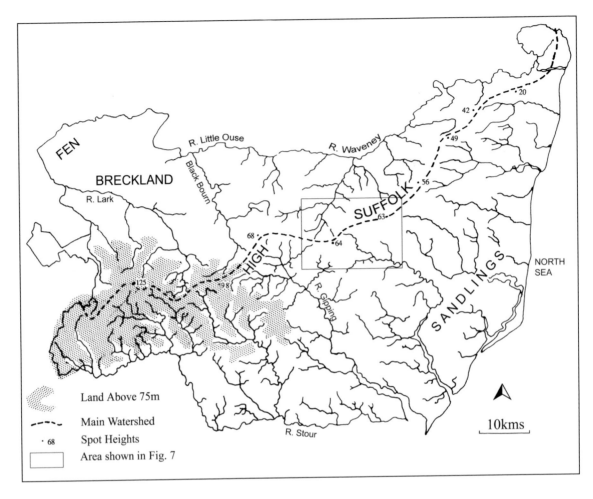

FEN

BRECKLAND

R. Little Ouse

R. Lark

Black Bourn

R. Waveney

SUFFOLK

HIGH

42

·49

56

·63

·20

68

·64

R. Gipping

·125

·98

SANDLINGS

NORTH
SEA

Land Above 75m

Main Watershed

· 68   Spot Heights

Area shown in Fig. 7

R. Stour

10kms

was well-wooded in the early Middle Ages, and particularly so in the north and east, where the level interfluves give rise to the most intractable soils (Warner 1987, 18–24). Here, at the end of the eighteenth century, large areas were under pasture, with extensive commons and greens, many of which may originally have been wooded (Dymond 2003, xi; Warner 1987, 5–7); these had become the focus of green-side settlements possibly as early as the ninth century, but certainly by the twelfth or thirteenth century, by which time their boundaries may have become fixed (Warner 1987, 2). There are also a large number of medieval moated sites; their presence reflects both the nature of the till, which made moat construction both effective (due to its impermeable nature) and advantageous (as a means of drainage, for food supply and for aesthetic appearance), and the nature of medieval tenure, which here was characterised by large numbers of free tenants and small manors (Martin 1999a; 1999b).

In the north-west the chalk is covered with glacial wind-blown sands giving rise to the dry soils of Breckland, which in the medieval period were exploited under an idiosyncratic system of sheep–corn husbandry supple-

FIGURE 55.
Suffolk's cultural landscape owes much to the physical character of the county. High Suffolk, the watershed region, was characterised in the medieval period by early enclosure, dispersed settlement around greens, moated sites, woodland and deer parks.

mented by commercial rabbit farming (Bailey 1988, 1–20). Probably cleared of woodland in the prehistoric period, Domesday records no woodland here at all (Darby 1971, 180). The land-use pattern in Breckland is, to some extent, mirrored by the coastal strip (the Sandlings), which is also characterised by sandy soils, here formed on ancient marine sands overlain with glacial out-wash and river gravels from the former periglacial course of the river Thames. In the medieval period both Breckland and the Sandlings were characterised by low population densities (Todd and Dymond 1999, 80–1). However, in con-trast to the till plateau, there is an absence of moated sites, a situation which is almost certainly due to geology rather than tenurial patterns, for Domesday shows that in the hundreds of the Sandlings the proportion of free peasantry was similarly high to that on the till plateau, and in some cases was higher (Darby 1971, 361). Areas of common heath were extensive here, in some cases also becoming settlement foci, as was the case with greens in High Suffolk (Williamson 2005, 76–80). The geographical distribution of Suffolk's parks is biased towards the till uplands (Figure 56), with just a few outside this area, and, as such, is congruent with the distribution pattern of Domesday woodland, greens and moated sites (Martin 1999a; 1999b). This was far from accidental, for common factors underlie these patterns.

Towards establishing a chronology of imparking: four contributory sources

Documentary evidence

Parks are first recorded in Suffolk in 1086 on five manors in Domesday Book: Bentley, Ixworth, Eye, Dennington and Leiston (LDB, 287r; 438v; 320r; 311v; 328r). The further recording of new parks is then rare until the mid-thir-teenth and fourteenth centuries when a burgeoning of numbers (56 per cent of the total) occurs as a result of increased references to parks in the records of medieval government. In Suffolk, parks mainly make their documentary debuts as a result of park-breaking events recorded in the Patent Rolls, and in the extents of manors contained in inquisitions *post mortem* (IPM) of ten-ants-in-chief (Cantor 1983, 70–1). This is in contrast to many other counties, where licences to impark form a major source for evidence of imparking. These licences, technically a requirement in royal forest, are almost absent in Suffolk, as no part of the county was subject to forest law.

The park-breaking complaints and the IPM extents clearly indicate that parks were established working resource-units that had probably existed for some time prior to their first appearance in the documentary record. The Pat-ent Rolls consistently refer to deer and other animals stolen and in one case, at Haughley, note that a park-keeper was killed (CPR 1316–17, 428); in the extents, the value of trees and presence (or absence) of deer is often recorded. What these documents emphatically do *not* do is provide dating evidence for actual park creation. As a result, closer examination of the documentary evidence and landscape context is essential in order to establish a more reliable chronol-ogy of imparking. What has become clear as a result of research in Suffolk is

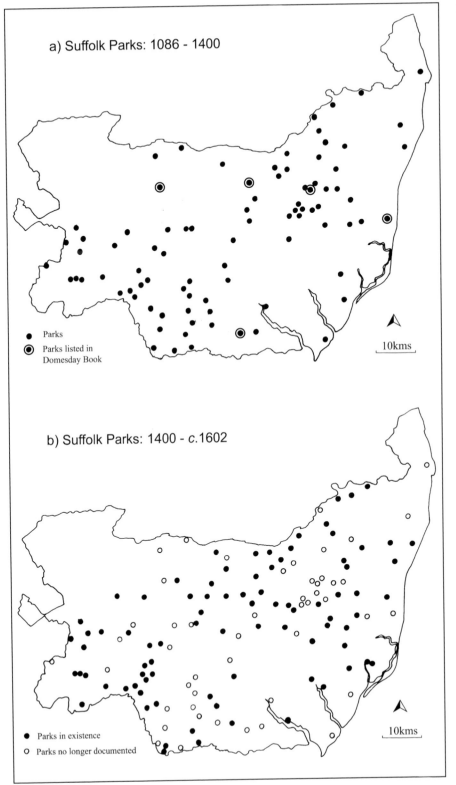

a) Suffolk Parks: 1086 - 1400

- • Parks
- ⊙ Parks listed in
  Domesday Book

10kms

b) Suffolk Parks: 1400 - *c*.1602

- • Parks in existence
- ○ Parks no longer documented

10kms

FIGURE 56.
Distribution of Suffolk
parks 1086–*c*.1602,
showing the large
numbers of parks no
longer documented
in the period
1400–*c*.1602, and
the expansion of the
distribution onto the
lighter soils of the
Sandlings and the
Breckland edge.

that charter evidence or manorial records invariably provide evidence for parks that pre-dates references in state documents. This not only highlights the importance of local research in order to obtain a more reliable and complete picture, but leads to a revision of the chronology for Suffolk, which points to imparking being a probable characteristic of the twelfth century, and probably part of a continuum from (at least) the Conquest onwards.

Three examples demonstrate the point. First, at Kelsale (Figure 57), initial lists give dates of 1314 and 1276 for the first reference to the park (Farrer 1923; Cantor 1983, 70). Documentary references continue through to the early seventeenth century, when the park was broken up into fields (SRO/I JA2/7/2). In 1276, however, the park was at least seventy or more years old as a charter dated 1189x1217 records that Roger (II) Bigod exchanged 21 acres and 1 rood of land in Wrabton and Kelsale which he 'enclosed within his park of Kelsale' (Brown 1987, no. 493, 22). So what was its likely date of origin? In 1086, Kelsale was the *caput* of Roger (I) Bigod's Suffolk fief. It was most probably a shrieval manor, held TRE by the former sheriff, Norman, and in Bigod possession in Roger's capacity as sheriff; Roger, therefore, probably came into possession in the early 1070s when he took up the shrievalty (Warner 1996, 188–91) and may have been consolidating Kelsale with the neighbouring two-carucate manor held TRE by Wulfeva, which he probably acquired at a similar time. There seems little doubt that Roger (I) Bigod would have sought to have his own hunting grounds; it was, after all, a mark of the prestige he sought. The question that really has to be asked is why he is *not* recorded as possessing any parks in Domesday Book, and especially at what was his most important manor, where he was already boasting a market 'by the king's gift' (LDB, 330v). That a park is not recorded is not evidence that one did not exist, of course. If it was not there before his acquisition of the manor, then it is highly likely to have been a creation of Roger (I) Bigod as part of his *caput* development. And if Roger (I) was not responsible for the creation of the park, then either his heir Hugh Bigod or Roger (II) Bigod must have imparked Kelsale at some point between 1107 and 1217.

A second example relates to another Bigod park, that at Butenhagh (Butenhae, Botenhawe, Buttrehagh) in Saxtead, near Framlingham, which is identifiable with former Botenhall Wood, which lay on the boundary with Dennington. Again, early listings produced a date from the Patent Rolls of 1300, when it was included in a list of Bigod parks into which 'persons entered … and carried away deer' (CPR 1292–1301, 631). The 1270 IPM extent of Roger (III) Bigod refers to Butenhagh as a 'pasture', which may suggest that it was not perceived or used as a park at that date (CIPM 1, no. 744). However, a charter dated before 1107 refers to land 'lying in [Roger (I) Bigod's] park called Butenhae next to the land of Henry Roscelin in Dennington' (Brown 1986, no. 125, 102). In this instance it would seem that Butenhae was considered to be a park some 200 years earlier than its first mention as such in the royal rolls.

Thirdly, at Hundon, on the large demesne manor of the de Clares, early

listing gives a first date for the Great Park as 1210 (Cantor 1983, 70), but again, local records produced a first date of 1090, 120 years earlier (Harper-Bill and Mortimer 1982, no. 70, 54).

Landscape evidence

Extrapolation from these and other examples suggests that chronologies of imparking based solely on state documents may be flawed and could give unreliable patterns, leading to misinterpretation of the processes at work. Charter evidence is not always available, however, and investigation of the landscape context presents another source of evidence for the likely timing of imparkment.

Suffolk's parks do not have the large relict bank-and-ditch boundaries of parks in some counties; in fact so few examples have survived that it is uncertain whether many Suffolk parks ever had the very large banks and ditches seen elsewhere. Where remains do exist, for example along the boundary of the Great Park at Framlingham, they are in general low banks degraded by natural erosion (Figure 58). Field boundaries in High Suffolk commonly have substantial ditches (owing to the nature of the soils and topography), and are not necessarily evidence of early boundaries. This means that in locating parks, other evidence – an understanding of the likely location for a park, documentary evidence, field names, property boundaries and cartographic sources – take on a greater importance.

Examples of two parks located in the watershed region illustrate the point.

Rishangles Park was situated in the parish of Thorndon (Figure 59). The first reference in the documentary record to the park's existence occurs in 1288, with a park-breaking event, when Edmund, Earl of Cornwall held the manor as part of the Honor of Eye (CPR 1281–92, 298). Documentary references continue through the fourteenth and fifteenth centuries, with the park probably disparked in the late sixteenth century. West of Thorndon is the parish of Wetheringsett, in which lay a park belonging to the bishop of Ely. Wetheringsett Park was first recorded in 1251 in the Ely Coucher Book along with a number of the bishop's other parks (CUL EDR G3/27 fol. 183). In 1297 there is a record of park-breaking 'touching those who entered the park of William Bishop of Ely at Wetheringsett, hunted therein and carried away deer' (CPR 1292–1301, 227). The creation of the parks at Rishangles and Wetheringsett must, obviously, pre-date their first appearance in documents, but how much older they are than is suggested by the documentary evidence is not clear.

An examination of the landscape history of these two parishes (which is similar to parishes elsewhere in the county, such as Kelsale, Hoxne and Hundon) reveals a pattern of topography and land use which can be seen working together, and which can be used to propose a model for the process of landscape development in the area of which imparkment was a component.

As indicated above, the watershed which runs across High Suffolk displays a uniformity of both physical and cultural landscape components: broad

FIGURE 58.
Framlingham Park boundary from inside the former park. The low bank (about 3 feet high) which formed part of the eastern boundary of the Great Park can be seen along the hedgeline. Very few former park boundaries in Suffolk have relict banks and ditches.

C. E. HOPPITT

level interfluves, heavy, poorly drained, cold soils, extensive greens, dispersed moated sites, and formerly, large areas of woodland. Domesday Book indicates that the watershed area was well wooded; it is here that some of the largest quantities of woodland were recorded for the county (Darby 1971, 180). Some of this woodland may be secondary, having regenerated following the retreat of settlement and agriculture from these (physically) marginal areas following the Roman withdrawal. Expansion back into these areas appears to have been occurring from the seventh century, but in the post-Domesday period it took on a specific form, in which churches, manorial complexes, villages and arable were located on lower slopes, and greens, woods, dispersed 'pioneer' settlement and minor manors (many of them moated) were located on the higher parts. These latter areas comprised manorial 'waste', which was in the main peripheral and uncultivated but which nevertheless formed an important resource base for the manor in the form of wood, wood pasture and open grazing land (Warner 1987, 5–7; Rackham 1999b, 64–5). It is here that the parks are found.

In Thorndon, for example, the church, manor house and village-cluster are on lower ground associated with a former small elongated green, and a number of moated sites and farms are situated on the higher ground. Two of these moated sites, Hestley Hall and Lampits Farm, are identifiable with minor Domesday landholdings (LDB 429r; 323r) and are evidence that these areas of manorial waste were being brought into cultivation by free tenants at least by the mid- to late eleventh century.

As population continued to expand in the twelfth and thirteenth centuries, so more land was taken out of the common waste and the pressure on this resource base thus increased. The designation of woods and wood pastures as parks (as in the case of Butenhae, above) may be, in part, evidence of a reaction to these diminishing resources, as well as of an increasing desire for exclusive game preserves. Thus lords may have been ring-fencing existing woodland and wood pasture as a means of retaining and conserving the resource for the demesne; at the same time some of these (by then) exclusive woodlands could also have been managed as parks.

The parks of Rishangles and Wetheringsett have every appearance of being enclosed from the common or wood pasture; each is surrounded by what appear to be remnants of more extensive greens (Figure 60), and their creation may thus have occurred during this period of settlement expansion. Thorndon was one of Robert Malet's Domesday demesne manors, part of the Honor of Eye. The Malet fief *does* record parks – indeed, three of the five Domesday parks (Dennington, Eye and Leiston) were Malet's parks. This would imply that Rishangles Park is post-1086 in origin: if so, who imparked it and when? It could have been Malet – he held the Honor until his death in *c.*1106, at which point it reverted to the Crown. Other possible imparkers include William Martel, who held the Honor from King Stephen, and Henry Duke of Lotharinga and Count of Louvain, who was granted the manor by King Richard I. The Honor remained with Henry for twenty-two years between 1198 and 1229. Although largely an absentee, he did appear to take 'an interest and pride in his English lands …' and we are told that '… he ordered the enclosure of Eye park' (Brown 1994, 32). Eye park was, however, already recorded in 1086, and he was probably ordering reparations to the park pales, but this suggests that he may have been interested in imparking and he is, therefore, probably a strong contender as the creator of Rishangles Park, which would support an early, rather than a later, thirteenth-century origin.

In the case of Wetheringsett, the same landscape context applies – church and village-cluster were similarly located on low ground, and on higher ground to the south were large greens and numerous moated sites. The park appears to have been carved out of this area of common land. Wetheringsett was one of eight Suffolk manors of the estate of the bishopric of Ely, which was established in 1109. During this period of population growth, the Ely estate was expanding its land under cultivation, and its income (as a result of the new rents) rose almost exponentially between 1086 and the late thirteenth century (Miller 1951, 94–7). The bishop's status, as well as this growing wealth, would have provided an appropriate socio-economic context for imparking, which is paralleled by the actions and circumstances of other ecclesiastical institutions.

At Homersfield, for example, the bishop of Norwich's earliest recorded Suffolk park was brought to light in a park-breaking event which Bishop Herbert de Losinga took as a personal slight, writing to his monks (sometime before 1119) concerning 'certain evil-minded men who … broke into my park at Homersfield in the night, and killed the only deer which I had there, and having thrown away his head with feet and intestines committed an abominable theft by carrying off the carcase …'. He goes on to deliver excommunication and puts a heavy curse on the perpetrators: '… May the flesh of those who have devoured my stag rot, as the flesh of Herod rotted … Let them have the Anathema Maranatha unless they shall come to a better mind and make me some reparation. Amen Amen Amen' (Goulbourn and Symonds 1878, 170). Other parks are found in association with episcopal palaces and occupying peripheral locations bordering greens, and thus may also date from the period before the thirteenth century. In the adjacent parish of South Elmham St Cross the park dates from at least 1316 (CPR 1313–17, 503); its location is coincident with a lacuna within the distribution of medieval finds from fieldwalking (Hardy with Martin 1987, 232–5). It may in fact be coincident with Herbert de Losinga's Homersfield park, which is still to be located. A new park at neighbouring South Elmham St James was recorded from 1326 (TNA:PRO SC6/1141/1). At Hoxne (site of the bishop's see from the tenth to the late eleventh century), the park's first record occurs in 1325 (TNA:PRO SC6/1141/1); a new park and palace were established on a lower, less exposed and perhaps more aesthetically pleasing site by the river Dove by the beginning of the fifteenth century (NRO DCN 44/141/1).

By the early twelfth century the abbot of Bury St Edmunds had parks at

Semer, Chelsworth and Bradfield St Clare (Monk's Park), and at Elmsett in Long Melford by 1180 (Douglas 1932, 112–13). Later documents record parks at Redgrave (SRO/B P551/1066), Great Barton (Caley 1817, 472), Chevington (Gage 1838, 323) and Woolpit (SRO/B E3/15 51/1.1), and possibly also at Cockfield (SRO/B IC500/2/25 ff.82v–83). It is almost certain that some of these were the parks referred to by the chronicler Jocelin of Brakelond who noted (*c*.1200) that Abbot Samson '… made many parks, which he filled with beasts, and had a huntsman and dogs. And whenever any important guest arrived, he used to sit with his monks in some retired grove, and watch the coursing for a while …' (Jane 1907, 43–4). The use of the term 'retired grove' sets an aesthetic tone, evoking an appreciation of the ambience of the setting as well as the spectacle of the hunting. There is every reason to see parks as having such a wider recreational usage beyond hunting and the chase. Despite the restrictions on their own hunting, the ecclesiastics of East Anglia clearly had no problem with park ownership, and the evidence points to these parks being in place from at least the early twelfth century.

Landscape evidence for the chronology of imparking may also be present in the relationship between parks and parish boundaries. In Suffolk, many parish boundaries date from the late Anglo-Saxon period (J. Martin 1999, 24) and some may follow even more ancient divisions; they were probably fully established by the twelfth century. As a consequence of the peripheral location of parks, they are often found adjacent to parish boundaries, and in some cases their presence is acknowledged by the boundary; in other words, the feature, whether early wood or later park, was already a part of the landscape when the boundary was being defined. This is the case at Holbrook (first date *c*.1300), where the park is almost entirely surrounded by a section of the parish boundary and appears to form an outlier from the rest of the parish. Southwood Park seems to have been congruent with the parish boundary; at Fakenham the boundary deviates around the boundary of the site of the former park, Fakenham Wood, as do the boundaries at Framlingham and other sites. In some locations the problem lies in distinguishing accurately between situations in which the boundary took account of the park, and those in which the park was slotted up against the boundary, where the landholding was peripheral. There are later parks which show the latter pattern, for example that at Wingfield, where the park was almost certainly not enclosed until the late fourteenth century, when Michael de la Pole obtained a licence to crenellate and impark on his properties at Wingfield, Huntingfield and Sternfield (CPR 1381–5, 555). The park at Badingham, probably late thirteenth- or early fourteenth-century in date, is similarly positioned up against the parish boundary (first date 1309: Cal IPM vol.VI, no. 519).

There are also parks that straddle parish boundaries. Staverton Park (first date 1268: TNA:PRO SC6/1005/7), which may have a claim as a very early Anglo-Saxon hunting ground, lies across the parish boundary of Wantisden and Eyke (Williamson 2005, 107); in the west of the county the park of Badmondisfield, in Wickhambrook (first date 1282: CPR 1281–92, 73), straddled

FIGURE 59.
Views across the sites
of the former parks
at Wetheringsett
(above) and Rishangles
(below), showing the
characteristic flat
landscape associated
with parks on the
clayland interfluve.
Wetheringsett was a
park of the bishop of
Ely, first recorded in
the Ely Coucher book
in 1251, although its
creation may date from
the twelfth century.
Rishangles Park (in
Thorndon) was first
recorded in 1288 but
is likely to have been
established by the early
thirteenth century. The
hedgeline on the left
of the picture marks
the western boundary.
C. E. HOPPITT

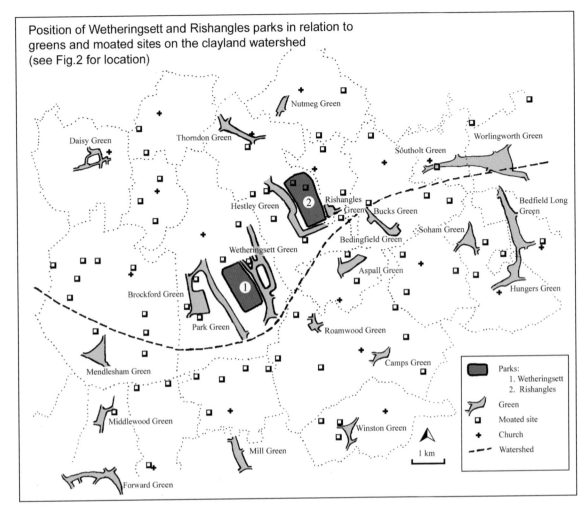

Position of Wetheringsett and Rishangles parks in relation to greens and moated sites on the clayland watershed (see Fig.2 for location)

Nutmeg Green

Thorndon Green

Daisy Green

Worlingworth Green

Southolt Green

Hestley Green

Rishangles Green

Bedfield Long Green

Bucks Green

Soham Green

Bedingfield Green

Wetheringsett Green

Aspall Green

Hungers Green

Brockford Green

Park Green

Roamwood Green

Mendlesham Green

Camps Green

Middlewood Green

Winston Green

Mill Green

Forward Green

Parks:
1. Wetheringsett
2. Rishangles

Green

Moated site

Church

Watershed

1 km

the boundary with neighbouring Lidgate. In both cases the adjacent manors were in the possession of the same manorial lord (Bigod at Staverton; de Hastings, Earls of Pembroke, at Badmondisfield). Cropley Park, in Lidgate itself (first date 1316: CPR 1313–17, 503), also the property of de Hastings, probably straddled the county boundary with Cambridgeshire and the parish of Ashley to the west. In these cases, the ecclesiastical boundary appears to take no account of the manorial resource (wood or park), which remained as an integral land-use unit, but did take account of it for tithe, which, as we shall see below, could vary either side of the parish boundary.

Tithes

A number of parks, including Hoxne Old Park, Hundon, Wetheringsett and Rishangles, largely maintained their integrity as land units through to the nineteenth century, when the tithe apportionments record property boundaries that conform to the likely size and shape of the former parks. In addition, in some cases the property was also exempt from tithe payments or paid a *modus decimandi* or composition instead (an alternative or a mutually agreed payment). One nineteenth-century writer stated that 'the real definition of a park' was that it was tithe-free (Grigor 1841, 190).

Tithe-free status was accorded, first, to natural resources, and woodland came into that category, being 'part of the inheritance of the land' (Clarke 1887, 63). Deer were similarly considered in law to be *ferae naturae* (beasts of nature), but park deer and produce from parks were not tithe-free. Thus at Eye in 1260 the seneschal was ordered to pay tithe on hay 'cut and sold' within the park, and later there is an order to 'give the prior [of Eye] the tithe of shoulders of game in each of his parks within [the seneschal's] bailiwick' (which probably included the park of Rishangles). In 1308, the Eye Priory Cartulary lists the lesser tithes, which included 'bracken, pannage, agistment of cattle in the park at Eye ... and tithes of game if they are in the park' (Brown 1992, no. 157, no. 159, 136–7; Brown 1994, no. 396, 120). Secondly, tithe-free status could be due to ownership. Religious houses were exempted from tithe payments on land they held at 1160, and after this some monastic land was later rendered tithe-free by the purchase of Papal Bulls (Selden 1618, 120–1; Clarke 1887, 98); but when there was change of ownership, tithe payment became due. The nineteenth-century tithe commissioners rarely seemed to know the reason for the exemptions they met in the field, recording tithe-free status as 'by presumption of the law' (Whalley 1838, 320).

The land of many former parks, however, was not exempt from tithe payments, and where it was there is considerable variation across the county, suggesting that the process was not clear-cut, as Grigor asserted (Hoppitt 1992, vol. II, 80–102). The former abbots' park at Bradfield St Clare (Monk's Park) was largely tithe-free, as were a number of other woods in the parish, described in the tithe award as 'tithe-free by prescription ...' as part of '... the Old Wood' (SRO/B T105/1, 2). Those parcels of the former park that had been cleared of wood *were* subject to tithe. Thus, in this case, the tithe-free status appears to have been related to land use rather than land ownership. In Long Melford Sir Robert Cordell was in dispute over the tithes of his park in the seventeenth century, refusing to pay tithes on land that was former monastic demesne. In the arguments it was noted that various pieces of land had been subject to tithe, in particular the area of Melford Park Farm, 'anciently the park belonging to the Abbot of Bury' (SRO/B FL 509/3/15 243). All or most of the area of the parks at Wetheringsett, Rishangles, and South Elmham St Cross were recorded as paying a *modus*. The site of the park of Badmondisfield, straddling the parish boundaries of Wickhambrook and Lidgate, was exempt from great tithes in Wickhambrook, but in Lidgate paid a *modus* of 2/6d (SRO/B 1201/5; Q/RI 43a; T128/1, 2). Sir Robert Drury, the owner of the park of Hawstead, which was imparked quite late (in 1509), gave to the rector annually a buck and a doe in lieu of tithe for the demesne lands (Cullum 1784, 204), suggesting that land which had been cultivated and was now imparked, and therefore 'unproductive', could become tithe-exempt as a consequence. The composition was presumably agreed between the two parties. In the nineteenth century the pasture in the area of the former park was exempt from tithe (SRO/B T15431/1, 2).

Where the land of former parks was accorded exemption from paying tithe in the nineteenth century, it is possible that this status was acquired as early as the twelfth century, or before that time if the exemption arose from woodland land use. The nineteenth-century tithe awards can thus provide evidence for land-ownership patterns as well as tithe-free status, both of which may be useful in identifying parks in the landscape as well as contributing to the chronology of imparkment in the county.

Manorial works and obligations

In some cases, the maintenance of park pales or the position of parker was undertaken by manorial tenants as part of the obligations of their villein status. Towards the end of the twelfth century and into the thirteenth, there is evidence that manorial lords were reconfirming the tenurial obligations in the surveys and extents of their manors; therefore, a date for the origin of these obligations is most likely to lie in the twelfth century or earlier. By the end of the fourteenth century many tenurial obligations had been commuted to money payments, or even removed entirely – especially after the population decline and subsequent unfavourable socio-economic conditions in the period after the Black Death (Aston 1987, 254–6; Bailey 2002, 31–9). While some of the work may have been part of more general obligations to the lord, the occurrence of specific park labour services may be indicative of imparking before the twelfth or thirteenth centuries, as they are unlikely to have originated *after* the mid-fourteenth century, by which time it would have been difficult to put new obligations in place.

On a number of occasions such works are recorded for parks. At Hoxne in 1327 repairs to the daub on the park lodge cost 5d and eight works, and ditching round the park cost 3d and forty works (NRO DCN 95/5). At Easty Park in Hundon in 1390, 268 perches of new hedging was done at a rate of one work per perch (TNA:PRO SC6/1000/3); at Framlingham in 1287 customary services and works of the tenants included 'Winter Works ... two parkers for the Great Park 68 works; one parker for Botenhagh and one parker for Frithagh 68 works; two parkers for Newhagh and Bradhagh 34 works' (TNA:PRO SC6/997/5). In the 1550s, repair of the park pales was recorded as the responsibility of the holders of Crane's, Verdon's and Hayward's tenements (Loder 1798, 390). Court rolls for Walsham le Willows record in 1328 that 'Richard Wade pays 3d fine to be relieved of his office and not to be the parker this year ...' and 'William Coppelowe ... elected to be the parker after Michaelmas is amerced 12d because he did not perform his duties and concealed wrongdoers in the said wood and trespass there with beasts' (Lock 2002, 108). At Eye, an entry in the Close Rolls demonstrates very clearly how manorial lords were able to utilise the human resources at their disposal. In 1314 the men of the vills of Brundish, Tannington, Badingham, Dennington, Laxfield and Stradbroke were recorded as responsible for the repair of 355 perches of pale

which was 'sufficient to enclose the park', and they were to take oaks from the park to carry out the work (CCR 1313–18, 108). This arrangement was still live in the sixteenth century, when an inquiry and survey of the park reconfirmed the responsibility (TNA:PRO E/178 2202 33 Eliz I). These vills were all demesne manors of Robert Malet's Domesday holding (except for Brundish, which was probably included within either Tannington or Dennington). By 1314, although still part of the Honor of Eye, these manors had changed in the character of their tenure; they were now either being leased at farm or split into knight's fees. It seems most likely that this system of upkeep dates from the origin of the park, perhaps from the period 1069–71, when the fief came into the hands of William Malet. It may be, as has been argued elsewhere, that these obligations date from the pre-Conquest period; if that were the case, then again the chronology of even these earliest parks may need reviewing (Liddiard 2003, 16–17).

There is also evidence of hereditary parkers in the county, particularly associated with the vills of Tannington, Dennington and Brundish, belonging to the Honor of Eye. Domesday Book records tenants-in-chief across the country who appear to have hereditary roles as *venatores* (huntsmen), some of which roles may have a pre-Conquest origin (Keats-Rohan 1999, 174, 365, 437). Where such hereditary roles occur in later contexts, it may be that these, too, have much earlier origins. In the early fourteenth century Margary, sister of the deceased John le Parker of Rishangles, inherited from him lands and tenements and 'the bailiwick of the custody of the park of Rishangles' (CPR 1313–17, 170). As Rishangles is one of the parks associated with the Honor of Eye, this may be a further indication of an early date for this park.

Suffolk's later parks

During the fourteenth century a large number of parks disappear from the documentary record, many of them parks for which there are few documentary references (Figures 54 and 56). Some of the old established parks continued in existence, with many being disparked in the early seventeenth century, such as Eye, Kelsale, Hundon and Framlingham (Figure 61). The dissolution of the monasteries gave the opportunity for new landholders to acquire old parks, as at Chevington and Redgrave, where Sir Thomas Kitson and Sir Nicholas Bacon became the respective owners. In some places completely new parks were established, as at Hengrave, where Kitson obtained a licence to impark in 1587 (CPR 29 Eliz I No 1073; SRO/B 528/31). Many of these new owners were not from the ranks of the aristocracy but, like Kitson and Bacon, came from wealthy merchant and lawyer families, who no doubt hoped to confirm their social standing and their implied (or hoped-for) nobility by demonstrating control over the landscape through the acquisition of their own hunting grounds.

Where new parks were established, they demonstrate a subtly different locational pattern to the early parks. On the macro-scale there is a change away from an almost entirely clayland/High Suffolk distribution; many of the new parks, such as Theberton (1522), Nacton (1510), Henham (1575), Hengrave (1587) and Sudbourne (1601), are founded on the lighter soils. One suggested reason for this change is that in the fifteenth and sixteenth centuries these areas were relatively poor and depopulated, providing 'ideal places for rising and affluent families to acquire [land] … because land could be bought and reorganised, and the risks of opposition were not high' (Dymond and Virgoe 1986, 80).

At the micro-scale, many of the early parks were located at a distance from the manorial hall to which they were linked; this pattern resulted from the imparking of peripheral woodland resources. Of the later parks, the majority are located at or close to the manorial complex. Imparkment at this time was no longer being controlled by the location of the woodland resource; Westhorpe (1450), Hawstead (1509), Theberton (1522), Framsden (1525), Smallbridge in Bures (1575) and Hengrave (1587) all follow this latter pattern, indicating a change in the factors behind the decision-making involved in imparkment. This move away from the high peripheral location is confirmed by the change in relative altitude between parks and the manorial complex to which they were attached. Early parks are notable for the higher altitude at which they are situated, compared with their manorial sites; later parks are generally located at similar heights to their manorial complexes (Hoppitt 1992, vol. I, III–12). Essentially there is a change in emphasis; increased importance was now attached to the park as a landscape feature and recreational area which could be viewed and accessed from, and which enhanced, the capital messuage.

Pre-Conquest parks

So far there has been an implicit assumption here that imparking was a Norman phenomenon, but with some implication that early parks could have been established in the pre-Conquest period. Hunting was not some novel activity exclusive to the Norman incomers; the English had an infrastructure in place to support their hunting, in particular enclosures (*hagan* or deerhays), which, it has been argued, may have fulfilled the same function as parks (Liddiard 2003).

Domesday Book recorded five parks in Suffolk at Eye, Leiston, Dennington, Bentley and Ixworth. There was no requirement to list parks in the Domesday returns, and thus it is impossible to be categorical about the accuracy of the data. As indicated above, Roger (I) Bigod, one of the wealthiest tenants-in-chief, appears, here in his Suffolk heartland, to have had no parks. It seems unlikely that this was the case. Likewise, Richard fitzGilbert, Lord of Clare, another of the country's wealthiest landholders, had no parks recorded across his fief, although his Great Park at Hundon is recorded by 1090 (Harper-Bill and Mortimer 1982, no. 70, 54) and almost certainly existed at the time of Domesday.

While there is no direct evidence, there is every reason to suppose that these early-recorded parks were, or at least could have been, pre-Conquest in origin. The example of the obligations of the demesne manors of the Honor of Eye, in particular, may be indicative of much earlier arrangements. The landholders who preceded the great Domesday tenants-in-chief were all of equally high status as their Norman successors; for example, Bentley was formerly a manor of Earl Gyrth, brother of Harold Godwinson, and the Malet holding was formerly held by Edric of Laxfield, who, although little is known about him, clearly moved in powerful circles and was extremely wealthy (Clarke 1994, 115). In the Suffolk Domesday there are no *deer-hagan* listed, but there are *haga* place-names. One of these (*Bricticeshaga*, LDB 433v) was a wood, and at another, Haughley (*Hagala*, LDB 408v) a park was established by 1262 (CPR 1266–72, 737). The term *haga*, in the forms *hagh*, *hegh* and *haugh*, meaning a hedge, and later an enclosed wood, is used widely to name woods across the county, and there are a number of deerhaugh names recorded in medieval and post-medieval contexts which may be indicative of pre-Conquest deer enclosures, for example at Colston in Badingham (BL Add Ms 19091), and at Chediston, Debenham, Little Stonham, and Monk Soham (S. Podd pers. comm.).

Conclusion

The distribution of parks in Suffolk reflects the choices made by landholders with regard to locating their parks on their major demesne manors, possibly reflecting at the same time a response to the diminishing resources of woodland and pasture during the rapid population growth of the twelfth and

thirteenth centuries and the opportunity to create exclusive hunting grounds.
At the micro-scale the siting of parks was dictated by topography, in that available woodland and pasture resources were located on the high interfluves where the soils were unsuitable for arable, and were thus also peripheral to the vills to which they pertained. This pattern provides a useful predictive tool for the investigation of sites of as-yet unlocated parks. The documentary evidence for the county confirms the existence of two major periods of imparking in the county, the first from about 1086 to the end of the fourteenth century and the second beginning in the sixteenth century. In many counties the chronology for imparking is based upon the dates of licences to impark; however, this evidence is lacking in Suffolk. Other comparable evidence – complaints with regard to park-breaking and IPM extents – provide evidence for the existence, but not the actual creation, of parks. Where further detailed local documentary and landscape research has been undertaken it is clear that some parks may have been in existence up to 100 years before their first appearance in state documents; in other cases it may have been even longer, and some parks could have been deer enclosures in the pre-Conquest period. Importantly, this research has demonstrated that in the case of Suffolk, and possibly, therefore, other counties, a chronology of imparking based solely on state documents may be unreliable, potentially leading to misinterpretation of the causal factors. This chapter thus further emphasises the importance of the investigation of local records and local landscape development in this area of research.

Notes

1. These end dates represent two key documents: Domesday Book (1086) and the *Chorography of Suffolk*, c.1602 (MacCullogh 1976).

CHAPTER NINE

Baronial and Manorial Parks in Medieval Cumbria

Angus J. L. Winchester

At one level, the place of parks in the economy, culture and landscape of medieval Cumbria was similar to that of parks in other parts of England. The chronology of imparking and disparking, the size and shape of Cumbrian parks and their multi-functional role in the manorial economy all mirror patterns found elsewhere (Stamper 1988), but there are aspects of their story which reflect the distinctive regional character of the counties of Cumberland, Westmorland and Lancashire North of the Sands. Cantor's gazetteer of deer parks records noticeably fewer parks in upland England – including Cumbria – than in most lowland counties (mapped in Rackham 1986, 124). That pattern is explained in part by the absence of parks in barren tracts of uninhabited mountain and moorland but it also reflects the influence of distinctive patterns of lordship and land tenure in many upland areas. Tenurial patterns in medieval Cumbria therefore form the starting point of this regional survey.

The distribution of deer parks in medieval Cumbria can only be understood in the context of the structure of baronial overlordship. Surrounding Carlisle was a core of royal land which included the great royal forest of Inglewood, stretching south to Penrith. Beyond this core, much of the region was held as large baronial estates. Several of these – the baronies of Greystoke, Kendal and Copeland, the honour of Cockermouth, and the liberties of Millom and Furness – were anchored to a *caput* in the lowlands but embraced a segment of the Lake District fells and dales, which was retained in hand and had the status of private forest or, more correctly, free chase (Winchester 1987, 14–22; Winchester 2005a). There are suggestions that in the twelfth century the baronial overlords possessed hunting rights across the whole of their estates, and that certainly appears to have been the case in Gilsland and in Copeland baronies, but by the 1290s they claimed rights of free chase over much more restricted areas in the uplands (Liddell 1966, 110–13; Todd 1997, 14). The combination of royal and baronial forest in Cumbria meant that large tracts of territory were retained, in theory at least, as hunting grounds. In practice, most of the private forests of the uplands were colonised by peasant communities and exploited as seigneurial pastures by the thirteenth century, though the designation as forest remained meaningful in a handful of cases through to the early modern period. Many of the parks to be discussed below were thus parks in forests, and the relationship between enclosed parks and wider hunting grounds runs as a theme through this chapter.

Parks and the pattern of lordship

The distribution of parks in Cumbria is shown in Figure 62.[1] In tenurial terms, they fall into three categories. First are the large parks attached (and often physically adjacent) to a castle at the heart of a baronial estate. The baronial lords also established further parks or other enclosures for the preservation of woodland and deer in their private forests: these form a second category. Finally, there were the parks created by lesser lords. In the lowland sections of the baronial estates, immediate lordship over most land was in the hands of manorial lords, many of whom shared in the fashion for creating parks on their estates in the thirteenth and fourteenth centuries. Each category is discussed in turn below.

Before embarking on this survey, however, it is perhaps necessary to dwell briefly on the matter of terminology. In medieval usage, the term 'park' had the broad meaning of an enclosure, specifically a private, seigneurial enclosure. In Cumbria, as elsewhere, it had a particular association with woodland, but not all 'parks' were deer parks in the conventional sense. Wooded 'parks' on the eastern shore of Coniston Water (Water Park, Parkamoor and Lawson Park) were described as 'herdwickes' (stock farms) in the sixteenth century (TNA:PRO DL 44/194); Oxen Park, nearby in Furness Fells, and 'Oxparke' in Caldbeck were presumably similar stock-rearing enclosures (CRO D/Lec/29/1; Farrer and Brownbill 1914, 384). 'Wood' and 'park' seem sometimes to have been used interchangeably to describe enclosed woodland, whether or not the enclosure was for deer. Brigwood, part of the baronial park at Brampton, was sometimes called a 'wood' and sometimes a 'park'. In the forest of Derwent-fells, the 'park' or 'wood' at Gatesgarth, at the head of Buttermere, recorded in the 1260s, was an enclosed wood pasture associated with a demesne stock-rearing farm, and had little connection with deer (Winchester 2003). Across the fells, on the shores of Derwentwater, Fawe Park and 'Scurlothyn Parke' were enclosed coppice woods in the fifteenth century (CRO D/Lec/29/4; TNA:PRO C 135/201/5). These examples illustrate the flexibility of the term 'park' and the need to question the exact nature of enclosures so called. A convergence between woodland and pasture, but not necessarily deer, appears to have been central to the concept encapsulated in a 'park'.

Baronial castle parks

The best-documented parks in Cumbria are the large parks which were found attached to most of the baronial seats by the later thirteenth century. Only the lowland baronies of Wigton and Burgh by Sands, on the Solway plain – in

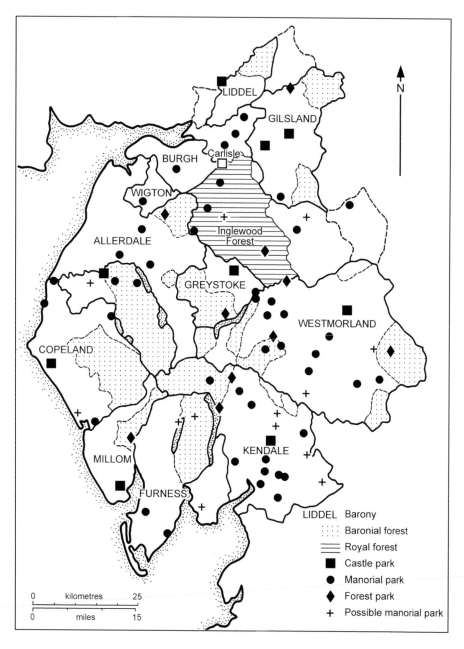

FIGURE 62.
Forests and parks in
medieval Cumbria.

neither of which was there a baronial castle – were without such parks. In most cases the baronial castle park balloons out from the castle, anchored to it at one extremity. At Egremont, a 300-acre park, recorded from 1294, embraced the valley of the river Ehen south of the castle (CCR 1288–96, 400–2). At Greystoke the two parks recorded in 1289 (identified as 'le Hevedpark' and Gillcambon in 1359) stretched away onto higher ground to the north and west of the castle (TNA:PRO C 133/53/13, m.4, C 135/146, m.9). Cockermouth Park, in existence by 1259, fanned out over rising ground east of the castle; while the park at Millom, recorded from 1337, rose over the hill north of the castle (TNA:PRO SC11/730, m.1; CIPM, 8, 67). The two parks at Kendal covered an area of at least 1,500 acres on the east bank of the river Kent, embracing the castle and stretching up onto the slopes of Hay Fell. There was already more than one park there by 1274, when Kendal Castle was valued 'with parks, fish ponds (*vivariis*) within the parks, herbage and fish traps (*cistis*) in the same' (TNA:PRO C 133/5/10). In 1310 one park was described as being 'around the castle' and there was a second and (to judge from the valuation placed on the herbage) larger park as well (TNA:PRO C 134/17/5; also Farrer 1923, 15).

In the baronies of Westmorland and Gilsland, large parks lay close to but separate from the baronial seat. In Westmorland the baronial park, recorded from 1314, lay 2 miles east of the castle at Appleby, at Flakebridge (CIPM 5, no. 533). In Gilsland, the park and the adjacent 'Brigwood' (itself referred to as 'a park with deer' in 1383, but as a wood in 1295 and 1486) covered over 1,000 acres between the rivers Irthing and Gelt, stretching east from their confluence towards Brampton (CIPM 15, 381; CIPM 3, 184; CIPM ser.2, 1, no. 157; Graham 1934, 47). After the original baronial seat at Irthington, across the river to the west of the park, was replaced by Naworth Castle, 4 miles to the east, probably in the fourteenth century, a new park was created around the castle. Described in 1603 as covering 442 acres and enclosed with a stone wall and a pale, Naworth Park was probably enclosed in the sixteenth century, as it was not referred to in an inquisition *post mortem* of 1486 and the first place-name reference dates to the late sixteenth century (Graham 1934, 31; Armstrong *et al.* 1950–2, vol. 1, 67).

With the exception of Naworth, most of these baronial parks appear to have originated before 1300: the earliest references are generally in inquisitions and estate records from the later thirteenth or fourteenth century. There are hints that most postdate the foundation of the castles to which they are attached: some appear as uncomfortable, rather artificial appendages to the castle, a narrow neck linking castle and park, as at Egremont or (less strikingly) Millom and Greystoke. The only baronial castles to lie surrounded by their parks were comparatively late creations: Kendal, where the new castle of the early thirteenth century replaced a motte and bailey in a cramped location on the west side of the town, and, as we have seen, Naworth, the fourteenth-century replacement for the motte at Irthington. Most of the other castle parks were probably late twelfth- or thirteenth-century additions to the landscape of baronial overlordship.

Forest parks

More numerous than the castle parks were the parks and other analogous enclosures for deer in the extensive areas of Cumbria which had the status of royal forest or private chase. Parks were a feature of royal forests and the great royal forest of Inglewood, centred on woodland between Chalk Beck and the river Eden to the south of Carlisle, was no exception. It was, according to the

Lanercost Chronicle, 'a goodly great forest, full of woods, red deer and fallow, wild swine, and all manner of wild beasts' (Cox 1905, 90). It contained several launds, but only one of them, at Plumpton on the east bank of the river Petterill, was imparked. The 'hay' of Plumpton Hay had been recognised as a separate entity from an early date and had become a 'park' by the later thirteenth century, when a commission of enquiry of 1274 reported that it had been enclosed in the reign of Henry III (CPR 1272–81, 69).

The other major lowland forest in Cumbria, the baronial forest of Whinfell, attached to the lord of Westmorland barony's castle at Brougham, also contained a park. It remained a notable feature of the Eden valley landscape into the seventeenth century, when Thomas Denton called it 'the larg[e] park or forest of Whinfeild, well shaded with wood & well stocked with red & fallow deer' (Denton 2003, 401). Denton's ambiguity over whether Whinfell was a forest or a park is mirrored in earlier sources, which use the terms 'forest', 'park' and 'wood', but there was certainly a park there in the mid-thirteenth century, when it contained game (*bestias*) but was said to be poorly enclosed (Smith 1967, vol. 2, 132; CIM 1, no. 436). The park had two deer leaps, through which, it was claimed in 1285, deer were driven into Whinfell from the nearby royal forest of Inglewood (Parker 1910, 8). The exact location of the park pale remains unclear, but the park, described in 1403 as the 'close of the forest', appears to have encompassed most but not all of a larger entity known as the 'forest, moor and pasture' of Whinfell (CIPM 18, 259).

Most of the retained hunting forests or chases of the baronial overlords in Cumbria were in the uplands. Although some fallow deer are recorded in the upland forests, the predominant species of the uplands was the red deer (and presumably, though these are rarely mentioned, the humbler roe), which roamed widely across the fells and dales. These remote valleys, deep in the hills, could be managed as deer forests without the need for enclosed parks to preserve the game, as the survival of herds of deer in the seventeenth century demonstrates. Geltsdale forest in the north Pennines, Wasdale and Ennerdale forests in the western Lake District and Martindale forest in the hills between Ullswater and Haweswater all supported significant herds of red deer (Denton 2003, 81, 98, 350, 396).

Parks and other enclosures for deer were features of upland forests and chases across northern England. Examples outside Cumbria include the parks of Leagram and Radholme in Bowland forest; Musbury Park in the forest of Rossendale; and the bishop of Durham's great park in his forest of Weardale (Shaw 1956, 425–36; Tupling 1927, 15–16; Drury 1978, 93–103). In Cumbria, many of the baronial estates possessed not only a large park attached to their castle but also, by the fourteenth century, at least one park in the upland forest. Such upland/lowland pairings can be seen in Millom seigniory, between the castle park at Millom and the forest park at Ulpha in the Duddon valley; in Greystoke barony, between the parks attached to the castle at Greystoke and Gowbarrow Park in the baronial forest on the shores of Ullswater; in Kendal barony, between the castle parks at Kendal and the forest park at Troutbeck;

and in Westmorland barony, between Flakebridge Park near Appleby and the Oldpark in Stainmoor forest. In origin, the upland parks were probably akin to the parks in royal forests, areas set aside to preserve an environment in which deer could thrive as demesne stock-rearing and peasant colonisation put pressure on the habitat of the deer in the twelfth and thirteenth centuries.

Manorial parks

Parks created by the Cumbrian overlords, whether attached to castles or within private forests, are comparatively well documented. Establishing the number, extent and chronology of the parks enclosed by the lesser, manorial lords is more difficult. Extents and surveys of subinfeudated manors are comparatively rare, partly because the framework of baronial overlordship meant that many subinfeudated manors were not tenancies in chief of the Crown and hence were rarely the subject of an inquisition *post mortem*. The limitations of the medieval documentary evidence often make it difficult to establish whether post-medieval place-names such as Parkgate or Parkhead record the former presence of a deer park or refer to a later or other form of 'park'.

Over fifty manorial parks can be identified in Cumbria's medieval documentary record (Figure 62). In most cases documentary mention of a park is complemented by one or more minor place-names recording its presence. For example, the licence granted to John de Harrington in 1341 to impark 300 acres of wood, moor and marsh in the manor of Aldingham in Furness can confidently be linked to the park attached to Gleaston Castle, the memory of which survives in the names Gleaston Park and Colt Park (Farrer and Brownbill 1914, 321). In other cases, particularly where the primary source is a licence to impark, the evidence is less clear. Most of the licences date from the middle decades of the fourteenth century and may reflect Crown attempts to raise revenue rather than a real surge in park creation in the decades leading up to the Black Death. In at least one instance, Setterah Park in the Lowther valley, a park is recorded by 1289, though a licence was not granted until 1339 (Winchester 1987, 105). In five other cases (Drigg, Eaglesfield, Highhead, Renwick and Roundthwaite), all dating from 1338, a licence is the only evidence for the existence of a park and in these instances the presence of a park is to be doubted (CPR 1338–40, 94, 119). The distribution of manorial parks mapped in Figure 62 must therefore be provisional: it is almost certainly incomplete but (by including places where the only evidence comes from a licence to impark) may also include some doubtful instances.

Manorial parks varied hugely in size and the character of the terrain they enclosed. Kentmere Park covered over 700 acres of rough fell land; Barton Park *c*.180 acres of wooded hillside; Setterah and Torpenhow parks similar acreages in the lowlands flanking the Lakeland hills. It may be assumed that most contained significant woodland. In some cases it was explicitly stated that woodland was imparked, as in the licence granted in 1337 to Robert Vipont, lord of Alston in the north Pennines, to impark the wood of Wanwood (CPR

1334–38, 550). The dual uses to which manorial parks were put can be inferred from manorial extents, where they are nearly always valued as pasture, probably suggesting that they rapidly became exploited as enclosed grazing grounds. Only rarely are deer mentioned, though the description of Wythop Park as a *parcus sine feris* ('a park without game') in 1475 may imply that this was unusual and that a park would normally have contained at least some deer (CRO D/Lec, box 302). Rydal Park, one of the few manorial parks in the Lake District proper, was said to have been 'well replenish'd with fallow-deer' until the mid-sixteenth century and the memory of the presence of deer in several other manorial parks in southern Westmorland, such as Barbon, Preston Patrick, Selside and Skelsmergh, persisted into the late seventeenth century (Porter and Collingwood 1928, 86; Ewbank 1963, 30, 43, 98–9).

Like their baronial counterparts, most manorial parks were physically adjacent to the lord's hall, forming landscapes of privilege and exclusion at the heart of the estate. Some contained tangible expressions of lordly power: Seawood Park, one of the parks belonging to Gleaston Castle in Furness, housed the courthouse where the manor courts were held (TNA:PRO E 317/ Lancs/18 ff.25–6).

Analogous enclosures: hays, fences and friths

As well as parks, there were other enclosures associated with game preservation in hunting forests. In order to set Cumbrian parks into a wider context, these are considered briefly below. As we have seen, the baronial overlords appear to have retained hunting rights over wide areas in the twelfth centuries, but their hunting grounds shrank subsequently, first to the upland portions of their estates claimed as free chases in the late thirteenth century; then, in practice at least, to the remote, unsettled parts of these free chases, as colonisation and demesne stock-rearing populated the dales with people and livestock.

The retreat in the extent of land over which the baronial lords claimed hunting rights may provide the context for the creation of baronial parks. Some baronial castle parks appear to have been carved out of a wider area of land over which the lord retained hunting rights. The clearest evidence of this comes from Kendal, where the parks attached to the castle lay within a larger area known as the 'hay' of Kendal, described as part of the private forest of the barons of Kendal in 1272 (Farrer 1923, 176). 'Hay' (Latin *haia*; OE *haga*) is now recognised as a term used to describe a hunting enclosure and is probably synonymous with *parcus* ('park') in Domesday Book (Hooke 1989; Liddiard 2003). Hay Fell, Hutton in the Hay and Hayclose all lay beyond the park boundary at Kendal, suggesting that the park there formed the core of a wider hunting ground which had some sort of separate identity and, presumably, a physical outer boundary. Place-name evidence suggests a similar pattern at Cockermouth, where the hill called The Hay lay adjacent to but beyond the pale of Cockermouth Park. On the margins of the forest belonging to Greystoke barony, perhaps in the vicinity of Greystoke Park, there was 'a several hay near the forest (*haya seperabilis iuxta dictam forestam*) where no one may enter without the lord's licence', which may have been a similar enclosure, though it was valued solely as grazing for livestock in 1254 (TNA: PRO C132/16/9, m.3).

The concept of a 'hay' wider than a park was not unique to the baronial parks: the reference to woodland described as 'le Heyinga extra parcum de Barton' in an agreement over pannage rights in 1279 perhaps suggests a wider 'hay' beyond the manorial park there (Ragg 1910, 448–9). It is impossible to say how great the antiquity of these 'hays' was, but they are perhaps to be compared with Plumpton Hay in the royal forest of Inglewood, which can be traced back to the twelfth century: the keepership of 'the King's hay of Plumpton' was said in 1212 to have been granted out by Henry I (Wilson 1901, 421). Are we seeing in these areas to which the term 'hay' was applied a memory of baronial hunting enclosures pre-dating the formal enclosure of parks?

Another term associated with game preservation in the upland forests and perhaps used as a synonym for 'park' was 'frith'. Derived from OE *fyrhð(e)*, usually translated as 'woodland', 'frith' seems to have a particular association with hunting forests in northern England, as in the names Duffield Frith and Leek Frith in the north Midlands, where it is used as a synonym for 'forest' (Wiltshire *et al.* 2005, 44; Page 1905, 398; Greenslade 1996, 7, 5, 80). The phrase 'the Foreste wele Frythede', describing the scene for a hunt in the late medieval Arthurian romance set in Inglewood Forest (Amours 1897, 117), suggests that it had a particular sense indicating 'enclosure', and the alliterative phrase 'forest and frith' (which is used as a township name in Harwood Forest in upper Teesdale) may thus contrast unenclosed forest with enclosed 'frith' (Amours 1897, 330; *cf.* Gelling 1984, 191–2). There is a possible echo of this sense in the wording of Gospatrick's writ, the sole surviving pre-Conquest charter from Cumbria, which grants freedom 'on weald, on freyð, on heyninga', perhaps to be translated 'in open woodland, in enclosed wood and in enclosed cultivated land' (Armstrong *et al.* 1950–2, vol.3, xxvii–xxx; Harmer 1952, 419–24; *cf.* Gelling 1984, 223). If this interpretation is correct, a 'frith' may have been an enclosed, and probably wooded, section of a forest.

The term frith occurs in several locations in the upland forests of the Lake District. In the forest of Copeland, parts of the unenclosed high fells – the western slopes of the Scafell massif (Scafell itself, Kettle Cove and Slightside) and Caw Fell, between Ennerdale and Wasdale – were deemed to be the lord's 'fences' or 'friths' in the fifteenth and sixteenth centuries, even though there is no evidence of physical enclosure. In Wasdale there were also two 'friths' which did take the form of large enclosed banks of fellside: Bowderdale, on the north shore of Wastwater, and the 'newe frithe', a walled enclosure on the slopes of Lingmell, full of underwood, which was enclosed from the common in the mid-sixteenth century 'for [the lord's] deare for the better preservation of his game there'.[2] Fellside enclosures on the south side of Ennerdale (known as the Side and the Coves) appear to have had a similar status. Although there were still deer in these 'fences' in the seventeenth century, they had long been used for grazing livestock (CRO D/Lec, box 94). The monks of Calder Abbey had grazing rights in the fences on the Wasdale fells and, within a generation of enclosure, the 'new frith' at Wasdalehead had been let for grazing (Alnwick Castle MSS, X.II.3: box 3(a): estate accounts, 1470–1; box 4). 'Frith' also appears in association with active attempts to preserve deer in Martindale forest, to the south-east of Ullswater, where five areas of land, including two substantial pastures totalling 140 acres and a 6-acre pasture called the 'olde frithe' were reserved by the lord in 1589 for the sustenance of 30 fallow deer and 20 red deer – though the actual numbers in the forest at that time were said to be 28 red and 16 fallow (TNA:PRO LR2/212, f.28). The term is also encountered in connection with parks: the baronial park of Flakebridge, near Appleby, recorded as 'Flackebridge frith' in 1684, was associated with the minor place-names Frith Beck and Frith Lane; the stream forming the eastern boundary of Gowbarrow Park on Ullswater was formerly called 'Frith Beck' (Smith 1967, vol. 2, 105; Clarke 1789, 42); Frith Wood lay in or close to the park in Naddle/Thornthwaite Forest; and Frith Hall in Ulpha Park in the seigniory of Millom. This assemblage of evidence suggests that the term 'frith' might be used as an alternative description of a deer enclosure in an upland forest but also to refer to a section, perhaps especially wooded, within a park. The enclosed friths in Wasdale appear to have been to all intents and purposes deer parks by another name, as may have been the park-like enclosures called Low Frith and High Frith, attached to Pendragon Castle in the chase of Mallerstang.

There may have been a chronological pattern to the use of these various terms – hay, park, frith – in Cumbria across the medieval centuries. 'Hay' appears to precede 'park' (though in the absence of early records it is impossible to know whether there were 'hays' in pre-Conquest Cumbria), while 'frith' may represent the transfer of a term meaning 'enclosed woodland' to synonymous use with 'deer park' in the later medieval centuries.

Parks and estate economy

The place of the baronial castle parks in the economy of the larger landed estates is illustrated by Cockermouth Park, for which later thirteenth-century park-keepers' accounts survive. Although not a continuous series, the accounts demonstrate the mixed land use and variety of parkland resources from which the lords derived income (TNA:PRO SC 6/824/7–15). When first recorded in 1259, the park at Cockermouth was said to contain around 100 deer, the terminology (*damos et damas*, rather than *cervus/cerva*) suggesting that this was a herd of fallow deer (TNA:PRO SC11/730, m.1). The park was attached to the castle on the south side of the river Derwent, stretching for 1.5 miles upstream and covering 690 acres. The park-keeper's core duties were to repair the paling and to look after the deer. Being wooden, the park boundary required constant maintenance. When major repairs were undertaken in 1277–8, the accounts give an indication of the structure of the park pale: 4,960 stakes were cut, along with 360 'reylles' and 1,300 'strukes' (planks?); part of the pale was

constructed with two rails and part with only one (TNA:PRO SC6/824/10).
During winter the park-keeper cut branches as fodder for the deer and he
accounted for any losses from the herd. The accounts contain no explicit references to hunting, which is not surprising as they cover a period when the
Cockermouth estate was in the hands of the widowed Countess Isabella de
Fortibus and was a distant outpost of an extensive estate run from Radstone
(Northants). Nevertheless, by order of the countess, the park-keeper made
gifts of deer to others: ten, including three to the sheriff of Cumberland, in
1277–8, and a dozen to another Cumbrian landowner, Matilda de Vaux, lady
of Gilsland, in 1280–1 (TNA:PRO SC 6/824/10/12).

Sustaining a herd of deer was only part of the function of the park at
Cockermouth. Regular income came from sales of parkland resources to neighbouring communities. The major sources of income were pannage (payments
for the right to fatten pigs on acorns in the autumn), herbage or agistment
(payments for putting livestock to graze in the park) and sales of deadwood as
fuel. On top of these repeated sales, the park also yielded smaller amounts of
income from other products: honey, bracken, bark, rushes, timber. In all these
sources of external income, but particularly the sales of fuel wood, the park's
proximity to the thriving borough of Cockermouth would have ensured high
demand. The park was thus by no means a closed game reserve, but rather
a valuable tract of woodland and pasture for the local community, which
provided fluctuating but regular income to the lord's coffers.

However, the accounts also record a brief period during which Countess
Isabella's officers intensified the use of the park by exploiting it directly, at the
expense of income from these sales. The repairs to the park pale in 1277–8
presaged major change. The income from sales of deadwood in that and the
following year were substantially higher than in previous or later years, perhaps
suggesting a more determined cropping (perhaps even clearance) of woodland. In 1278–9 the account noted that 'the whole park is newly divided into
closes (*resicit in claustura*)' (TNA:PRO SC6/824/11). Two years later income
from sales was very low and there are indications that parts of the park were
being farmed: the castle reeve bought in cattle, made a new close in the park
for stocking purposes (*ratione instauri*) and accounted for the mowing of 4
acres of hay meadow in the park. The two other surviving accounts from the
1280s suggest that the major use of the park in those years was direct stock
farming. In 1282–3 the countess's cattle and horses (40 cattle and a herd of
13 mares, 2 colts and 10 foals) grazed in the park. By the end of the decade
the cattle had gone but the stud remained and had grown in size to contain
a stallion and two other 'horses', 10 mares and 15 colts and foals (TNA:PRO
SC6/824/12–14). This episode of demesne farming in the park was short-lived,
cut short by the death of Countess Isabella in 1293 and the escheat of the
Cockermouth estate to the Crown. The later surviving account rolls show
a return to indirect exploitation through agistment and sales of deadwood
(TNA:PRO SC6/824/15, E199/7/3).

The story of Cockermouth Park in the later thirteenth century provides a rare glimpse of the place of a park in the economy of a Cumbrian estate and illustrates the dual role of many parks, combining an attempt to maintain a herd of deer with a diversity of other means of exploiting the resources of an enclosed area of woodland and pasture. The later medieval history of the park is less well documented. Although the lords of Cockermouth were largely absentees, the castle was substantially enlarged *c.*1400 by Henry Percy, first earl of Northumberland, who had inherited the estate from his first wife. He gave the castle an imposing gatehouse displaying the arms of five families through whom the estate had descended. Such ostentatious expenditure may have been accompanied by further expenditure to create the 'stone wall around the park', which was under repair in 1442 (Curwen 1911, 142–3; CRO D/Lec/29/2). It may be that an enclosure close to the castle called the 'Deer Orchard', which existed by the mid-sixteenth century, recalls a deliberate attempt to keep deer within sight of the castle and represents the dominance of aesthetics over economic use in a section of the park close to the castle (Figure 63; CRO D/Lons/L5/2/24/1, 218).

Sixteenth-century surveys of surviving castle parks provide glimpses of the wood-pasture landscape at that time. The park at Cockermouth retained its parkland character, being described in 1570 as 'a great large ground not empaled … in the nature of a chace very well replenyshed with wood and tymbre', a description confirmed by the representation of the park on a pictorial map of Cockermouth *c.*1600 (Figure 63; TNA:PRO E164.37, f.20). In addition to the Deer Orchard, other sections of the park close to the castle (their

FIGURE 63.
Cockermouth Park, shown on the remarkable pictorial map of *c.*1600. The survival of a wood-pasture landscape is clearly indicated.

CUMBRIA RECORD OFFICE

FIGURE 64.
Troutbeck Park, in
the heart of the Lake
District. A baronial
forest park at the head
of a Lakeland valley,
enclosed before 1274.

names – Horse Close, Wheat Close – suggesting agricultural uses) had been
separated from the 'Grett Park' by 1560 (CRO D/Lons/L5/2/24/1, 218). Likewise, in 1576 Kendal Park contained both wood pasture and a number of
separate closes. The park's 630 acres were said to contain almost 450 oak trees,
'growinge dispersedly … which have bene lopped and shred for Browse for the
deere' and a similar number of 'doterde' oaks, not fit for timber (TNA:PRO
E 310/25/146). By 1604 the two great parks at Greystoke were yielding the
considerable annual sum of over £100 from agistment and had been divided
for accounting purposes (and, probably, on the ground) into at least seven
sections of pasture: over half the agistment income came from summer grazing ('le sommerground') in Gilcambon Park (CRO D/HG/21). The picture
painted by these documents suggests that many of the baronial castle parks
retained both their seigneurial character and their landscape quality as wood
pasture, but were being exploited primarily for grazing rather than as game
reserves or pleasure grounds.

A similar picture emerges from the forest parks. By the mid-fourteenth
century Plumpton Park in Inglewood forest appears to have been exploited
increasingly as a grazing ground. It was enclosed with a stone wall over the
years 1332–5 at great expense (the full cost was over £185) and subsequent
accounts show that it was being managed as an agistment ground for horses
and cattle. Income from agistment and attachments (payments for infringing
forest rights, often by taking wood) remained high across the middle decades
of the century, suggesting that by then the use of the park as a resource by

neighbouring communities was of greater importance than its original function as a game preserve (Young 1979, 116–20; Cox 1905, 94). Likewise, the 'Oldparke' in Whinfell forest was still wooded and paled in 1442 and was used as grazing both for demesne livestock and by agistment (CRO (Kendal) WD/Hoth, box 45). Both Plumpton Park and Whinfell Park thus fulfilled a dual function, expressing seigneurial power as the haunt of herds of deer but also serving as valuable reserves of pasture in a pastoral economy.

Parks in the upland forests represented one of the few areas (demesne stock farms or 'vaccaries' were another) where effective seigneurial control remained by 1300. Here again, lordly control was expressed principally through exploitation to yield income from the sale of pasture for livestock. For example, the herbage of the rocky and wild park at the head of Troutbeck in the forest of Kendal barony (Figure 64) was said to be worth £3 6s 8d a year, over and above the cost of sustaining the deer, in 1283 (Farrer 1924, 40). Indeed, it is doubtful whether we should view the seigneurial enclosures in the baronial forests as traditional deer parks: there is little evidence of active management of herds of fallow deer, nor of hunting or lordly entertainment. The parks, fences and friths, most of which appear to have contained more woodland than survived on the open fells, provided some protection for deer in the face of competition from the growing herds and flocks. But the overwhelming impression is that by the fourteenth and fifteenth centuries the primary value of these fellside enclosures to absentee lords was as grazing grounds, and the main activity was the exploitation of their potential to generate income from

agistment and sales of pasture. There is thus a difficulty in deciding whether parks in the upland forests are to be considered 'deer parks' in the normal sense or, rather, the last vestiges of the private forests, physically separated as seigneurial reserves, ostensibly for the preservation of deer but actually to create private demesne pastures.

Parks in the Cumbrian landscape

Whether a park survives as a feature of the modern landscape is largely determined by the long-term history of the estate to which it belonged. In the Cumbrian context the key factor is the decline in the number of resident lords, a process which had begun by the fourteenth century, by which time many of the baronial overlords were also non-resident. Good numbers of the lesser gentry families remained resident until the sixteenth century but their numbers declined rapidly across the seventeenth and eighteenth (Winchester 2005b, 34–7). Non-residence increased the likelihood that a park would be divided up and leased as farmland, while the paucity of post-medieval country houses in Cumbria meant that comparatively few medieval parks enjoyed a reincarnation as landscape parks in the post-medieval centuries, the parks at Lowther and Levens being the principal exceptions. In a handful of cases, where a medieval park remained intact as a large grazing ground, vestiges of the wood-pasture landscape of the medieval deer park survive. These tend to be remote parks in the pastoral uplands, such as Askerton Park on the sour, wet hills on the Border and Troutbeck Park (Figure 64), deep in the heart of the Lake District.

Two of the most impressive surviving park walls in Cumbria surround very late manorial parks, which represent a final flowering of the medieval tradition. These are at Wharton and Ravenstonedale (Figure 65), near Kirkby Stephen, where an aspiring social climber, Thomas the first Lord Wharton, consolidated his estates after acquiring extensive former monastic property. The creation of both his parks involved the dispossession of tenants by offering them other land in exchange, allowing Wharton to enclose land which had formerly been part of the farming resource of the local community. At Wharton, in the mid-1540s, he threw a wall around a roughly circular area of 210 acres surrounding Wharton Hall; at Ravenstonedale he enclosed a larger, similarly rounded block of land covering both sides of the valley north of the village in 1560–1. His parks were statements of power; the process of clearing them of tenants ensuring his survival in local folk memory, while the separation of his manor house at Wharton Hall behind the park wall physically reinforced the social distance he sought from his tenants. Both parks were surrounded by high limestone walls, which survive in parts to almost 10 feet in height, suggesting that they were indeed intended to confine herds of deer; but the parks were also valuable pastures. When surveyed in 1560, Wharton Park was said to consist largely of grassland (*prata*) and was valued at £23 6s 8d, over and above the grazing of 300 deer. Ravenstonedale Park, then newly enclosed, was valued as grazing for fat cattle and oxen (Blackett-Ord 1986; Hoyle 1995; CRO D/Lons/L5/2/24/1, pp. 2, 31). The dual economy of the deer park is thus in evidence again, stressing that preserving game and rearing livestock in the same enclosure were not necessarily incompatible in a pastoral region such as Cumbria.

Few Cumbrian parks have left marks in the modern landscape as dramatic as the remarkable park wall at Ravenstonedale. Rather more – but still comparatively few – survive as a line in the landscape, even where the fabric of the pale has gone. Some fellside parks (for example, Kentmere Park and Barton Park) survive as large, round-cornered enclosures. The outer boundaries of some lowland parks stand out as a dominant field boundary marking out the line of the former park pale, as at Setterah Park, near Helton, and the parks at Torpenhow (an oval adjoining the hall at the east end of the village) and Kirkoswald (where the line of the pale determines the southern section of the parish boundary). But in the majority of cases, only a minor place-name records the former existence of a park. The reduction in the number of parks can be traced to the disruptions of the late medieval centuries.

The troubled fourteenth century saw the disappearance of several Cumbrian parks as the disruptive effects of Border hostilities exacerbated the economic dislocation caused by livestock disease, climatic deterioration and pestilence. As early as 1300, the baronial park attached to Liddel Strength, hard on the Border, was said to contain no deer and, though it had previously yielded income from herbage, was then worth nothing 'because of the war' (TNA:PRO C133/94/3, m.2). But outright destruction was probably rare. Three examples from western Cumberland illustrate the processes involved in the conversion of a former park to farmland, apparently more by accident of lordly circumstance than by deliberate policy.

The first is the castle park at Egremont, *caput* of the barony of Copeland. By the mid-thirteenth century, Copeland had become an outpost of the extensive landholdings of the de Multon family, whose base was in Lincolnshire, and there is little evidence of direct lordly involvement in Egremont. By the time John de Multon, the last of the line, died in 1334, the park at Egremont was described as unenclosed and without underwood, and worth only 20 shillings yearly for summer herbage, the low valuation being attributed to the lack of enclosure (TNA:PRO C135/41/1). It appears that it had already ceased to function as a park; indeed, the southern section of the park had already been separated when dower was assigned in 1294 (CCR 1288–96, 40–2). After de Multon's death, the barony was divided between his three sisters in a partition which apportioned the baronial demesnes between them in considerable detail. Whether the 1294 division of the park persisted until the partition after John de Multon's death is unclear but at that partition the park (described as 'wood') was divided into three and was subsequently leased as farmland (CCR 1337–9, 476, 486, 494).[3] The legacy of the partition – the accident of an absentee landowner's failure to produce a male heir almost seven centuries ago – is still visible in the landscape today (Figure 66). The outer boundary of the

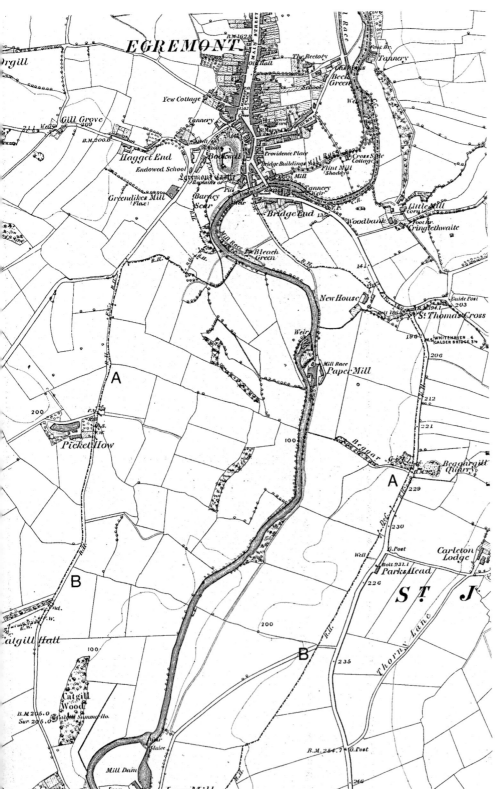

FIGURE 66.
Egremont Park *c.*1860.
The outer boundary of
the park is followed,
in large part, by the
parish boundary. A–A
and B–B mark the
divisions dating from
the partition of the
baronial demesnes in
1338.

park, enclosing the valley of the river Ehen downstream from Egremont, coincides with a road on the western and part of the eastern sides. Two dominant field boundaries running east–west and taking the form of massive earthern hedgebanks (Figure 67), represent the division of the park between the three heiresses, the internal field boundaries the subsequent parcelling out of each share into farmland.

A second example, also illustrating the accidents of inheritance, is the park at Loweswater, enclosed by Thomas de Lucy and his father in the thirteenth century (Figure 68). Loweswater had been hived off from Copeland barony in 1230 and had thus gained a separate identity as an estate held in chief of the Crown. It became known as the manor of 'Balnes', taking its name from Bowness, the rounded headland on the shore of Crummock Water on which the manor house stood. A park surrounding the headland was enclosed in two stages, first by de Lucy's father in the middle decades of the century, then by Thomas de Lucy himself in the 1280s (Wilson 1915, no. 106). When de Lucy's son, Anthony, obtained a grant of Cockermouth Castle and honour from the Crown in 1323, Loweswater came to be administered from there and the

FIGURE 67.
Egremont Park: the massive earthen bank of one of the field boundaries, dating from the 1338 partition.

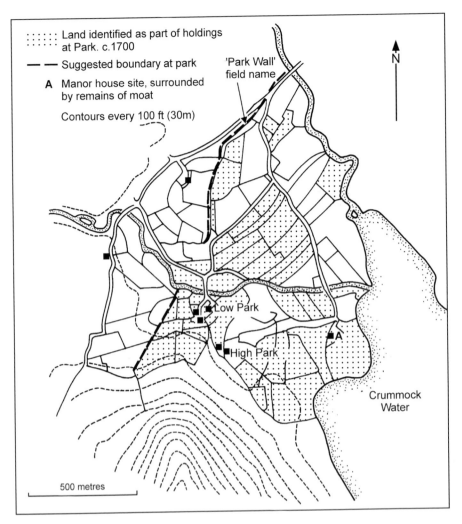

Land identified as part of holdings at Park. c.1700

— — Suggested boundary at park

A Manor house site, surrounded by remains of moat

Contours every 100 ft (30m)

'Park Wall' field name

N

Low Park

High Park

A

Crummock Water

500 metres

manor house and park at Bowness became superfluous. The park had been let to tenants by 1437, resulting in the creation of the farming hamlets of Low Park and High Park. The nineteenth-century field name 'Park Wall' presumably records the outer boundary of the de Lucys' park but the post-medieval landscape shows little indication of its former status as a park: the strip-like fields suggest the existence of a small open-field system, though whether this pre-dated or postdated the imparking of the area is impossible to say.

A similarly complete obliteration of a manorial park took place a few miles away, at Embleton, near Cockermouth (Figure 69). Thomas de Lucy, the feudal superior, had granted Thomas de Ireby, lord of Embleton, licence to enclose a park *c*.1285, in exchange for the right to take two deer from it each year (Wilson 1915, 568–9). How long the park continued to contain game is unclear: the inquisition after de Ireby's death in 1308 merely refers to a 'close', valued as herbage (TNA:PRO C 134/2/10). It may thus have already lost its identity as a park by 1322 when almost half of the houses in Embleton were burnt in the Scottish raid of that year (TNA:PRO C134/75/7). The park had disappeared as a landscape feature by the post-medieval centuries, no hint of a park pale surviving in the field pattern. Its location can, however, be reconstructed from nineteenth-century field names containing the element 'Park', which form a block stretching south-west from the site of the manor house (which survives as an earthwork in a field named 'Hallgarth').

By the seventeenth century most of the baronial castle parks had been broken up and leased as farmland: only those at Millom, Greystoke and Naworth continued to be stocked with deer (Denton 2003, 70, 350; Fleming 1962, 54). The presence of a resident landlord played a major part: although Greystoke belonged to the absentee earls of Arundel, both Millom and Naworth were the principal seats of resident lords – the Hudlestons and the Howards

FIGURE 69.
The 'lost' medieval park of Embleton.

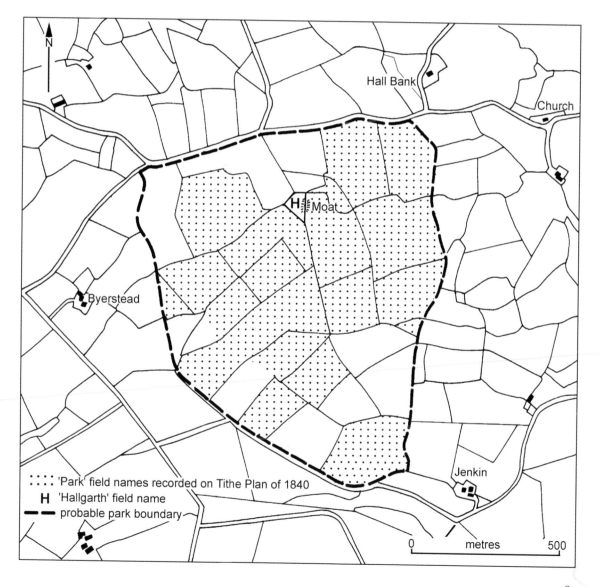

respectively. As with the baronial parks, most of the surviving manorial parks were associated with resident gentry families. In Furness, there were parks with substantial herds of fallow deer at Coniston, Kirkby and Holker, the seats of the Fleming, Kirkby and Preston families (Fleming 1962, 29, 32–3). Thomas Denton, describing Cumberland and Westmorland in 1687–8, recorded, among others, the Pennington family's park at Muncaster, stocked with deer and rabbits; the walled park of the Curwens at Workington, where the deer were 'large & fatt in grease time'; Sir Wilfred Lawson's three parks at Isel, where there were 'severall great heards of red & fallow deer'; and Lord Wharton's park at Wharton, where the deer were large and very fat. By the late seventeenth century deer had become a fashionable accessory in the designed landscapes of post-medieval country houses. In addition to these survivals of medieval parkland landscapes, Denton records the case of Sir John Ballantine of Crookdake, near Wigton, who had altered the house and landscaped the garden and had created, adjacent to the house, 'a little parkett, about 20 or 30 acres of ground, enclosed with a stone wall to hem in a few deer' (Denton 2003, 78, 110, 144, 189, 404). In describing Cumberland in the 1680s, Denton thus captures both the survival of traditional medieval parks and the transition to a new form of lordly pleasure ground.

Notes

1. Parks mapped in Figure 62 have been identified from documentary sources. I should like to record my thanks to Harry Hawkins of Penrith for giving me access to his list of Cumbrian parks, which formed an invaluable starting point. However, I take full responsibility for errors or omissions on this map, which must be considered to be provisional.

2. Liddell 1966, 128; quotation is from CRO D/Lec/265/551. Bowderdale is recorded as a 'close' in 1541 (CRO D/Lec/20/14) and as a separate agistment ground from 1513 (CRO D/Lons/W8/12/51, pp. 235, 238). Fifteenth-century references to 'le frith & le fenc in Wacedale' (e.g. in 1478: CRO D/Lec/29/6) probably refer to the high fells, since Bowderdale was not within that part of the forest covered by the Percy archives at that date.

3. That the 'wood' of Egremont was synonymous with the park is made clear by the third entry cited here, which gives Elizabeth, wife of Walter Bermingham one-third of the wood 'to the castle on the north'. Later estate records confirm that the three divisions of the park were each held of the descendants of the different sisters. The Lucy share had been leased in two parts by the 1470s (Alnwick Castle muniments, X.II.3a; CRO D/Lec/29/6); the Fitzwalter share had been let as four holdings by 1547 (CRO D/Lec/314/38, ff. 48v–49).

Bibliography

Albarella, U. and Thomas, R. (2002) 'They dined on crane: bird consumption, wild fowling and status in medieval England', *Acta Zoologica Cracoviensia* **45**, 23–38.

Alexander, K. N. A. (1998) 'The links between forest history and biodiversity: the invertebrate fauna of ancient pasture-woodlands in Britain and its conservation' in eds K. J. Kirby and C. Watkins, *The Ecological History of European Forests*, CAB International, Wallingford, 73–80

Almond, R. (2003) *Medieval Hunting*, Sutton, Stroud.

Alston, L. (1992) 'Lamarsh Park, the origin and management of a medieval park', *Colchester Archaeological Group Annual Bulletin* **35**, 3–16.

Amours, F. J. ed. (1897) *Scottish Alliterative Poems in Riming Stanzas*, Scottish Text Society **27** and **38**, William Blackwood and Sons, Edinburgh.

Andrén, A. (1997) 'Paradise lost: looking for deer parks in medieval Denmark and Sweden' in eds. H. Andersson, P. Carelli and L. Ersgård, *Visions of the Past: Trends and Traditions in Swedish Archaeology*, Central Board of National Antiquities, Stockholm, 469–90.

Anon. (1836) 'Narrative of the reception in England of Louis Seigneur de la Gruthuyse', *Archaeologia* **26**, 275–80.

Armitage-Smith, S. ed. (1911) *John of Gaunt's Register 1372–1376*, 2 vols, Camden Society 3rd series **20–1**, London, 1911.

Armstrong, A. M., Mawer, A., Stenton, F. M., and Dickens, B. (1950–2) *The Place-Names of Cumberland*, 3 vols, English Place-Name Society XX–XXII, Cambridge University Press, Cambridge.

Ashcroft, M. ed. (1988) *The Memorandum Book of Richard Cholmeley of Brandsby 1602–1623*, North Yorkshire County Record Office Publications **44**, Northallerton.

Askwith, E. and Harrison, B. J. D. (1975) 'The medieval landscape [of the Bedale area]', *North Yorkshire County Record Office Journal* **2**, 51–59.

Astill, G. (2002) 'Windsor in the context of medieval Berkshire' in eds L. Keen and E. Scarff, *Windsor: Medieval Archaeology, Art and Architecture of the Thames Valley*, British Archaeological Association Conference Transactions **25**, Leeds, 1–14.

Aston, T. H. ed. (1987) *Landlords, Peasants and Politics in Medieval England*, Cambridge University Press, Cambridge.

Austin, D. (1978) 'Excavations at Okehampton deer park, Devon, 1976–1978', *Proceedings of the Devon Archaeological Society* **36**, 191–239.

Austin, D., Daggett, R. H. and Walker, M. J. C. (1980) 'Farms and fields in Okehampton Park, Devon: the problems of studying medieval landscape', *Landscape History* **2**, 39–57.

Ayton, A. (1994) *Knights and Warhorses: Military Service and the English Aristocracy under Edward III*, Boydell & Brewer, Woodbridge.

Baildon, W. P. ed. (1901) *Court Rolls of the Manor of Wakefield, vol. 1, 1274–1297*, Yorkshire Archaeological Society Record Series **29**, Leeds.

Baildon, W. P. ed. (1906) *Court Rolls of the Manor of Wakefield, vol. 2, 1297–1309*, Yorkshire Archaeological Society Record Series **36**, Leeds.

Bailey, M. (1988) 'The rabbit and the Medieval East Anglian Economy', *Agricultural History Review* **36**, 1, 1–20.

Bailey, M. (1989) *A Marginal Economy? East Anglian Breckland in the Later Middle Ages*, Cambridge University Press, Cambridge.

Bailey, M. (2002) *The English Manor*, Manchester University Press, Manchester.

Bailey, M., Brooker, J. and Flood, S. eds (1998) *Hertfordshire Lay Subsidy Rolls 1307 and 1334*, Hertfordshire Record Society, Hertford.

Baillie-Grohman, Wm. A. and F. eds (1904) *The Master of Game, by Edward, Second Duke of York. The Oldest English Book on Hunting*, Ballantyne, Hanson and Co., London.

Barron, W. R. J. (1987) *English Medieval Romance*, Longman, London.

Barron, W. R. J. ed. (1998) *Sir Gawain and the Green Knight*, revised edition, Manchester University Press, Manchester.

Bates, A. (n.d.) 'The animal bones from the Stansted excavations 1999 to 2001', unpublished report for Framework Archaeology.

Bateson, P. and Bradshaw, E. L. (1997) 'Physiological effects of hunting red deer (*Cervus elaphus*)', *Proceedings of the Royal Society of London B* **264**, 1707–1714.

Bennett, M. J. (1987) 'Careerism in late medieval England' in eds J. Rosenthal, and C. Richmond, *People, Politics and Community in the Later Middle Ages*, Alan Sutton, Gloucester, 19–39.

Bent, D. C. (1977–8) 'The animal remains', in ed. P. Liddle, 'A late medieval enclosure in Donnington Park', *Transactions of the Leicestershire Archaeological and Historical Society* **53**, 8–29, 14–15.

Beresford, M. W. (1954) *The Lost Villages of England*, Lutterworth Press, London.

Beresford, M. (1957) *History on the Ground: Six Studies in Maps and Landscapes*, Methuen, London.

Beswick, P. and Rotherham, I. D. eds (1993) *Ancient Woodlands: Their Archaeology and Ecology: A Coincidence of Interest*, Landscape Archaeology and Ecology 1, Landscape Conservation Forum, Sheffield.

Bettey, J. H. (1993) *Estates and the English Countryside*, Batsford, London.

Bettey, J. (2000) 'Downlands' in ed. J. Thirsk, *The English Rural Landscape*, Oxford University Press, Oxford, 27–49.

Bice, G. ed. (trans. J. P. Tallon) (1978) *Medieval Hunting Scenes* ('The Hunting Book' of Gaston Phoebus), Miller Graphics, Geneva.

Bigmore, P. (forthcoming) 'Ancient Woodland' in ed. D. Short, *An Historical Atlas of Hertfordshire*, Hertfordshire Publications, Hatfield.

Bilikowski, K. (1983) *Hampshire's Countryside Heritage: Historic Parks and Gardens*, Hampshire County Council, Winchester.

Birch, W. de Gray (1885) *Cartularium Saxonicum: A Collection of Charters Relating to Anglo-Saxon History*, vol. 1, reprinted 1964, Whitley and Co, London.

Birrell, J. (1982) 'Who poached the King's deer? A study in 13th century crime', *Midland History* **7**, 9–25.

Birrell, J. R. (1990–1) 'The forest and the chase in medieval Staffordshire', *Staffordshire Studies* **3**, 23–50.

Birrell, J. (1992) 'Deer and deer farming in medieval England', *Agricultural History Review* **40**, 2, 112–26.

Birrell, J. (1996a) 'Peasant deer poachers in the medieval forest' in eds R. Britnell and J. Hatcher, *Progress and Problems in Medieval England: Essays in Honour of Edward Miller*, Cambridge University Press, Cambridge, 68–88.

Birrell, J. (1996b) 'Hunting and the royal forest', in ed. S. Cavaciocchi, *L'uomo e la foresta: secc. XIII–XVIII: atti della "Ventisettesima settimana di studi", 8–13 maggio 1995*, Le Monnier, Florence, 437–57.

Birrell, J. (2006) 'Procuring, preparing and serving venison in late medieval England' in eds C. Woolgar, D. Serjeantson and T. Waldron, *Food in Medieval England: History and Archaeology*, Oxford University Press, Oxford, 176–88.

Blackett-Ord, M. (1986) 'Lord Wharton's deer park walls', *Transactions of Cumberland and Westmorland Antiquarian & Archaeological Society*, new series **86**, 133–9.

Bibliography

Blockmans, W. and Janse, A. eds (1999) *Showing Status: Representations of Social Positions in the Late Middle Ages*, Medieval Texts and Cultures of Northern Europe **2**, Turnhout.

Bond, C.J. and Iles, R. (1991) 'Early gardens in Avon and Somerset' in ed. A.E.Brown, *Garden Archaeology*, Council for British Archaeology, London, 36–52.

Bond, J. (1994) 'Forests, chases, warrens and parks in medieval Wessex' in eds M.Aston and C.Lewis, *The Medieval Landscape of Wessex*, Oxbow Monograph **46**, Oxford, 115–58.

Bond, J. (1998) *Somerset Parks and Gardens: A Landscape History*, Somerset Books, Tiverton.

Bond, J. (2004) *Monastic Landscapes*, Tempus, Stroud.

Bond, J. and Tiller, K. (1997) *Blenheim: Landscape for a Palace*, Sutton Publishing, Stroud.

Britnell, R.H. (1997) *The Closing of the Middle Ages? England, 1471–1529*, Blackwell, Oxford.

Brooker, J. (n.d.) 'The place names of Hertfordshire and their relationship to landscape and settlement', Hertfordshire Archives and Local Studies, County Hall, Hatfield.

Brown, P. ed. (1986) *Sibton Abbey Cartulary and Charters Part II*, Suffolk Charters **8**, Boydell & Brewer, Woodbridge.

Brown, P. ed. (1987) *Sibton Abbey Cartulary & Charters Part III*, Suffolk Charters **9**, Boydell & Brewer, Woodbridge.

Brown, V. ed. (1992) *Eye Priory Cartulary and Charters Part I*, Suffolk Charters **12**, Boydell & Brewer, Woodbridge.

Brown, V. (1994) *Eye Priory Cartulary and Charters Part II*, Suffolk Charters **13**, Boydell & Brewer, Woodbridge.

Brown, W. ed. (1902) *Yorkshire Inquisitions: III*, Yorkshire Archaeological Society Record Series **31**, Leeds.

Buckland, P.C. (1975) 'Synanthropy and the death-watch; a discussion', *Naturalist* **100**, 37–42.

Buckland, P.C. (1979) *Thorne Moors: A Palaeoecological Study of a Bronze Age Site*, Occasional Publication **8**, Department of Geography, University of Birmingham, Birmingham.

Busby, K. (1987) 'The character and the setting' in eds N.J.Lacy, D.Kelly and K.Busby, *The Legacy of Chrétien de Troyes*, Editions Rodopi B.V., Amsterdam, 57–89.

Cahn, W. (1991) 'Medieval landscape and the encyclopaedic tradition', *Yale French Studies* **80**, 11–24.

Caley, J. ed. (1817) *Valor Ecclesiasticus*, vol.III, Record Commission, London.

Callou, C. (2003) *De la Garenne au Clapier: Etude Archéozoologique du Lapin en Europe Occidental*, Mémoires du Muséum National d'Histoire Naturelle, Tome **189**, Publications Scientifiques du Muséum, Paris.

Calendar of Liberate Rolls 1260–1267, 1961.

Calkins, R.G. (1986) 'Piero de' Crescenzi and the medieval garden' in ed. E.MacDougall, *Medieval Gardens*, Dumbarton Oaks Research Library and Collection, Washington, 157–73.

Campbell, B.M.S. (2005) 'The agrarian problem in the early fourteenth century', *Past and Present* **188**, 3–70.

Campbell, K. (1999) 'Time to "leap the fence": historic parks and gardens' in eds G.Chitty and D.Baker, *Managing Historic Sites and Buildings: Reconciling Presentation and Preservation*, Routledge, London, 127–40.

Cantor, L.M. (1962) 'The medieval parks of south Staffordshire', *Transactions and Proceedings of the Birmingham Archaeological Society* **80**, 1–9.

Cantor, L.M. (1982) 'Forests, chases, parks and warrens' in ed. L.M.Cantor, *The English Medieval Landscape*, Croom Helm, London, 56–85.

Cantor, L.M. (1983) *The Medieval Parks of England. A Gazetteer*, Loughborough University, Loughborough.

Cantor, L.M. and Hatherly, J.M. (1979) 'The medieval parks of England', *Geography* **64**, 71–85.

Cantor, L.M. and Wilson, J.D. (1961) 'The mediaeval deer-parks of Dorset: I', *Dorset Natural History and Archaeology Society* **83**, 109–16.

Carpenter, C. (1992) *Locality and Polity. A Study of Warwickshire Landed Society, 1401–1499*, Cambridge University Press, Cambridge.

Cartmill, M. (1993) *A View to a Death in the Morning: Hunting and Nature Through History*, Harvard University Press, Cambridge.

Chambers, W. ed. J. Harris (1772) *A Dissertation on Oriental Gardening*, Gregg International, London.

Chicoyne, R.A. (1998) *Selcoup Signes: Magic, Reason and Social Order in William of Palerne*, unpublished MA thesis, McGill University, Montreal.

Chisholm, H. ed. (1910–11; 11th edn) *The Encyclopedia Britannica*, 29 vols, Cambridge University Press, Cambridge.

Clanchy, M.T. (1979) *From Memory to Written Record: England 1066–1307*, Edward Arnold, London.

Clarke, H.W. (1887) *The History of Tithes*, George Redway, London.

Clarke, J. (1789; 2nd edn) *A Survey of the Lakes of Cumberland, Westmorland and Lancashire*, London.

Clarke, P. (1994) *The English Nobility under Edward the Confessor*, Clarendon Press, Oxford.

Clay, C.T. ed. (1926) *Yorkshire Deeds: V*, Yorkshire Archaeological Society Record Series **69**, Leeds.

Coates, B.E. (1960) *The Development and Distribution of the Landscape Parks in the East and West Ridings*, unpublished PhD thesis, University of Leeds.

Coates, B.E. (1969) 'Parks in transition: medieval deer-park to modern landscape park', *Transactions of the Hunter Archaeological Society* **9**, 132–50.

Colt Hoare, R., and Nichols, J.G. (1837) *The Modern History of South Wiltshire: Vol.5, Pt 1, Containing the Hundred of Alderbury*, John Bowyer Nichols and Son, London.

Colvin, H.M. (1963) *History of the King's Works*, HMSO, London.

Colvin, H.M. (1986) 'Royal gardens in medieval England' in ed. E.MacDougall, *Medieval Gardens*, Dumbarton Oaks Research Library and Collection, Washington, 9–22.

Corbet, G.B. and Harris, S. eds (1991) *The Handbook of British Mammals*, Blackwell Scientific, Oxford.

Coss, P.R. (1991) *Lordship, Knighthood and Locality. A Study in English Society c.1180– c. 1280*, Cambridge University Press, Cambridge.

Coss, P. (1998) *The Lady in Medieval England 1000–1500*, Wrens Park, Stroud.

Coss, P.R. (2003) *The Origins of the English Gentry*, Cambridge University Press, Cambridge.

Coss, P.R. ed. (1980) *The Langley Cartulary*, Dugdale Society **32**, Stratford-upon-Avon.

Coss, P.R. and Keen, M. eds (2002) *Heraldry, Pageantry and Social Display in Medieval England*, Boydell & Brewer, Woodbridge.

Coulson, C.L.H. (1979) 'Structural symbolism in medieval castle architecture', *Journal of the British Archaeological Association* **132**, 73–90.

Coulson, C.L.H. (1982) 'Hierarchism in conventual crenellation. An essay in the sociology and metaphysics of medieval fortification', *Medieval Archaeology* **26**, 69–100.

Coulson, C.L.H. (2003) *Castles in Medieval Society. Fortresses in England, France and Ireland in the Central Middle Ages*, Oxford University Press, Oxford.

Coulton, G.G. (1925) *The Medieval Village*, Cambridge University Press, Cambridge.

Cox, J.C. (1905) *The Royal Forests of England*, Methuen, London.

Coy, J. (1980) 'The animal bones' in 'A Middle Saxon iron smelting site at Ramsbury, Wiltshire', *Medieval Archaeology* **24**, 41–9.

Crawford, O.G.S. (1953) *Archaeology in the Field*, Dent, London.

Creighton, O. (2002) *Castles and Landscapes*, Continuum, London.

Crook, D. (2002) 'The development of private parks in medieval Nottinghamshire', *Transactions of the Thorton Society of Nottinghamshire* **106**, 73–80.

Crossley, A. ed. (1990) 'Blenheim Park to 1705' in A History of the County of Oxford: Volume 12: Wootton Hundred (South) including Woodstock, 439–48.

Bibliography

Crouch, D. (1982) 'Geoffrey de Clinton and Roger, Earl of Warwick: new men and magnates in the reign of Henry I', *Bulletin of the Institute of Historical Research* **55**, 113–23.

Crouch, D. (1992) *The Image of Aristocracy in Britain, 1000–1300*, Routledge, London.

Crouch, D. (1996) 'The local influence of the Earls of Warwick, 1088–1242: a study in decline and resourcefulness', *Midland History* **21**, 1–22.

Cullum, J. (1784) *History and Antiquities of Hawsted in the County of Suffolk*, J. Nichols, London.

Cummins, J. (1988) *The Hound and the Hawk: The Art of Medieval Hunting*, Wiedenfeld and Nicholson, London.

Cummins, J. (2002) 'Veneurs s'en vont en Paradis: medieval hunting and the "natural" landscape' in eds J. Howe and M. Wolfe, *Inventing Medieval Landscapes: Senses of Place in Western Europe*, University Press of Florida, Gainesville, 33–56.

Cummins, J. (1988) *The Hound and the Hawk: The Art of Medieval Hunting*, Wiedenfeld and Nicholson, London.

Curwen, J. F. (1911) 'Cockermouth castle', *Transactions of Cumberland and Westmorland Antiquarian and Archaeological Society*, new series **11**, 129–58.

Dalby, D. (1965) *Lexicon of the Medieval German Hunt*, Walter de Gruyter, Berlin.

Dale, M. K. (1962) 'The city of New Salisbury' in ed. E. Crittall, *A History of Wiltshire*, vol. 6, The Victoria history of the counties of England, The Institute of Historical Research, Oxford University Press, Oxford, 69–194.

Dam, P. van (2002) 'New habitats for the rabbit in northern Europe, 1300–1600' in eds J. Howe and M. Wolfe, *Inventing Medieval Landscapes: Senses of Place in Western Europe*, University Press of Florida, Gainesville, 57–69.

Danielsson, B. ed. (1977) *William Twiti: The Art of Hunting 1327*, Cynegetica Anglica 1, Stockholm Studies in English 37, Almqvist and Wiksell International, Stockholm.

Darby, H. C. (1971; 3rd edn) *The Domesday Geography of Eastern England*, Cambridge University Press, Cambridge.

Darby, H. C. and Campbell, E. M. J. eds (1962) *The Domesday Geography of South-East England*, Cambridge University Press, Cambridge.

Darbyshire, H. S. and Lumb, G. D. (1934) *The History of Methley*, Publications of the Thoresby Society **35**.

Davies, R. R. (1987) *Conquest, Coexistence and Change. Wales 1063–1415*, Clarendon Press, Oxford.

Davies, R. T. ed. (1964) *Medieval English Lyrics: A Critical Anthology*, Northwestern University Press, Evanston, Illinois.

Davis, R. H. C. (1989) *The Medieval Warhorse: Origin, Development and Redevelopment*, Thames and Hudson, London.

Dean, R. M. (2001) 'Social change and hunting during the Pueblo III to Pueblo IV transition, east-central Arizona', *Journal of Field Archaeology* **28**, 271–85.

Dennison, E. ed. (2005) *The Story of Sheriff Hutton Park*, William Sessions, York.

Denton, T., ed. A. J. L. Winchester with M. Wane (2003) *Thomas Denton: a Perambulation of Cumberland 1687–8*, Surtees Society **207**, Boydell & Brewer, Woodbridge.

Douglas, D. C. ed. (1932) *Feudal Documents from the Abbey of Bury St Edmunds*, Oxford University Press, London.

Drury, J. L. (1978) 'Durham palatinate forest law and administration, specially in Weardale up to 1440', *Archaeologia Aeliana* 5th series **6**, 87–105.

Du Boulay, F. R. H. (1970) *An Age of Ambition. English Society in the Late Middle Ages*, Nelson, London.

Duceppe-Lamarre, F. (2001) 'Le parc à gibier d'Hesdin. Mises au point et nouvelles orientations de recherches', *Revue du Nord – Archéologie* **83**, 343, 175–84.

Dyer, C. (1988) 'Documentary evidence: problems and enquiries' in eds G. Astill and A. Grant, *The Countryside of Medieval England*, Blackwell, Oxford, 12–35.

Dyer, C.C. (1991) 'The West Midlands' in ed. E. Miller, *The Agrarian History of England and Wales, Vol. III, 1348–1500*, Cambridge University Press, Cambridge, 222–38.

Dyer, C.C. (1994) *Everyday Life in Medieval England*, Hambledon Press, London.

Dymond, D. (2003) *Hodskinson's Map of Suffolk in 1783*, Larks Press, Dereham.

Dymond, D. and Virgoe, R. (1986) 'The reduced population and wealth of early fifteenth-century Suffolk', *Proceedings of the Suffolk Institute of Archaeology* **36**, 73–100.

England, G. and Pollard, A. ed. (1897) *The Towneley Plays*, Early English Text Society, Extra Series 71, Kegan Paul, Trench, Trübner, London.

Evans, I.M. and Lawrence, H. (1979) *Christopher Saxton, Elizabethan Map-Maker*, Wakefield Historical Publications 4, Wakefield.

Everson, P., Brown, G. and Stocker, D. (2000) 'The castle earthworks and landscape context' in ed. P. Ellis, *Ludgershall Castle: A Report on the Excavations by Peter Addyman 1964–1972*, Wiltshire Archaeological and Natural History Society, Devizes, 97–119.

Ewbank, J.M. ed. (1963) *Antiquary on Horseback*, Cumberland and Westmorland Antiquarian and Archaeological Society Extra Series **XIX**, Titus Wilson, Kendal.

Fairweather, J. (2005) *Liber Eliensis: A History of the Isle of Ely from the Seventh Century to the Twelfth*, Boydell & Brewer, Woodbridge.

Farrer, E. (1923) *Suffolk Deer Parks*, a series of newspaper articles drawn together as SRO/I S712.644.

Farrer, W. (1923) *Records Relating to the Barony of Kendale Vol. I*, Cumberland and Westmorland Antiquarian and Archaeological Society Record Series **IV**, Titus Wilson, Kendal.

Farrer, W. (1924) *Records Relating to the Barony of Kendale Vol. II*, Cumberland and Westmorland Antiquarian and Archaeological Society Record Series **V**, Titus Wilson, Kendal.

Farrer, W. and Brownbill, J. eds (1914) *The Victoria history of the county of Lancaster*, vol. 8, Victoria history of the counties of England, Constable, London.

Faull, M.L. and Moorhouse, S. eds (1981) *West Yorkshire: An Archaeological Survey to A.D. 1500*, 4 vols, West Yorkshire Metropolitan County Council, Wakefield.

Fisher, E.J. (1954) *Some Yorkshire Estates of the Percies 1450–1650*, unpublished DPhil thesis, University of Leeds.

Fleming, A (1998) *Swaledale: Valley of the Wild River*, Edinburgh University Press, Edinburgh.

Fleming, D. (1962) 'Sir Daniel Fleming's description of Cumberland, Westmorland and Furness, 1671' in ed. E. Hughes, *Fleming-Senhouse Papers*, Cumberland County Council Record Series 2, The Courts, Carlisle.

Fowler, G.H. ed. (1937) 'Calendar of Inquisitions Post Mortem No. II', *Bedfordshire Historical Record Society* **19**, 111–70.

Fowler, J. (2002) *Landscapes and Lives. The Scottish Forest Through the Ages*, Canongate Books, Edinburgh.

Franklin, P. (1989) 'Thornbury woodlands and deer parks, part 1: the Earls of Gloucester's deer parks', *Transactions of the Bristol and Gloucester Archaeological Society* **107**, 149–69.

Fryde, E.B. (1988) *William de la Pole. Merchant and King's Banker († 1366)*, Hambledon Press, London.

Gage, J. (1838) *The History and Antiquities of Suffolk: Thingoe Hundred*, John Deck, Bury St Edmunds.

Gardiner, J. ed. (2000) *Who's Who in British History*, Collins and Brown Ltd, London.

Gelling, M. (1984) *Place-Names in the Landscape*, Dent, London.

Gilchrist, R. (1999) *Gender and Archaeology: Contesting the Past*, Routledge, London.

Given-Wilson, C. (1987) *The English Nobility in the Late Middle Ages*, Routledge, London.

Goulbourn, G.M. and Symonds, H. eds (1878) *The Life Letters and Sermons of Herbert de Losinga*, Oxford and London.

Graham, T.H.B. ed. (1934) *The Barony of Gilsland: Lord William Howard's survey taken in 1603*, Cumberland and Westmorland Antiquarian and Archaeological Society Extra Series **XVI**, Kendal.

Bibliography

Greenslade, M.W. ed. (1996) *The Victoria history of the county of Stafford*, vol.7, Victoria history of the counties of England, Oxford University Press, Oxford.

Greenway, D.E. and Sayers, J.E. eds (1989) *Jocelin of Brakelond. Chronicle of the Abbey of Bury St. Edmunds*, Oxford University Press, Oxford.

Grigor, J. (1841) *The Eastern Arboretum*, London.

Hale, W.H. (1858) *The Domesday of St Paul's of the year MCCXXII*, Camden Society Old Series **69**, London.

Hall, G.M. (1938) *A History of Bushey*, Bournehall Press, Bushey.

Harding, P.T. and Rose, F. (1986) *Pasture-Woodlands in Lowland Britain: A review of their importance for wildlife conservation*, Institute of Terrestrial Ecology, Monks Wood Experimental Station, Huntingdon.

Harding, P.T. and Wall, T. eds (2000) *Moccas: An English Deer Park*, English Nature, Peterborough.

Hardy, M.with Martin, E. (1987) 'Field surveys: South Elmham', *Proceedings of the Suffolk Institute of Archaeology* **36**, 232–5.

Harmer, F.E. (1952) *Anglo-Saxon Writs*, Manchester University Press, Manchester.

Harper-Bill, C. and Mortimer, R. eds (1982) *Stoke by Clare Cartulary Part I*, Suffolk Charters **4**, Boydell & Brewer, Woodbridge.

Harris, R.C., Helliwell, T.R., Singleton, W., Stickland, N. and Naylor, J.R.J. (1999) *The Physiological Response of Red Deer (Cervus elaphus) to Prolonged Exercise undertaken during Hunting*, R & W Publications, Newmarket.

Harriss, G.L. (2005) *Shaping the Nation. England 1360–1461*, Clarendon Press, Oxford.

Harwood, T.E. (1929) *Windsor Old and New*, privately published, London.

Harvey, J. (1981) *Medieval Gardens*, Batsford, London.

Hatherly, J.M. and Cantor, L.M. (1979–80) 'The medieval parks of Berkshire', *Berkshire Archaeological Journal* **70**, 67–80.

Hayman, R. (2003) *Trees. Woodlands and Western Civilization*, Hambledon and London, London.

Hearne, T. ed. (1745) *Johannis Rossi, Historia Regum Angliae*, Oxford.

Hebditch, M.J. ed. (1948) *Yorkshire Deeds: IX*, Yorkshire Archaeological Society Record Series **111**, Leeds.

Henisch, B.A. (2002) 'Private pleasures: painted gardens on the manuscript page' in eds J.Howe and M.Wolfe, *Inventing Medieval Landscapes: Senses of Place in Western Europe*, University Press of Florida, Gainesville, 150–68.

Herring, P. (2003) 'Cornish medieval deer parks' in ed. R.Wilson-North, *The Lie of the Land: Aspects of the Archaeology and History of the Designed Landscape in the South West of England*, The Mint Press, Exeter, 34–50.

Heslop, T.A. (1987) 'English seals in the thirteenth and fourteenth centuries', in eds J.Alexander and P.Binski, *Age of Chivalry: Art in Plantagenet England, 1200–1400*, Royal Academy of Arts, London, 114–17.

Hewitt, H.J. (1983) *The Horse in Medieval England*, Allen, London.

Hey, D. (1975) 'The parks at Tankersley and Wortley', *Yorkshire Archaeological Journal* **47**, 109–20.

Hey, D. and Rodwell, J. (2006) 'Wombwell: the landscape history of a South Yorkshire township', *Landscapes* **7.2**, *forthcoming*.

Higham, N.J. (2004) *A Frontier Landscape: The North West in the Middle Ages*, Windgather Press, Macclesfield.

Hooke, D. (1989) 'Pre-Conquest woodland: its distribution and usage', *Agricultural History Review* **37**, **2**, 113–29.

Hope, W.H. St. J. (1914) 'A palatinate seal of John, Earl of Warenne, Surrey and Stratherne, 1305–1347', *Surrey Archaeological Collections* **27**, 123–7.

Hoppitt, R. (1992) *A Study of the Development of Parks in Suffolk from the Eleventh to the Seventeenth Century*, 2 vols, unpublished PhD thesis, University of East Anglia.

Hoppitt, R. (1999) 'Deer Parks 1086–*c*.1600' in eds D. Dymond and E. Martin, *An Historical Atlas of Suffolk*, Suffolk County Council, Lavenham, 66–7.

Howes, L. L. (2002) 'Narrative time and literary landscapes in Middle English poetry' in eds J. Howe and M. Wolfe, *Inventing Medieval Landscapes: Senses of Place in Western Europe*, University Press of Florida, Gainesville, 192–207.

Hoyle, R. W. (1991) 'Thomas Lord Darcy and the Rothwell tenants *c*.1526–1534', *Yorkshire Archaeological Journal* **63**, 85–108.

Hoyle, R. W. (1995) 'Thomas first Lord Wharton's parks at Ravenstonedale and Wharton', *Transactions of Cumberland and Westmorland Antiquarian & Archaeological Society*, new series **95**, 111–18.

Hunn, J. R. (1994) *Reconstruction and Measurement of Landscape Change: A Study of Six Parishes in the St Albans Area*, British Archaeological Reports British Series **236**, Oxford.

Hyland, A. (1999) *The Horse in the Middle Ages*, Sutton, Stroud.

Illingworth, W. and Caley, J. eds (1812 and 1818) *Rotuli Hundredorum temp. Hen. III & Edw. I*, 2 vols, Record Commission, London.

Ingrem, C. (n.d.) *Assessment of the animal remains from Bishopstone, Sussex*, unpublished report to the Sussex Archaeological Society, 2005.

James, P. W., Hawksworth, D. L. and Rose, F. (1977) 'Lichen communities in the British Isles: a preliminary conspectus' in ed. M. R. D. Seaward, *Lichen Ecology*, Academic Press, London, 295–413.

James, T. B. (1990) *The Palaces of Medieval England: Royalty, Nobility, the Episcopate and their Residences from Edward the Confessor to Henry VIII*, Seaby, London.

James, T. B. and Gerrard, C. (forthcoming) *Clarendon: Landscape of Kings*, Windgather Press, Macclesfield.

Jane, L. C. ed. (1907) The Chronicle of Jocelin of Brakelond Monk of St. Edmundsbury: A Picture of Monastic and Social Life in the XIIth Century, Chatto and Windus, London.

Johnson, C. ed. (1950) *The Course of the Exchequer by Richard son of Nigel, Treasurer of England and Bishop of London*, Thomas Nelson and Sons, London.

Johnson, M. (2002) *Behind the Castle Gate: From Medieval to Renaissance*, Routledge, London.

Jones, R. T. and Ruben, I. (1987) 'Animal bones, with some notes on the effects of differential sampling' in eds G. Beresford and J. Geddes, *Goltho: The Development of an Early Medieval Manor c.850–1150*, Historic Buildings and Monuments Commission for England, London, 197–200.

Jourdain, F. C. R. (1905) 'Mammals' in ed. W. Page, *Victoria County History of Derby*, vol. 1, Street, London, 150–8.

Jones, J. and Jones, M. (2005) *Historic Parks and Gardens in and around South Yorkshire*, Wharncliffe Books, Barnsley.

Jones, M. (1996) 'Deer in South Yorkshire: an historical perspective', in eds M. Jones, I. D. Rotherham and A. J. McCarthy, 'Deer or the New Woodlands?', *The Journal of Practical Ecology and Conservation* Special Publication 1, 11–26.

Jones, M., Rotherham, I. D. and McCarthy, A. J. eds (1996) 'Deer or the New Woodlands?', *The Journal of Practical Ecology and Conservation* Special Publication 1.

Keats-Rohan, K. S. B. (1999) *Domesday People: A Prosopography of Persons Occurring in English Documents, 1066–1166, I Domesday Book*, Boydell & Brewer, Woodbridge.

Keevil, G. D. (2000) *Medieval Palaces. An Archaeology*, Tempus Publishing, Stroud.

Kendall, H. P. (1918) 'Elphaborough Hall and Errenden Park', *Transactions of the Halifax Antiquarian Society*, 1–33.

King Alfred's College Consultancy (1996) *Clarendon Park, Salisbury, Wiltshire: Archaeology, History and Ecology – English Heritage Survey Grant for Presentation vols I–II*, English Heritage Project Number 1750, unpublished, Winchester.

Kirby, K. J. and Drake, C. M. eds (1993) *Dead Wood Matters: The Ecology and Conservation of Saproxylic Invertebrates in Britain*, English Nature Science 7, English Nature, Peterborough.

Bibliography

Kirkby, J.W. ed. (1983) *The Manor and Borough of Leeds, 1425–1662: An Edition of Documents*, Publications of the Thoresby Society **57**, Leeds.

Lachaud, F. (2002) 'Dress and social status in England before the sumptuary laws', in eds P.Coss and L.Keen, *Heraldry, Pageantry and Social Display in Medieval England*, Boydell & Brewer, Woodbridge, 105–23.

Lacroix, P. (1874) *Manners, Customs and Dress in the Middle Ages and During the Renaissance Period*, Chapman and Hall, London.

Langdon, J. (1986) *Horses, Oxen and Technological Innovation: The Use of Draft Animals in English Farming from 1066–1500*, Cambridge University Press, Cambridge.

Lapsley, G.T. (1905) 'Text of the Boldon Book', in ed. W.Page, *The Victoria history of the county of Durham*, vol.1, Victoria history of the counties of England, Constable, London, 327–41.

Lasdun, S. (1991) *The English Park: Royal, Private and Public*, Andre Deutsch, London.

Lasdun, S. (1992) *The English Park: Royal, Private and Public*, Vendome Press, New York.

Lavelle, R. (2001) *Royal estates in Anglo-Saxon Wessex*, unpublished PhD thesis, University of Winchester.

Leadam, I.S. ed. (1893) 'The Inquisition of 1517: inclosures and evictions, II', *Transactions of the Royal Historical Society* new series 7, 127–292.

Lee, R. (1997) 'Hunting' in ed. T.Barfield, *The Dictionary of Anthropology*, Blackwell, Oxford, 252–3.

Le Patourel, J. ed. (1957) *Documents Relating to the Manor and Borough of Leeds, 1066–1400*, Publications of the Thoresby Society **45**, Leeds.

Levett, A.E. (1938) *Studies in Manorial History*, Oxford University Press, Oxford.

Liddiard, R. (2000a) *'Landscapes of Lordship': Norman Castles and the Countryside in Medieval Norfolk, 1066–1200*, British Archaeological Reports British Series **309**, Oxford.

Liddiard, R. (2000b) 'Castle Rising, Norfolk: a "landscape of lordship"?', *Anglo-Norman Studies* **22**, 169–86.

Liddiard, R. (2003) 'The deer parks of Domesday Book', *Landscapes* **4**, 1, 4–23.

Liddiard, R. (2005) *Castles in Context: Power, Symbolism and Landscape, 1066 to 1500*, Windgather, Macclesfield.

Liddell, W.H. (1966) 'The private forests of south-west Cumberland', *Transactions of Cumberland and Westmorland Antiquarian and Archaeological Society*, new series **66**, 106–30.

Lister, J. ed. (1930) *The Court Rolls of the Manor of Wakefield; IV, 1315–17*, Yorkshire Archaeological Society Record Series **78**, Leeds.

Lock, R. ed. (2002) *The Court Rolls of Walsham le Willows, 1351–1399*, Suffolk Records Society **45**, Boydell & Brewer, Woodbridge.

Locker, A.M. (1994) 'Animal bones' in M.Papworth, 'Lodge Farm, Kingston Lacy estate, Dorset', *Journal of the British Archaeological Association* **147**, 57–121, 107–10.

Loder, R. (1798) *History of Framlingham*, Woodbridge.

Lomas, R.A. (1978) 'The priory of Durham and its demesnes in the fourteenth and fifteenth centuries', *Economic History Review* **31**, 339–53.

Loyd, L.C. and Stenton, D.M. eds (1950) *Sir Christopher Hatton's Book of Seals*, Northamptonshire Record Society Publications, Clarendon Press, Oxford.

McFarlane, K.B. (1973) *The Nobility of Later Medieval England*, Clarendon Press, Oxford.

McLean, T. (1983) *The English at Play in the Middle Ages*, Kendal Press, Windsor Forest.

MacCullogh, D.N.J. ed. (1976) *Chorography of Suffolk*, Suffolk Records Society, Ipswich.

Manning, R.B. (1993) *Hunters and Poachers: A Cultural and Social History of Unlawful Hunting in England 1485–1640*, Clarendon Press, Oxford.

Martin, E. (1999a) 'Medieval moats' in eds D.Dymond and E.Martin, *An Historical Atlas of Suffolk*, Suffolk County Council, Lavenham, 60–1.

Martin, E. (1999b) 'Greens, commons and tyes' in eds D.Dymond and E.Martin, *An Historical Atlas of Suffolk*, Suffolk County Council, Lavenham, 62–3.

Martin, J. (1999) 'Ecclesiastical jurisdictions' in eds D. Dymond and E. Martin, *An Historical Atlas of Suffolk*, Suffolk County Council, Lavenham, 24–5.

Marvin, W. P. (1999) 'Slaughter and romance: hunting reserves in late medieval England' in eds B. Hanawalt and D. Wallace, *Medieval Crime and Social Control*, University of Minnesota Press, Minneapolis, 224–52.

Michelmore, D. J. H. (1979) 'The reconstruction of the early tenurial and territorial divisions of the landscape of northern England', *Landscape History* 1, 1–9.

Michelmore, D. J. H. (1981) 'Tenurial gazetter' in eds M. L. Faull and S. Moorhouse, *West Yorkshire: An Archaeological Survey to A.D. 1500*, West Yorkshire Metropolitan County Council, Wakefield, 294–576.

Mileson, S. A. (2005a) *Landscape, Power and Politics: The Place of the Park in Medieval English Society, c.1100–c.1535*, unpublished PhD thesis, University of Oxford.

Mileson, S. A. (2005b) 'The importance of parks in fifteenth-century society' in ed. L. Clark, *The Fifteenth Century V*, Boydell & Brewer, Woodbridge, 19–37.

Miller, E. (1951) *The Abbey and Bishopric of Ely: The Social History of an Ecclesiastical Estate from the Tenth Century to the Early Fourteenth Century*, Cambridge University Press, Cambridge.

Mitchell, S. (7th October 2006) 'Bambi bites back', *The Daily Telegraph*.

Moorhouse, S. (1978) 'Notes on the medieval park at Emley', *Sciant Presentes* **5**, 5–6.

Moorhouse, S. (1979) 'Documentary evidence for the landscape of the manor of Wakefield in the Middle Ages', *Landscape History* 1, 44–58.

Moorhouse, S. (1981) 'The rural medieval landscape' in eds M. L. Faull and S. Moorhouse, *West Yorkshire: An Archaeological Survey to A.D. 1500*, West Yorkshire Metropolitan County Council, Wakefield, 581–850.

Moorhouse, S. (1985) 'Permanent iron working sites in medieval West Yorkshire', *CBA Forum 1985*, 10–15.

Moorhouse, S. (1990) 'The quarrying of stone roofing slates and rubble in West Yorkshire during the Middle Ages' in ed. D. Parsons, *Stone: Quarrying and Building in Stone AD43–1525*, Phillimore and the Royal Archaeological Institute, Chichester, 126–48.

Moorhouse, S. (2003) 'The anatomy of the Yorkshire Dales: deciphering the medieval landscape' in eds T. G. Manby, S. Moorhouse and P. Ottaway, *The Archaeology of Yorkshire: An Assessment at the Beginning of the 21st Century*, Yorkshire Archaeological Society Occasional Paper **3**, 293–362.

Moorhouse, S. (2007a) 'An interdisciplinary approach to understanding past landscapes: processes and procedures' in ed. M. Atherdon, *Yorkshire Landscapes: Past and Future*, People, Landscapes and Cultural, Environmental, Educational and Research Centre, York St John College, York.

Moorhouse, S. (2007b) 'Buildings in the medieval landscape', *Yorkshire Buildings* **34**.

Moorhouse, S. (2007c) 'Minor buildings and features in the field systems of western Yorkshire', *Medieval Yorkshire* **36**.

Moorhouse, S. (2007d) 'The quarrying of building stone and stone artifacts in medieval Yorkshire: a multi-disciplinary approach' in ed. J. Klápstì, *Ruralia VI: Medieval Crafts and Industries*, Pamatky Archeologicke, Supplementum 18.

Morkill, J. W. (1891) 'The manor and park of Roundhay', *Publications of the Thoresby Society* **2**, 215–46.

Morris, J. ed. (1976) *Domesday Book: Hertfordshire*, Phillimore, Chichester.

Muir, R. (2005) *Ancient Trees Living Landscapes*, Tempus, Stroud.

Munby, L. M. ed. (1963) *The History of King's Langley*, Workers' Educational Association, King's Langley.

Munby, L. M. (1977) *The Hertfordshire Landscape*, Hodder and Stoughton, London.

Murphy, P. and Scaife, R. G. (1991) 'The environmental archaeology of gardens' in ed. A. E. Brown, *Garden Archaeology*, Council for British Archaeology, London, 83–99.

Bibliography

Neave, S. (1991) *Medieval Parks of East Yorkshire*, Centre for Regional and Local History, University of Hull, Beverley.

Neave, D. and Turnbull, D. (1992) *Landscaped Parks and Gardens of East Yorkshire*, Georgian Society for East Yorkshire, Bridlington.

Neville, J. (1999) *Representation of the Natural World in Old English Poetry*, Cambridge Studies in Anglo-Saxon England 27, Cambridge University Press, Cambridge.

Newcourt, R. (1708) *Repertorium ecclesiasticum parochiale Londinense*, I, B. Mote for C. Bateman, London.

Newell, A. (1915) 'Sowerby Ramble and Erringden Park', *Transactions of the Halifax Antiquarian Society*, 233–36.

Nishimura, M.M. and Nishimura, D. (forthcoming) 'Rabbits, warrens, and Warenne: the patronage of the Gorleston Psalter', in eds K. Smith and C. Krinsky, Festschrift for Lucy Freeman Sandler, Harvey Miller Press, London.

Norden, J. (1598, reprt 1903) *A Description of Hertfordshire*, G. Price and Son, Ware.

Oggins, R.S. (2004) *The Kings and Their Hawks: Falconry in Medieval England*, Yale, London.

O'Regan, H.J. (2002) 'From bear pits to zoos', *British Archaeology* **68**, 12–19.

Orme, N. (1992) 'Medieval hunting: fact and fancy' in ed. B. Hanawalt, *Chaucer's England: Literature in Historical Context*, University of Minnesota Press, Minneapolis, 133–53.

Page, W. ed. (1905) *The Victoria history of the county of Derby*, vol. I, Victoria history of the counties of England, London.

Page, W. (1908) 'Parishes: King's Langley' in ed. W. Page, *The Victoria History of the County of Hertford*, vol. 2, The Victoria history of the counties of England, Constable, London, 234–45.

Page, W. ed. (1914, reprt 1971) *The Victoria history of the county of Hertford*, vol. IV, Constable, London.

Panayotova, S. (2005) *The Macclesfield Psalter*, The Fitzwilliam Museum, Cambridge.

Parker, F.H.M. (1910) 'Inglewood Forest Parts V and VI', *Transactions of Cumberland and Westmorland Antiquarian and Archaeological Society*, new series **10**, 1–28.

Pastoureau, M. (1993) *Traité d'Héraldique*, Picard, Paris.

Perlin, J. (1989) *A Forest Journey*, Harvard University Press, Massachusetts.

Peterken, G.F. (1981) *Woodland Conservation and Management*, Chapman and Hall, London.

Peterken, G.F. (1996) *Natural Woodland: Ecology and Conservation in Northern Temperate Regions*, Cambridge University Press, Cambridge.

Phibbs, J.L. (1991) 'The archaeology of parks – the wider perspective' in ed. A.E. Brown, *Garden Archaeology*, Council for British Archaeology, London, 118–22.

Pigott, C.D. (1993) 'The History and Ecology of Ancient Woodlands', *Landscape Archaeology and Ecology* **1**, 1–11.

Platt, C. (1976) *The English Medieval Town*, Secker and Warburg, London.

Pluskowski, A.G. (2006) *Wolves and the Wilderness in the Middle Ages*, Boydell & Brewer, Woodbridge.

Pollard, A.J. (1990) *North-Eastern England during the Wars of the Roses: Lay Society, War and Politics, 1450–1500*, Clarendon Press, Oxford.

Pollard, A.J. (2004) *Imagining Robin Hood: The Late-Medieval Stories in Historical Context*, Routledge, New York.

Poole, K. (in prep.) 'Bird introductions' in eds T.P. O'Connor and N. Sykes, *Extinctions and Invasions: A Social History of British Fauna*, Windgather Press, Macclesfield.

Porter, R.E. and Collingwood, W.G. eds (1928) *The Memoirs of Sir Daniel Fleming*, Cumberland and Westmorland Antiquarian and Archaeological Society Tract Series **XI**, Titus Wilson, Kendal.

Poulton, R. (2005) *A Medieval Royal Complex at Guildford: Excavations at the Castle and Palace*, Surrey Archaeological Society, Guildford.

Preece, R. and Fraser, D. (2000) 'The status of animals in Biblical and Christian thought: a study of colliding values', *Society and Animals* **8** (3), 245–63.

Purvis, J.S. ed. (1936) *The Chartulary of the Augustinian Priory of St John the Evangelist of the Park of Healaugh*, Yorkshire Archaeological Society Record Series **92**.

Rackham, O. (1976) *Trees and Woodland in the British Landscape*, Dent, London.

Rackham, O. (1978) 'Archaeology and land-use history' in ed. D.Corke, *Epping Forest: The Natural Aspects?*, Essex Naturalist new series **2**, 16–57.

Rackham, O. (1980) *Ancient Woodland: its History, Vegetation and Uses in England*, Edward Arnold, London.

Rackham, O. (1986) *The History of the Countryside*, Dent, London.

Rackham, O. (1990; revised edn) *Trees and Woodland in the British Landscape*, Phoenix Press, London.

Rackham, O. (1993; 2nd edn) *The Last Forest: the Story of Hatfield Forest*, Dent, London.

Rackham, O. (1999a, first pub.1986) *The History of the Countryside*, Phoenix, London.

Rackham, O. (1999b) 'Medieval woods' in eds D.Dymond and E.Martin, *An Historical Atlas of Suffolk*, Suffolk County Council, Lavenham, 64–5.

Rackham, O. (2000) *The History of the Countryside*, Phoenix, London.

Rackham, O. (2002) 'The medieval countryside of England: botany and archaeology' in eds J.Howe and M.Wolfe, *Inventing Medieval Landscapes: Senses of Place in Western Europe*, University Press of Florida, Gainesville, 13–32.

Rackham, O. (2004) 'Pre-Existing Trees and Woods in Country-House Parks', *Landscapes* **5** (2), 1–16.

Radley, J. (1961) 'Holly as a winter feed', *Agricultural History Review* **9**, 89–92.

Ragg, F.W. (1910) 'De Lancaster', *Transactions of Cumberland and Westmorland Antiquarian and Archaeological Society*, new series **10**, 395–494.

Read, H. (1999) *Veteran Trees: A guide to good management*, English Nature, Peterborough.

Recarte, J.M., Vincent, J.P. and Hewison, A.J.M. (1998) 'Flight responses of park fallow deer to the human observer', *Behavioural Processes* **44**, 65–72.

Redmonds, G. (2004) *Names and History: People, Places and Things*, Hambledon and London, London.

Richardson, A. (2005) The Forest, Park and Palace of Clarendon c.1200–c.1650: Reconstructing an Actual, Conceptual and Documented Wiltshire Landscape, British Archaeological Reports British Series **387**, Oxford.

Richardson, A. (2006) '"Hedging, ditching and other improper occupations": royal landscapes and their meaning under Edward II and Edward III' in ed. J.Hamilton, *Fourteenth Century England* **4**, The Boydell Press, Woodbridge, 26–42.

Rigby, S.H. (1995) *English Society in the Later Middle Ages. Class, Status and Gender*, Macmillan, Basingstoke.

Riley, H.T. ed. (1867, repub. 1965) *Gesta Abbatum Monasterii Sancti Albani*, vol.1, HMSO, London.

Riley, H.T. ed. (1870, reprt 1965) *Annales Monasterii S.Albani a Johanne Amundesham AD 1421–1444*, vol.1, HMSO, London.

Rimington, F.C. (1970) 'The early deer parks of north-east Yorkshire, Part I, Introduction', *Transactions of the Scarborough and District Archaeological Society* **13**, 3–16.

Rimington, F.C. (1971) 'The early deer parks of north-east Yorkshire, Part II, Catalogue', *Transactions of the Scarborough and District Archaeological Society* **14**, 1–16.

Rimington, F.C. (1972) 'The early deer parks of north-east Yorkshire, Part II, Catalogue', *Transactions of the Scarborough and District Archaeological Society* **15**, 33–6.

Rimington, F.C. (1973) 'The early deer parks of north-east Yorkshire, Part II, Catalogue', *Transactions of the Scarborough and District Archaeological Society* **16**, 21–3.

Rimington, F.C. (1974) 'The early deer parks of north-east Yorkshire, Part II, Catalogue', *Transactions of the Scarborough and District Archaeological Society* **17**, 5–10.

Rimington, F. C. (1975) 'The early deer parks of north-east Yorkshire, Part II, Catalogue', *Transactions of the Scarborough and District Archaeological Society* **18**, 9–13.

Rimington, F. C. (1976) 'The early deer parks of north-east Yorkshire, Part II, Catalogue', *Transactions of the Scarborough and District Archaeological Society* **19**, 23–6.

Rimington, F. C. (1977) 'The early deer parks of north-east Yorkshire, Part II, Catalogue', *Transactions of the Scarborough and District Archaeological Society* **20**, 31–8.

Rimington, F. C. (1978) 'The early deer parks of north-east Yorkshire, Part II, Catalogue', *Transactions of the Scarborough and District Archaeological Society* **21**, 24–8.

Ritvo, H. (1987) *The Animal Estate: The English and Other Creatures in the Victorian Age*, Harvard University Press, Cambridge.

Roberts, E. (1988) 'The bishop of Winchester's deer parks in Hampshire, 1200–1400', *Proceedings of the Hampshire Field Club and Archaeological Society* **44**, 67–86.

Roberts, E. (1995) 'Edward III's lodge at Odiham, Hampshire', *Medieval Archaeology* **39**, 91–106.

Roberts, J. (1997) *Royal Landscape: The Gardens and Parks of Windsor*, Yale University Press, London.

Rollins, J. (2003) *Land Marks: Impressions of England's National Nature Reserves*, English Nature, Peterborough.

Rooney, A. (1993) *Hunting in Middle English Literature*, Boydell & Brewer, Woodbridge.

Rose, F. (1974) 'The epiphytes of oak' in eds M. G. Morris and F. H. Perring, *The British Oak: Its History and Natural History*, Classey, Faringdon, 250–73.

Rose, F. (1976) 'Lichenological indicators of age and environmental continuity in woodlands' in eds D. H. Brown, D. L. Hawksworth and R. H. Bailey, *Lichenology: Progress and Problems*, Academic Press, London.

Rose, F. and James, P. W. (1974) 'Regional studies on the British lichen flora, 1. The corticolous and lignicolous species of the New Forest, Hampshire', *Lichenologist* **6**, 1–72.

Rowe, A. (forthcoming) *Medieval Parks in Hertfordshire*, Hertfordshire Publications, Hatfield.

Rowland, B. (1978) *Birds with Human Souls: A Guide to Bird Symbolism*, University of Tennessee Press, Knoxville.

Rowley, T. (1986), *The High Middle Ages 1200–1550*, Routledge, London.

Ryan, P. (2000) 'Woodham Walter Hall – its site and setting', *Essex Archaeology and History* **30**, 178–95.

Sadler, P. (1990) 'Osteological Remains' in ed. J. R. Fairbrother, *Faccombe Netherton: Excavations of a Saxon and Medieval Manorial Complex II*, British Museum Occasional Paper **74**, British Museum, London.

Salisbury, J. E. (1994) *The Beast Within: Animals in the Middle Ages*, Routledge, London.

Saunders, C. J. (1993) *The Forest of Medieval Romance: Avernus, Broceliande, Arden*, D. S. Brewer, Cambridge.

Sayce, R. U. (1946) 'Traps and snares', *Montgomery Collections* **49**, 37–73.

Selden, J. (1618) *The Historie of Tithe*, London.

Shaw, R. C. (1956) *The Royal Forest of Lancaster*, Preston.

Shirley, E. P. (1867) *Some Account of English Deer Parks*, John Murray, London.

Slade, C. F. and Lambrick, G. eds (1990–2) *Two Cartularies of Abingdon Abbey*, 2 vols, Oxford Historical Society new series **32** and **33**.

Smirke, E. (1848) 'On certain obscure words in charters, rentals, accounts etc, of property in the west of England [part 2]', *Archaeological Journal* **5**, 118–24.

Smith, A. H. ed. (1961) *The Place-Names of the West Riding of Yorkshire Part IV: Barkston Ash, Skyrack and Ainsty Wapentakes*, English Place-Name Society XXXIII, Cambridge University Press, Cambridge.

Smith, A. H. ed. (1962) *The Place-Names of the West Riding of Yorkshire Part VII: Introduction, Bibliography, River-Names and Analysis*, English Place-Name Society XXXVI, Cambridge University Press, Cambridge.

Smith, A.H. (1967) *The Place-Names of Westmorland*, 2 vols, English Place-Name Society XLII–XLIII, Cambridge University Press, Cambridge.

Smout, T.C. ed. (2003) *People and Woods in Scotland*, Edinburgh University Press, Edinburgh.

Speight, M. (1989) *Saproxylic invertebrates and their conservation*, Nature and Environment Series 42, Council of Europe, Strasbourg.

Spray, M. and Smith, D.J. (1977) 'The rise and fall of the holly in the Sheffield region', *Transactions of the Hunter Archaeological Society* 10, 239–51.

Squires, A.E. and Humphrey, W. (1986) *The Medieval Parks of Charnwood Forest*, Sycamore Press, Melton Mowbray.

Stamper, P. (1988) 'Woods and parks' in eds G. Astill and A. Grant, *The Countryside of Medieval England*, Blackwell, Oxford, 128–48.

Stannard, J. (1986) 'Alimentary and medicinal uses of plants' in ed. E. MacDougall, *Medieval Gardens*, Dumbarton Oaks Research Library and Collection, Washington, 69–113.

Steane, J. (1993) *The Archaeology of the Medieval English Monarchy*, Batsford, London.

Steane, J. (2001) *The Archaeology of Power: England and Northern Europe A.D. 800–1600*, Tempus, Stroud.

Steel, T.M. (1979) 'Holden park, a study', *Yorkshire Archaeological Society* MS1325, unpublished manuscript.

Stephens, W.B. *A History of the County of Warwick: vol. 8, The City of Coventry and the Borough of Warwick*, Victoria history of the counties of England, Institute of Historical Research, Oxford University Press, London.

Stocker, D. and Stocker, M. (1996) 'Sacred profanity: the theology of rabbit breeding and the symbolic landscape of the warren', *World Archaeology* 28 (2), 265–72.

Stockstad, M. (1986) 'The garden as art' in ed. E. MacDougall, *Medieval Gardens*, Dumbarton Oaks Research Library and Collection, Washington, 176–85.

Swanton, M. ed. (1993) *Anglo-Saxon Prose*, Everyman, London.

Sykes, N.J. (2004) 'The introduction of fallow deer (*Dama dama*) to Britain: a zooarchaeological perspective', *Environmental Archaeology* 9, 75–83.

Sykes, N.J. (2005a) 'Hunting for the Normans: zooarchaeological evidence for medieval identity' in ed. A. Pluskowski, *Just Skin and Bones? New Perspectives on Human–Animal Relations in the Historical Past*, British Archaeological Reports International Series 1410, Oxford, 73–80.

Sykes, N.J. (2005b) 'The dynamics of status symbols: wildfowl exploitation in England AD 410–1550', *Archaeological Journal* 161, 82–105.

Sykes, N.J., White, J., Hayes, T. and Palmer, M. (2006) 'Tracking animals using strontium isotopes in teeth: the role of fallow deer (*Dama dama*) in Roman Britain', *Antiquity* 80, 948–59.

Sykes, N.J. (in press) 'Taking sides: the social life of venison in medieval England' in ed. A. Pluskowski, *Breaking and Shaping Beastly Bodies: Animals as Material Culture in the Middle Ages*, Oxbow Books, Oxford, 150–61.

Sykes, NJ. (in prep.) *The Norman Conquest: A Zooarchaeological Perspective*, British Archaeological Reports International Series, Oxford.

Taigel, A. and Williamson, T. (1993) *Parks and Gardens*, Batsford, London.

Taylor, C. (2000) 'Medieval ornamental landscapes', *Landscapes* 1, 38–55.

Taylor, C.C. (2004) 'Ravensdale park, Derbyshire, and medieval deer coursing', *Landscape History* 26, 37–57.

Taylor, T. (1886) *The History of Wakefield: The Rectory Manor*, Wakefield.

Tebbutt, C.F. (1974) 'King's Standing, Ashdown Forest', *Sussex Archaeological Collections* 112, 30–3.

Thomas, K. (1983) *Man and the Natural World. Changing Attitudes in England 1500–1800*, Allen Lane, London.

Thomas, R. (2006) 'Chasing the ideal. Ritual, pragmatism and the later medieval hunt' in ed. A.G. Pluskowski, *Breaking and Shaping Beastly Bodies: Animals as Material Culture in the Middle Ages*, Oxbow Books, Oxford, 126–49.

Thorn, F. and Thorn, C. eds (1986) *Domesday Book, 25, Shropshire*, Phillimore, Chichester.

Ticehurst, N.F. (1957) *The Mute Swan in England*, Cleaver-Hume Press, London.

Todd, H. and Dymond, D. (1999) 'Population Densities 1327 and 1524' in eds D. Dymond and E. Martin, *An Historical Atlas of Suffolk*, Suffolk County Council, Lavenham, 80–2.

Todd, J.M. ed. (1997) *The Lanercost Cartulary*, Surtees Society **203**, Gateshead.

Tufto, J., Anderson, R. and Linnell, J. (1996) 'Habitat use and ecological correlates of home range size in a small cervid: roe deer', *The Journal of Animal Ecology* **65** (6), 715–24.

Tupling, G.H. (1927) *The Economic History of Rossendale*, Chetham Society new series **86**.

Turton, R.B. ed. (1895) *The Honour and Forest of Pickering [II]*, North Riding Record Series new series **2**.

Turton, R.B. ed. (1896) *The Honour and Forest of Pickering [III]*, North Riding Record Series new series **3**.

Turton, R.B. ed. (1897) *The Honour and Forest of Pickering [IV]*, North Riding Record Series new series **4**.

Underwood, G. (2002) 'Guildford park', *Surrey History* **6.4**, 208–20.

van Buren, A.H. (1986) 'Reality and literary romance in the park of Hesdin', in ed. E. MacDougall, *Medieval Gardens*, Dumbarton Oaks Research Library and Collection, Washington, 117–34.

Veale, E.M. (2003) *The English Fur Trade in the Later Middle Ages*, London Record Society, London.

Vellacott, C.H. (1912) 'Mining and smelting [medieval]', in ed. W. Page, *The Victoria County History of the County of York*, vol. 2, 338–55.

Vera, F. (2000) *Grazing Ecology and Forest History*, CABI Publishing, Oxford.

Villy, F. (1921) 'The site of Norton Tower, Rylstone', *Bradford Antiquary* new series **4**, 179–89.

Waites, B. (1964) 'Medieval iron working in north-east Yorkshire', *Geography* **49**, 33–43.

Walker, J.W. ed. (1945) *Court Rolls of the Manor of Wakefield: V, 1322–1331*, Yorkshire Archaeological Society Record Series **109**, Leeds.

Wallsgrove, S. (2004/5) 'Wedgnock park, Warwick: its creation and loss', *Warwickshire History* **12** (6), 239–52.

Warner, P. (1987) *Greens, Commons and Clayland Colonization*, Leicester University Press, Leicester.

Warner, P. (1996) *The Origins of Suffolk*, Manchester University Press, Manchester.

Watkins, A. (1993) 'The woodland economy of the forest of Arden in the later middle ages', *Midland History* **18**, 19–36.

Watts, J.L. (1996) *Henry VI and the Politics of Kingship*, Cambridge University Press, Cambridge.

Watts, K. (1998) 'Some Wiltshire deer parks', *Wiltshire Archaeological and Natural History Magazine* **91**, 90–102.

Way, T. (1997) *A Study of the Impact of Imparkment on the Social Landscape of Cambridgeshire and Huntingdonshire from c1080 to 1760*, British Archaeological Reports British Series **258**, Oxford.

Whalley, G.H. (1838) *The Tithe Act and the Tithe Amendment Act with Notes*, Shaw and Sons, London.

Whitaker, J. (1892) *A Descriptive List of the Deer-Parks and Paddocks of England*, Ballantyne, Hanson and Co., London.

Whitehead, G.K. (1964) *The Deer of Great Britain and Ireland*, Routledge, London.

Whitehead, G.K. (1980) *Hunting and Stalking Deer in Britain Through the Ages*, Batsford, London.

Whyte, I.D. (2002) *Landscape and History Since 1500*, Reaktion Books, London.

Wickham, C. (1994) 'European forests in the early middle ages: landscape and land clearance' in ed. C.Wickham, *Land and Power: Studies in Italian and European Social History, 400–1200*, British School at Rome, London, 155–99.

Williamson, T. (2000) *The Origins of Hertfordshire*, Manchester University Press, Manchester.

Williamson, T. (2005) *Sandlands: The Suffolk Coast and Heaths*, Windgather Press, Macclesfield.

Williamson, T. (2006) *The Archaeology of Rabbit Warrens*, Shire, Princes Risborough.

Williamson, T. and Bellamy, L. (1987) *Property and Landscape: A Social History of Land Ownership and the English Countryside*, George Philip, London.

Wilson, C. (2002) 'The royal lodgings of Edward III at Windsor Castle' in eds L.Keen and E. Scarff, *Windsor: Medieval Archaeology, Art and Architecture of the Thames Valley*, British Archaeological Association Conference Transactions 25, Leeds, 15–94.

Wilson, J. ed. (1901) *The Victoria history of the county of Cumberland*, vol.1, Victoria history of the counties of England, Constable, London.

Wilson, J. ed. (1915) *The Register of the Priory of St Bees*, Surtees Society 126, Durham.

Wilson, J. D.T. and Cantor, L. M. (1969) 'A medieval park site at Closworth', *Notes and Queries for Somerset and Dorset* 29, 49–51.

Wiltshire, M., Woore, S., Crisp, B. and Rich, B. (2005) *Duffield Frith: History and Evolution of the Landscape of a Medieval Derbyshire Forest*, Landmark Publishing, Ashbourne.

Winchester, A.J.L. (1987) *Landscape and Society in Medieval Cumbria*, John Donald, Edinburgh.

Winchester, A.J.L. (2003) 'Demesne livestock farming in the Lake District: the vaccary at Gatesgarth, Buttermere, in the later thirteenth century', *Transactions of Cumberland and Westmorland Antiquarian & Archaeological Society*, third series 3, 109–18.

Winchester, A.J.L. (2005a) 'The moorland forests of medieval England' in eds I.D.Whyte and A.J.L.Winchester, *Society, Landscape and Environment in Upland Britain*, Society for Landscape Studies, Birmingham, 21–34.

Winchester, A.J.L. (2005b) 'Regional identity in the Lake Counties: land tenure and the Cumbrian landscape,' *Northern History* 42 (1), 29–48.

Woolgar, C.M. (1999) *The Great Household in Late Medieval England*, Yale University Press, New Haven.

Woolgar, C.M. ed. (1993) *Household Accounts from Medieval England Part 2; Diet Accounts (ii) Cash, Corn and Stock Accounts Wardrobe Accounts Catalogue*, Records of Social and Economic History, New Series XVIII, The British Academy, Oxford University Press.

Woolley, L. (2002) *Medieval Life and Leisure in the Devonshire Hunting Tapesteries*, V&A, London.

Yalden, D. (1999) *The History of British Mammals*, T. & A.D.Poyser, London.

Young, C.R. (1979) *The Royal Forests of Medieval England*, Leicester University Press, Leicester.

Index

....

Entries in bold refer to the figures